PHOTOSHOP

RESTORATION & RETOUCHING

KATRIN EISMANN

New Riders

201 West 103rd Street,
Indianapolis, Indiana 46290

EXECUTIVE EDITOR
Beth Millett

MANAGING EDITOR
Thomas Hayes

PROJECT EDITOR
Heather McNeill

COPY EDITOR
Kay Hoskin

INDEXER
Aamir Burki

PROOFREADER
Harvey Stanbrough

TECHNICAL EDITOR
Julieanne Kost

TEAM COORDINATOR
Julie Otto

INTERIOR DESIGNER
Anne Jones

COVER DESIGNER
Anne Jones

PRODUCTION
Trina Wurst

For Instructors

This book was built around the techniques that I have taught over the years to the numerous students in my digital and creative imaging classes. I hope that this book can help you teach Photoshop as well, and that the examples and images I have provided will help you learn and demonstrate the concepts and techniques of retouching and restoration. As a teacher, I'm sure you know how much time and work is involved in creating exercises and preparing materials that fulfill all the needs of a classroom. I ask now that you respect my work, and that of the many other professionals whose work I've featured in this book, by not copying pages of the book, distributing any of the images from the Web site, or otherwise reproducing the information, even if paraphrased, without proper attribution and permission. Of course, if each student owns a copy of the book then they can freely download and use the images from the Web site in the classroom. For information about educational sales of this book, please contact Greg Wiegand at Que Publishing, greg.wiegand@quepublishing.com.

TRADEMARKS

All terms mentioned in this book that are known to be trademarks or service marks have been appropriately capitalized. Que cannot attest to the accuracy of this information. Use of a term in this book should not be regarded as affecting the validity of any trademark or service mark.

Adobe, the Adobe logo, and Photoshop are registered trademarks of Adobe Systems, Incorporated.

Warning and Disclaimer

Every effort has been made to make this book as complete and as accurate as possible, but no warranty or fitness is implied. The information provided is on an "as is" basis. The author and the publisher shall have neither liability nor responsibility to any person or entity with respect to any loss or damages arising from the information contained in this book.

Contents at a Glance

Table of Contents

9

PORTRAIT RETOUCHING

10

GLAMOUR AND FASHION RETOUCHING

ABOUT THE AUTHOR

Katrin Eismann is an internationally respected lecturer and teacher on the subject of imaging, restoration, retouching, and the impact of emerging technologies upon professional photographers, artists, and educators. Her clients include Eastman Kodak, Apple, Adobe, American Film Institute, Professional Photography Association, and University of California Los Angeles. She received her Bachelor of Fine Arts degree in Photographic Illustration with a concentration in electronic still imaging from the Rochester Institute of Technology. She recently received her Masters of Fine Arts degree in design at the School of VISUAL ARTS in New York City.

Katrin co-authored *Web Design Studio Secrets*, *Adobe Photoshop Studio Secrets, 2nd Edition*, and *Real World Digital Photography*, and has written numerous articles for *Photo Electronic Imaging*, *IdN*, and *Popular Photography*. She speaks about creative imaging and restoration techniques at the Thunder Lizard Productions' Focus on Photoshop, HOW, PMA/DIMA, and PhotoPlus Expo conferences. She has been named a SGI Vanguard of Visual Computing, as well as guest artist at the La Pietra Hawaii School for Girls and a 1999 Guerin Visiting Scholar at the Marlborough School in Los Angeles, California. Katrin is also a regular contributor to the online Apple Master Class series.

In the future, Katrin would like to take photographs that do not require any color correction, retouching, cropping, dodging and burning, or enhancement of any kind. To learn more about Katrin and to see her creative work, please visit www.photoshopdiva.com. To learn more about the book, *Photoshop Restoration and Retouching*, please visit the book's supplemental Web site, www.digitalretouch.org.

DEDICATION

To the only person this side of the Atlantic who could and would put up with yet another 'Katrin Project' that enveloped our time, energy, and too many sunny weekends. Johnnie, I couldn't and wouldn't have achieved any of this without you. *Fore!*

To my family on the other side of the Atlantic—thank you for the images, memories, and understanding phone calls. *Send Schocki!*

ACKNOWLEDGMENTS

As many authors have recognized, writing a book initially seems like a secluded undertaking, but the very task of researching and seeking expert insights into any topic changes the process from solitary to collaborative. Over the years I have learned from countless Photoshop experts, engineers, artists, and students. Many have techniques featured throughout this book. Thank you to Mark Beckelman, Joel Becker, Rick Billings, David Blatner, Steve Broback, Russell Brown, Dan Caylor, Jane Conner-ziser, Bruce Fraser, Helene DeLillo, Mark Hamburg, Bob Hawkins, Julieanne Kost, Dan Margulis, Bert Monroy, Myke Ninness, Wayne Palmer, Herb Paynter, Marc Pawliger, Andrew Rodney, Shangara Singh, Eddie Tapp, Chris Tarantino, Laurie Thompson, Greg Vander Houwen, Lee Varis, Dennis Walker, John Warner, Lloyd Weller, and Ben Wilmore for putting up with yet another email, phone call, or question from me.

Thank you to the numerous people who have challenged me to explain more clearly, answer one more time, or demonstrate a technique again. This book is for you—all the attentive and curious students who have attended my hands-on workshops, sat in darkened lecture halls, or emailed me questions. This book would never have gotten off the ground without your enthusiasm and criticism. A technique that is complicated or poorly explained is worthless and, believe me, alert students will always let the teacher know if they don't get it. After answering the question, it is every teacher's job to think of a better way to share knowledge with tomorrow's students. Teaching and writing is not a 9–5 job—it requires tossing, turning, experimentation, observation, and trying again. In other words, over the years, I've learned from all my students as they dedicated themselves to learning Photoshop. Thank you.

Finally, I have no idea how any editor could ever put up with my sleep-deprived, determined-to-write-a-book-that-I-would-buy hysteria, as I obsessed about the tone of the book or whether to include this or that Photoshop technique. Beth Millett has the wherewithal to train for marathons, send personal notes of encouragement, and let me blow off steam as I watched the clock strike midnight yet again. Beth, one reason I decided to write this book was because of you. I hope you're as glad as I am that we went from lunch to contract to finished book.

TELL US WHAT YOU THINK!

As the reader of this book, you are our most important critic and commentator. We value your opinion and want to know what we're doing right, what we could do better, what areas you'd like to see us publish in, and any other words of wisdom you're willing to pass our way.

As associate publisher for New Riders, I welcome your comments. You can fax, email, or write me directly to let me know what you did or didn't like about this book—as well as what we can do to make our books stronger.

Please note that I cannot help you with technical problems related to the topic of this book, and that due to the high volume of mail I receive, I might not be able to reply to every message.

When you write, please be sure to include this book's title and author as well as your name and phone or fax number. I will carefully review your comments and share them with the author and editors who worked on the book.

Fax: 317-581-4663

Email: stephanie.wall@newriders.com

Mail: Stephanie Wall
        New Riders Publishing
        201 West 103rd Street
        Indianapolis, IN 46290 USA

FOREWORD

Digital imaging and the manipulation of photographs has certainly sent shock waves through the industry in the last ten years. The future and value of photography has been debated and its demise has been predicted by those who have been afraid that what makes photography so valuable— the ability to record a moment of time and bring it back to us later when we look at an image—has been destroyed by the opportunity to change that image for some ulterior motive. In addition to offering the opportunity to compromise the integrity of the photograph, the computer has forced us to look at too many immature composites that look like a young medium in desperate search of a mature vision. So often we have quickly dismissed an image that was obviously manipulated because the hand of the artist was much too visible and the message presented to us was much too obvious. Or, even more upsetting, the computer has enabled photographs to be altered so subtly that we did not know that they had been manipulated.

What the doomsayers have missed (though, certainly many of their concerns are legitimate) is that the computer is now allowing us to go back and restore and retouch old photographs and bring them back to life. Photography is the one medium that can give us these images at the time they were made and, in a perfect world, enable us to see and enjoy that same image many years later as well. Much of the human condition has been recorded by some form of light-sensitive material and much of this invaluable record is now disappearing because these older materials are deteriorating. The science of preserving photographs is relatively new. It really does not matter whether these images are of some important news or social event or merely the recording of a simple aspect of our social fabric and family histories. To add a new tool to our libraries, to our archives, and to our family albums that will help us preserve and restore these images is truly a gift.

Katrin Eismann is the perfect artist and technician to write this book. She combines the artistic ability to appreciate the value of the original image and the technical skills to do the restoration of antique images and retouching of contemporary images in a manner both delicate and respectful to that image. She understands that the most well-intentioned photographer, from the dedicated amateur to the seasoned professional, may miss an exposure, forget to check light temperature, or overlook a cluttered background. The techniques shown in this book will help you make a good image better and, most importantly, will enable you to show the image as you really meant it to be.

I first met Katrin in 1992 when I took a class in Photoshop from her at the Kodak Center for Creative Imaging in Camden, Maine. Her enthusiasm for the artistic and technical sides of photography and digital manipulation and retouching made a lasting impression on me, and I still think back to how much I learned that week. She brought her background as a photographic artist to everything we did and to everything she has done in her career. She is an artist who is in control of her medium and who has mastered the skills to carefully use the techniques available to add to her vision. Now, with her help, we can add these new tools and her understanding of how to use them respectfully to the medium that has meant so much to all of us.

Digital imaging is not something to be feared. It is simply a new tool to enable us to communicate our vision. The use of the computer offers us a new way of expressing ourselves, and the integrity of the image is solely dependent on the creator. In this book, the computer is shown as a way to help us go back to communicate the vision of the original photographer and bring these socially and personally important images back to life. We can now recreate parts of our social and personal histories so that we can relive them in a way that will add to the present quality of our lives.

Steve Simmons

Publisher and Editorial Director
CameraArts and *View Camera* magazines

INTRODUCTION

THE IMPORTANCE OF IMAGES

A few years ago I was watching a TV news report about a tornado that had flattened a neighborhood near Oklahoma City. As the camera crew neared a family, the interviewer asked, "Did you have a chance to save anything?" The woman sobbed, "The family photos are gone—the wedding pictures, the kids, the photos of the grandkids—all gone." Then last year, I was watching a news report on the fires that swept through Los Alamos, New Mexico. The news team interviewed a couple who had lived in the same home for thirty years. When asked if they had been able to save anything they replied, "All we took were the photographs." In both instances, the first item these people mentioned were their photographs. Objects without any great financial value, but with tremendous personal value.

Our photographs contain our memories and our legacy, and they connect us to our family and friends. Even if they are cracked, yellowed, or damaged, we don't throw them away. No matter how tattered or faded a photograph is, it still helps us remember and learn about the past. The combination of image, emotion, and memory fascinates me. With the addition of one component to this mixture—Photoshop—you can make faded colors rich again, remove damage, and clean up mold, making the images as clear and crisp as the day they were taken. With the skilled use of Adobe Photoshop as presented in this book, you can fight the ravages of time and, more importantly, share the memories with your family and friends.

I started working with an early version of Photoshop 1.0 in 1989, and since 1992 have been teaching digital imaging at workshops and schools around the world.

My students always surprise me with questions, challenges, and examples of taking what I've taught them and going much further than I imagined possible. Take a look at what Sean Melnick, a recent graduate of the School of VISUAL ARTS in New York City, started with **figure 1** and then what he created. **Figure 2** shows Sean's passion and perseverance to bring the individual pieces together with the careful use of layers, adjustment layers, and cloning. For Sean, more important than the actual image was the moment he showed the final print to his grandparents—their eyes lit up as they remembered everyone in the picture. Our photographs are our legacy.

figure 1

figure 2

As you can see by paging through the book, not all the pictures and examples featured in this book are historical. Many of the examples are contemporary—images that were captured with the latest digital cameras or came from leading photo studios. As a photographer, I always try to get the picture right before hitting the shutter, rather than using Photoshop as an afterthought to rescue a bad photograph. In other words, if I can create a better picture by fixing the lighting, hiring a professional makeup artist, or changing camera lenses or position, I'll always opt to make the extra effort to get the picture right in front of the lens.

THE IMPORTANCE OF LEARNING

A few years ago I decided to start playing golf. I'm athletic, coordinated, love being outside, and very dedicated after I put my mind to a challenge. I figured that with a few golf lessons, I would be able to enjoy an idyllic, relaxing round of golf with my husband John, who has been playing golf for thirty years. Little did I know how much went into a good golf swing—position of the feet, weight distribution, keeping your eye on the ball, hands relaxed yet firm, position of the club head, and that's all before you even start a back swing. It took two years and a lot of golf balls (and some significant frustration) before I even hit the ball solidly. One day, we were playing and I launched the ball with a 7 wood down the fairway and onto the green. I was stunned and remember thinking, "Wow! That's what a good golf swing feels like." Needless to say, I was hooked and, although I still hit plenty of bad shots, it's the good ones that keep me going out and practicing more.

Time and practice—you can't be good at a sport, cook a gourmet meal, or restore an image without it. There will be frustration, anger, and muttering, generally along the lines of "Why do I even bother… this looks terrible… I might as well just stop right now…." Please turn off that noisy, no-good critic (that we all have in our heads). Shut the voice down and keep practicing—just as you learned to master a hobby, sport, or language, you'll learn to master and enjoy Photoshop restoration and retouching.

© Melnick family archive

IS THIS BOOK RIGHT FOR YOU?

This book is right for you if you love images or work with photographs as a dedicated amateur or fulltime professional. You may be a historian, photographer, librarian, teacher, multimedia artist, designer, artist, or the grandmother who wants to share the best photos with the rest of the family. This book addresses salvaging historical images and righting the contemporary images that have gone wrong—the missed exposures, the poor color balance, the busy and distracting background, or the inevitable wrinkle, pimple, or extra pounds that are just driving you crazy every time you look at that photo.

This book is not for you if you don't have the time, curiosity, and patience to read through the examples, try them out and then—just as I push my students—take the techniques further by applying them to your own images.

You have three ways to learn the techniques in this book:

- By reading the examples and looking at the images.
- By downloading the images from the book's Web site, www.digitalretouch.org, and with the book in hand, recreating my steps.
- By taking the techniques shown here and applying them to your own images. As you work, you'll need to adjust some of the tool or filter settings to achieve optimal results. It is exactly at that moment, when you are working with your own images, that you're really learning how to restore and retouch images.

This is not an introductory book. To get the most out of it you should be comfortable with the fundamentals of Photoshop, know where the tools are and what they do, and common tasks, such as how to activate a layer or save a selection. As mentioned, I've been working with Photoshop for over ten years, and yet I still learned a lot by writing this book. In fact, I tried to write a book that I would want to buy or that would interest the many intermediate and advanced Photoshop users that are looking for in-depth and challenging learning materials.

In addition, you'll see that I did all of my work and took my screen captures on a Macintosh. If you're a Windows user, don't let that deter you from the book. Photoshop is, for all accounts and purposes, identical on the Macintosh and Windows platforms. All of the features discussed in the book are available on both platforms, and the interface is identical. When offering keyboard shortcuts, I give you both Macintosh and Windows commands, so you can use whichever is appropriate (there's more on this in Chapter 1, "The Tools and Essential Navigation").

THE STRUCTURE OF THE BOOK AND THE WEB SITE

This book is divided into three primary areas:

1. Working with Tone, Contrast, Exposure, and Color
2. Removing Dust and Mold and Repairing Damage
3. Professional Portrait and Fashion Retouching

In fact, the book is structured in the same way you should work with your images, starting with a brief overview of Photoshop essentials, file organization, and the tools a retoucher needs. It then works through tonal and color correction (the first things to focus on when retouching an image), followed by chapters on dust and damage removal, adding creative effects, doing portrait retouching, and the techniques professional retouchers use in the fashion and glamour business.

Each chapter starts with a brief overview of what will be covered in the chapter. I always start with a straightforward example that leads to more advanced examples. You may be tempted to jump to the more advanced sections right away, but I don't recommend it. My teaching and chapter structure serves the purpose of building up the tools and techniques in which the introductory examples serve as the foundation for the advanced examples. Similarly, the chapters on tonal and color correction serve as the foundation for the portrait and glamour retouching chapters. Do I expect you to sit down right now in the bookstore and read the book from cover to cover? Of course not—you should really pay for it first! Rather, take the book home, page through the chapters so you can see how the book and retouching workflow is structured, and then work your way through the book.

Rather than including a CD with the book, I opted to build a small supplemental Web site where you can download many of the tutorial images featured in the book. Please visit www.digitalretouch.org to download images, view the reader gallery, follow links to additional retouching resources, and to contact me. Each chapter (except for Chapter 1) has four to twelve images that you can download. I've included a low-resolution version that will expand to approximately 1MB and a higher-resolution version that will open to approximately 2-4MB. Use the low-resolution version if you are on a slower connection, are less patient, or aren't 100% sure you want to work though the exercise. Use the higher-resolution file if you are on a faster connection or are more patient than I am.

Note

The images on the book's companion Web site are for your personal use and should not be distributed by any other means.

Most of the images in the book originated from my or my husband's own image and photography collection. Numerous professional retouchers, teachers, and photographers have generously shared many of their images and examples, many of which are posted on the Web site. Throughout the book I did use some images from stock CD collections, and I would be breaking the fineprint contract that came with the CD collections if I posted them on the Web. Call me old-fashioned, but I respect International and US copyright laws—the copyright of all images remains with the originator, as noted throughout the book. Please do not email the publisher or me to request images that are not posted. I will not be able to send them to you. You really don't want me to go to jail do you?

In the cases where I didn't have permission to post specific images on the book's Web site, you can use similar images from your own photo albums or collections to follow along. Although you won't have the exact image I am using in the book, the problems being corrected are so universal that I am sure you'll be able to learn the techniques by working with similar images. After all, I'm sure you will be branching out to your own problem files sooner rather than later.

I would love to hear from you. Please email your comments about the book and Web site to me at katrin@digitalretouch.org. As mentioned, I am planning to build a reader's gallery on the Web site. Show me how you've taken the techniques in these pages and gone further with them. If you send me before-and-after files (please keep them small, 1MB in total) of the retouched image, I'll post it in the reader's gallery. Be sure to include information about how I can contact you; great examples of restoration and retouching may be fodder for the next edition of the book.

WHAT IS NOT COVERED IN THIS BOOK

Although this book was an ambitious project from the very start, there is a lot of Photoshop that I do not cover. I concentrated on the latest version of Photoshop 6.0. In case you are still working with versions 4.0, 5.0, or 5.5, you will still learn a lot from this book, because the most important tools for retouching—layers, Adjustment Layers, and Blending Modes—all go back that far. (And this book probably will still be useful long after the next release of Photoshop.) I do not work for Adobe but can highly recommend the upgrade to 6.0. I do not address Photoshop basics, I don't go down the toolbar, which would just bore you to death, and I don't cover complex selections or masking. I concentrated on image restoration and retouching and, with these words, I wish you a lot of fun as you bring back image memories and take your contemporary photographs to a higher level.

Best regards,

Katrin Eismann
katrin@digitalretouch.org
The Big Apple, New York City
01.01.01

Photoshop for Retouching

I

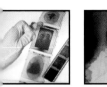

1

PHOTOSHOP ESSENTIALS

Put three people in a room, give them each a computer and 30 minutes, and I bet that they'll each come up with at least three different ways to solve the same Photoshop problem. The variety of approaches that Photoshop allows can at times be frustrating or invigorating, depending on how much you like to explore and experiment. So what separates a casual Photoshop user from a power user? In most cases it's experience and the ability to visualize the final outcome of the project. To power users, Photoshop is transparent—the interface practically disappears as they work to create the retouched or restored image. For novices, Photoshop can be so overwhelming that they get lost in finding tools, commands, and controls and, although they might get the image done, it will have taken them a lot longer than necessary.

Learning to move quickly through Photoshop helps you be a better retoucher because you will be able to concentrate on the image and not the software. In this chapter, you learn to be more efficient with Photoshop and, in the same vein, be a better Photoshop retoucher by

- Working with quick keys
- Using file navigation
- Discovering the importance of layers
- Developing file organization and workflow methods

Restoration and retouching is more than being a fast mouse clicker. A good retoucher understands that the images he is working with are very important to the client, a family member, or the person in the picture. Before you start a retouching project, take a moment to consider that the pixels represent real people and real events—they're more than a collection of dark and light specs of digital information. It's your job to bring back memories from faded, cracked, and damaged originals. This is a weighty responsibility, and keeping that in mind throughout the retouching process helps you see the image with empathy and care.

WORKING WITH QUICK KEYS

Photoshop was developed from the ground up to be used with two hands—one on the keyboard and one on the mouse. The time saved by using keyboard equivalents to access a tool or command and to navigate through a file will make you a more efficient retoucher. Additionally, using the keyboard rather the mouse reduces the total number of repetitive mouse clicks that can add up to the pain, aggravation, and lost productivity of repetitive-motion injury.

Knowing the keyboard commands to access tools, change settings, and control palettes enables you to concentrate on the image and be a better retoucher. For example, imagine you're retouching a file and need to access the Clone Stamp tool, increase the brush size, and change the brush opacity to 40%. The manual method would involve selecting the Clone Stamp tool, dragging to the brush size required, highlighting the Opacity value, and typing in 40. The command-key method entails tapping the letter S, tapping the right bracket to increase the brush size, and typing in the desired opacity with either the numerals on the top of your keyboard or on the extended keypad to the right of your keyboard. It's a much faster way to get the same results! Learning the essential key commands enables you to concentrate on the image rather than getting distracted by the tool settings.

Photoshop offers numerous methods to navigate through a file and a plethora of documented and undocumented quick keys. Do you need to know them all? Of course not. Should you learn how to activate the tools that you'll be using everyday?

Absolutely. If you use a Photoshop tool or command three or more times a day, learning its quick key both saves time and makes sense. Additionally, if you access a filter or sequence of commands more than three times a day, learning how to build a command key or action is also a good idea.

Tip

Look inside the box that Photoshop came in—the folded reference card has the most important shortcuts and key commands you'll ever need.

Photoshop is, for all accounts and purposes, identical on both the Macintosh and Windows platforms. Throughout the text I used both commands, beginning with the Macintosh command in parenthesis followed with the PC command in brackets. For example, undoing the last step would read (Cmd + Z) [Ctrl + Z]. In general, the Macintosh Cmd key is used where the PC Ctrl key would be, and you'll find that the Mac Option key maps to Alt. Control is used on the Mac where the right mouse button is used on Windows.

The following section covers the primary navigational shortcuts and command keys used throughout this book that will help you be a more efficient retoucher. More than 600 useful and undocumented Photoshop key commands and quick keys are cataloged in *Photoshop 6 Power Shortcuts* by Michael Ninness.

Learning the most useful Photoshop quick keys and navigation techniques takes fifteen minutes. To get the most out of the time, go to your computer, launch Photoshop, and open an at least 10Mb file. The reason I suggest practicing with a 10Mb file is that you will really appreciate the ease of navigation, discussed later, when you are working with an image that is larger than your monitor can display.

The Toolbar

Tapping the appropriate letter on the keyboard activates a specific tool in the Photoshop toolbar. In most cases, the first letter of the tool's name is the letter to tap, such as B for Brush and M for the Marquee tool. Of course, there are exceptions to the first letter rule, such as J for Airbrush and V for the Move tool. **Figure 1.1** spells out all of the letter commands to access each tool.

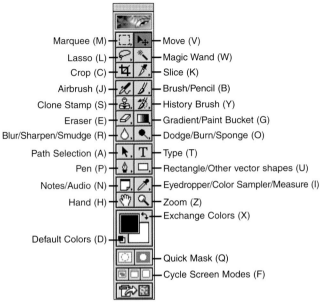

Marquee (M) — Move (V)
Lasso (L) — Magic Wand (W)
Crop (C) — Slice (K)
Airbrush (J) — Brush/Pencil (B)
Clone Stamp (S) — History Brush (Y)
Eraser (E) — Gradient/Paint Bucket (G)
Blur/Sharpen/Smudge (R) — Dodge/Burn/Sponge (O)
Path Selection (A) — Type (T)
Pen (P) — Rectangle/Other vector shapes (U)
Notes/Audio (N) — Eyedropper/Color Sampler/Measure (I)
Hand (H) — Zoom (Z)
— Exchange Colors (X)
Default Colors (D) —
— Quick Mask (Q)
— Cycle Screen Modes (F)

figure 1.1

The Photoshop toolbar with keyboard commands.

 Tip

To see and learn the tool tips, choose Edit > Preferences > General and turn on Show Tool Tips. As you hold the mouse over a tool, Photoshop shows the name and command key as shown in **figure 1.2**.

figure 1.2

Use the Tool tips to learn the most important keyboard quick keys.

As you can see in **figure 1.3**, some tools are nested. For example, the Dodge, Burn, and Sponge tools all share one spot on the toolbar. You can cycle through the tools by holding the Shift key as you press the key until you reach the desired tool. **Table 1.1** lists all the shortcuts you'll need.

figure 1.3

The Dodge, Burn, and Sponge tool are nested within one another.

If you would rather just press the key (without needing the Shift modifier) to cycle through a nested tool, select Edit > Preferences > General and uncheck Use Shift Key for Tool Switch.

table 1.1
Nested Retouching Tools

Marquee	Shift + M cycles between the Rectangular and Elliptical Marquee tools.
Lasso	Shift + L cycles through Lasso, Polygon, and Magnetic Lasso tools.
Brush and Pencil	Shift + B switches between the Brush and the Pencil tools.
Clone Stamp	Shift + S cycles through the Clone Stamp and Pattern Stamp tools.
History Brush	Shift + Y cycles through History and Art History Brush tools.
Gradient and Paint Bucket	Shift + G cycles between the Gradient Blend tool and the Paint Bucket tool.
Tonal tools	Shift + O cycles through the Dodge, Burn, and Sponge tools.
Sharpening tools	Shift + R cycles through the Sharpen, Blur, and Smudge tools.
Path Selection	Shift + A cycles through the Path Component Selection and the Direct Selection tools.
Pen tool	Shift + P cycles through the Pen and Freeform Pen tool.
Annotation	Shift + N switches between note or voice annotation.
Eyedropper and Measure	Shift + I cycles through the Eyedropper, Color Sampler, and Measure tools.

The Options Bar

When using any painting tool, change the opacity by simply typing in the required value—you don't need to highlight the opacity box. Just type the numbers, and the brush opacity or pressure will change. Use the left- and right-bracket keys to decrease and increase brush sizes.

Photoshop 5.0 and 5.5 had the Tool Options palette, which showed the various settings and controls for the tool you currently had selected. In Photoshop 6.0, these options (and many other features) are now housed in the Options bar. Position the Options bar at the top or bottom of your monitor and, to keep down monitor clutter, dock the palettes you use most often into the Palette Well, as shown in **figure 1.4**.

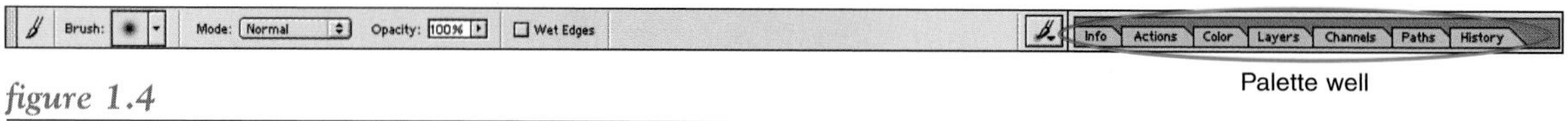

figure 1.4

Palette well

The Options bar reflects the controls of the active tool and includes the Palette Well where you can place often used palettes.

The Palettes and Function Keys

Adobe has assigned function keys to the most important palettes (listed in table 1.2). The function keys are the topmost row of buttons on your keyboard and they begin with the letter *F*; hence the nickname *f* keys. You can use them to hide and reveal palettes. I keep my palettes either on a second monitor or, when working on a laptop or single monitor system, I'll position the palettes to be as out of the way as possible. If the palettes are blocking the image, press Tab to hide all the palettes and the toolbar. Press Tab again to reveal all the palettes and toolbar, or press *f* keys to reveal individual palettes. Press Shift-Tab to hide the palettes, while keeping the toolbar visible.

table 1.2
f Keys to Show and Hide Palettes

Color palette	F6
Layer Palette	F7
Info palette	F8
Actions palette	F9

Not every palette has a function key. Docking palettes that don't have a function key together with palettes that do will give you access to every palette quickly. For example, dock the History and Actions palette together and then use F9 to open the Action palette and click the History palette tab to bring it to the forefront.

Taking a few moments to arrange the palettes and learn the function keys is similar to setting up your work space in a traditional studio—brushes go over here and camera equipment goes over there. Position the palettes in relationship to how often you use them, with the more important ones— Layers, Channels, and Info—close at hand.

Palette Tips

When working with a single monitor workstation, have as few palettes open as possible.

Decide on an ideal palette placement for your workflow. This saves time when hiding and showing palettes, because they will reappear exactly where you positioned them.

Press the Tab key to hide and show all palettes and the Toolbar at once.

Shift + Tab hides all palettes while keeping the Toolbar on screen.

Pull unnecessary nested palettes out of their groups and close them. For example, the Navigation palette is redundant if you use the navigational tips discussed later in this chapter. By separating and closing it, it won't pop up with the other docked palettes.

In case you close a palette and you forget the *f* key to make it appear again, use the Window menu to select the palette you want to see.

Context-Sensitive Menus

Every Photoshop tool includes context-sensitive menus that you access by (Control + clicking) [right-mouse clicking] directly on the image. These menus give you tremendous control over each tool. Rather than going through the menu of every tool in this book, I suggest you open an image and go through the context-sensitive menus of each tool. In exchange for that, I'll review the most important context menus you should be aware of. For some tools, the context-sensitive menu will change depending on the state of the tool or file at the time. For example, notice the difference of the context-sensitive menu for any selection tool with and without an active selection (as shown in **figures 1.5** and **1.6** respectively) and after using a filter (as seen in **figure 1.7**).

figure 1.5

Context-sensitive menu for any selection tool without an active selection.

figure 1.6

Context-sensitive menu for any selection tool with an active selection.

figure 1.7

Context-sensitive menu for any selection tool after applying a filter.

Brush Context and Controls

While using any painting tool (Airbrush, Clone Stamp, Brush, Pencil, History Brush, or Gradient tool), pressing (Shift + Control + click) [Shift + right click] menu contains options to edit the brush and to change the brush's Blending Mode (see **figure 1.8**). Use (Control + click) [right click] with any brush to make the Brush palette appear, as shown in **figure 1.9**.

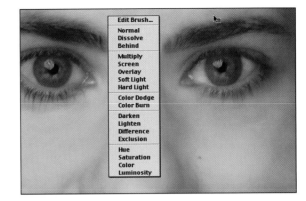

figure 1.8

The context-sensitive menu for all painting tools enables you to edit brushes and change blend modes.

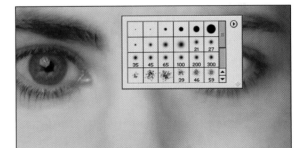

figure 1.9

Additional access to edit brushes on-the-fly.

To change brush size

- Left bracket decreases brush size while maintaining hardness and spacing settings.
- Right bracket increases brush size while maintaining hardness and spacing settings.
- Shift + left bracket decreases brush hardness while maintaining size and spacing.
- Shift + right bracket increases brush hardness while maintaining size and spacing.

Toning Tools Context-Sensitive Menus

The Dodge and Burn tools' context-sensitive menu enables you to change the tonal range affected (see **figure 1.10**), and the Sponge tool's context menu accesses the saturate/desaturate mode very quickly.

Magnifying Tools Context Menus

In addition to the techniques described below, use the context-sensitive menu of the Zoom tool to see quickly the image at useful views (see **figure 1.11**).

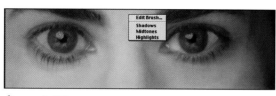

figure 1.10

The context-sensitive menu of the Dodge and Burn tools.

figure 1.11

Using the context-sensitive menu of the Zoom tool is one way to quickly zoom in and out of a file.

QUICK IMAGE NAVIGATION

Moving through a file and zooming in and out quickly and often is an essential skill for an efficient retoucher. Critical retouching is done at a 100% or 200% view (as shown in **figure 1.12**), which means that you are seeing only a small part of the entire file. This requires that you can easily zoom in and out of a file to see how the retouched area is blending in with the entire image.

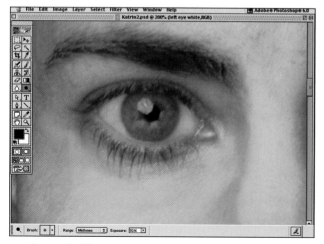

figure 1.12

Most critical retouching is done at 100% or 200% zoom, which allows you to see only a small portion of the file at one time.

Use any one of the following techniques to navigate through a file:

To go to 100% view to see the full resolution of the file

- Double-click on the Zoom tool (magnifying glass).
- (Cmd + Option + 0) [Ctrl + Alt + 0] That's a zero, not an oh.
- (Space + Ctrl + click) [Space + Right mouse click] and drag down to Actual Pixels.

To see the entire image
- Double-click the Hand tool.
- (Cmd + 0) [Ctrl + 0] That's a zero, not an oh.
- (Space + Ctl + click) [Space + Right mouse click] and drag down to Fit on Screen.

To zoom in on a specific area
- (Command + Space) [Ctrl + Space] and drag over the area you want to zoom into.

To pan through an image
- On both Macintosh and PC, holding down the Space bar converts any tool (except the Type tool, if you are actively entering text) into the Hand tool, allowing you to pan through an image. This works only if the image is larger than your monitor can display.

You can review an image that will not fit entirely on your monitor using only the keyboard. Starting in the upper-left corner, these shortcuts will adjust the viewing area one screen width or height at a time:

- Tap the Home key to jump to the upper-left corner.
- Tap the Page down to move down one monitor full.
- Tap the Page up to move up one monitor full.
- Tap (Cmd + page down) [Ctrl + page down] to move one monitor full to the right.
- Tap (Cmd + page up) [Ctrl + page up] to move one monitor full to the left.

The Workspace View

Your monitor is your worktable—keeping it organized and neat will pay off with time saved and frustration reduced. Learning to use every bit of your monitor real estate can make a small monitor feel a lot larger than it really is and make a large monitor feel even more expansive.

- Take advantage of your monitor real estate by working in either Full Screen Mode with Menu Bar or Full Screen Mode. Tap the (F) letter key to cycle through the viewing modes.

- Consider working with a second monitor. Keep all of your tools and palettes on the secondary monitor and dedicate the primary monitor to images. Since you'll be using this monitor for the palettes and not for making critical color or tonal adjustments, you might be able to get away with a lower-quality or used monitor.

- When cleaning up files, work at 100% or 200% view to see every pixel.

- Create a second view, as shown in **figure 1.13**. Select View > New View and position this second view so that you can reference it as you retouch. This is incredibly useful when retouching a person's face, as you can zoom in on an image detail and simultaneously keep an eye on how retouching the details is impacting the overall image.

If all these navigational tips are starting to get jumbled, remember, you don't need to sit down and memorize them all at once. Just try to learn the ones you use all the time—including the most often-used tools—also, learn how to hide and show palettes, and learn a few navigational tips and you'll be working like a power user in no time at all.

LEARNING THE IMPORTANCE OF LAYERS

With the introduction of layers in Photoshop 3.0, Adobe truly entered the world of professional image enhancement. For a retoucher, layers are the most important feature in Photoshop, and throughout this book you will be working with eight different types of layers:

- Background Layer: This is your original data and should be treated as carefully as your original prints or film. Never, ever retouch directly on the Background layer. It should remain as pristine as the day you scanned it. Do I sound adamant about this? You bet. The Background layer is your reference, your guide, your before and after. Do not touch it. To maintain the Background layer's integrity, either duplicate it or do a Save As to backup the original file before undertaking any color correction, retouching, or restoration.

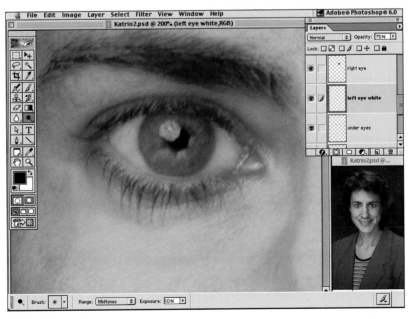

figure 1.13

A second view allows you to monitor how the retouching is impacting the overall image.

- Duplicate Layers: Duplicating any layer by dragging the layer to the New Layer icon creates an exact copy, in perfect registration, on which you can work and retouch without affecting the original data. Use the quick keys (Command + J) [Control + J] to quickly duplicate a layer.

- Copied Layers: Many times you don't want or need to duplicate the entire Background layer because you just need a part of a layer to work on. In those cases, select the part of the image you want to work on and select Layer > New > Layer via Copy. Photoshop will copy and paste the selection onto its own layer and keep the newly created layer information in perfect registration with the original data.

- Merged Layers: As the number of layers increases, it is often easier to work on a Work in Progress layer, which is a flattened layer created with all visible layers you have been retouching.

- Adjustment Layers: Introduced with Photoshop 4.0, adjustment layers enable you to apply global and selective tonal and color corrections. We'll be using them extensively in Chapters 5, 6, and 7 to do tonal, exposure, and color corrections.

- Empty Layers: Photoshop represents empty layers with a grid pattern. Think of these empty layers as a clear sheet of acetate on which you paint and clone without affecting the pixel data of the layers underneath.

- Neutral Layers: Photoshop doesn't show the blending mode neutral colors of white, gray, or black when used in combination with specific layer Blending Modes. We'll be using neutral layers to apply subtle and dramatic tonal improvements throughout the retouching process.

- Fill layers: New to Photoshop 6.0, fill layers enable you to add solid, gradient, or patterned fills as a separate layer. The solid color fill layer is useful when coloring and toning an image.

The best aspect of layers is that they all (with the exception of the Background layer) support Layer Masks, Blending Modes, opacity changes, and Advanced Blending Options—features you'll be working with throughout the book to retouch and restore images.

Layer Naming and Navigation

Layers enable you to build up a retouch. In many cases, a retouching project can take five, ten, twenty, or more layers to finish. Relying on the generic Photoshop name such as *Layer 1* or *Layer 1 copy* to identify layers is a sure way to be confused and frustrated as you try to find the layer you need to work on. It only takes a split second, but naming your layers as you build up a retouch enables you to identify and activate the correct layer quickly and easily. Look at the difference between the two layer stacks in **figure 1.14**. On the left you see the generically named layers, and on the right the layers have useful names, making it much easier to use and navigate through. Additionally, the context-sensitive menu of the Move tool gives you instant access to all the layers that have pixel information at the point where your mouse is at the moment. As seen in **figure 1.15**, (Control + clicking) [Right mouse clicking] shows all layer names in the file—even if the Layers palette is not open at the time.

In Photoshop 6.0, select Layers Properties from the Layers palette menu to name layers. Or you can (Control + click) [Conrol + click] the name of the layer to access the Layer Properties dialog box.

Working with Layer Sets

In Photoshop 6.0, you can create up to a total of 8,000 layers and layer effects, something that requires a way to organize and manage layers more efficiently. Layer sets, shown in **figure 1.16**, are folders in which you can place related layers. The folders can be expanded or collapsed, the layers can be moved around within the set, and layer sets can be moved around within the layer stack.

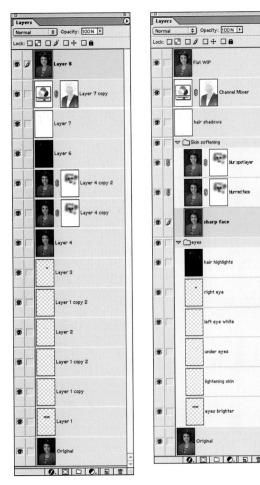

figure 1.14

The generic layer names in the palette on the left won't help you find your way through a complex retouch, but the ones on the right prove that naming your layers is a good habit to get into.

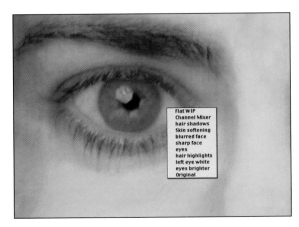

figure 1.15

The context sensitive menu of the Move tool shows you the layers that have pixel information at the cursor location.

figure 1.16

The many layers you create when retouching become much more manageable when they are grouped as layer sets.

There are two ways to create a layer set:

• Select New Layer Set from the Layers palette menu, name the layer set, and then drag the desired layers into the set.

• Link all the layers you would like in a layer set, and then select New Set from Linked in the Layers palette menu. All the linked layers will be placed into the newly created layer set.

There are three ways to delete a layer set:

• Drag the layer set to the trash can on the Layers palette to delete the entire layer set without showing a warning dialog box.

• Select Delete Layer Set from the Layers palette menu. The dialog box in **figure 1.17** then gives you choices to cancel the operation, delete the set, or to delete the set and the set's contents.

• (Cmd + drag) [Ctrl + drag] the layer set to the trash can to delete the layer set folder without deleting the contents of the layer set. The layers in the set remain in the document in the order they appeared in the set.

figure 1.17

You can delete the set (the folder) or the set and the contents.

You can color-code layers to quickly identify layer relationships and lock layers to prevent accidental edits to image data, transparency settings, and layer position. All in all, organizing, naming, or color-coding layers and layer sets takes only a moment but can save you a lot of time in hunting and searching for the layer you want to work on.

Creating and using consistent layers and layer set naming conventions is imperative to create an efficient workflow. If you work with a partner, on a team, or are part of a production workflow, you'll especially need to use layer names. Imagine you're working on a complicated retouching project and for some reason you can't come to work to finish the retouch. If the layers were well named, someone else on your team would be able to open the file, find the layers that need additional work, and finish the project. However, if the layers are all over the place, not named, or not in layer sets, it will take a while to even figure out where to begin. In the worst case scenario, a very important layer might be ruined or deleted. Enough said—name your layers!

Flattening and Discarding Layers

I'm a conservative Photoshop retoucher with a large hard drive. I don't throw away layers unless I know that they are absolutely wrong or unnecessary. Keep all production layers with a file because you'll never know if a mask or tidbit of information from a layer will be useful later on in the project. By clicking on the eyeball in the view column on the left side of the Layers palette, you can turn off a layer whenever you like. The only time I flatten an image is as the very last step before sending a file to the printer or taking a file into a page layout program.

FILE ORGANIZATION AND WORKFLOW ISSUES

Taking a few moments to organize your folders and files helps you to work more efficiently, saves time searching for files and projects, and also reduces the likelihood of deleting important files. For each project I work on, I create a Master Folder, and in that folder I make three folders—Scans, WIP, and Finals (see **figure 1.18**). As you can imagine, the scans go into the scan folder and those originals are never worked on. The Work-in-Progress folder contains all the layered files and versions of the retouch in progress. The third folder is where only flattened, sized, and sharpened files go. The finals folder only contains one version of the final file and not files that are obviously not done, such as "retouch_3_little_better_like_it_more_I_think_maybe_4b.tif."

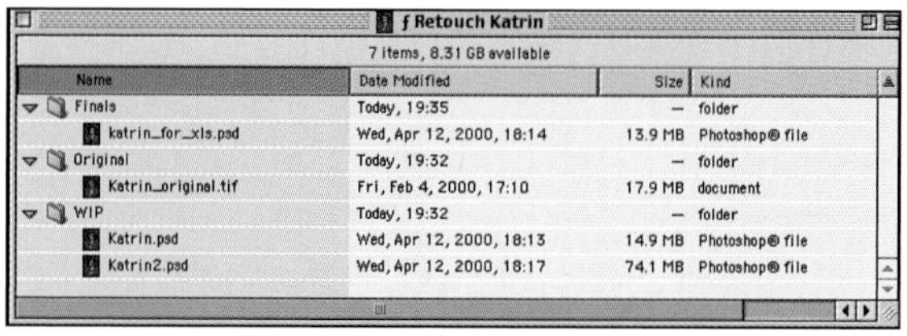

figure 1.18

Keep your working files organized as seen here.

N o t e

Although I work in a Macintosh working environment, I do exchange files with printers and clients that use PCs, which requires that I take those systems into account. I make it a habit of keeping filenames as short as possible, without spaces, and always have Photoshop add the three-letter file extension to the file when saving. Since you can tell Photoshop to add the extension automatically, there isn't any reason for Macintosh users not to use it. The PC system adds the file extension without this Preferences setting, so PC users don't need to worry about this detail.

The Retouching Workflow

Each retouching project is unique, requiring a sensitive eye and sympathetic mouse. Of course, each retoucher is just as unique, and over time you will devise your own retouching workflow.

The primary steps in my retouching workflow are

1. **Assess the original:** Study the original and identify the problems or areas that need enhancement, repair, or replacement. Never lift the mouse without first taking a few minutes to identify the character of either the image or the person in the photograph.

2. **Input:** Scan the original or have the original scanned by a professional service bureau. For additional information on image scanning, go to www.digitalretouch.org and download ch1_ScanningResolution.pdf.

3. **Develop a strategy:** Make a plan to outline the steps to do the retouch. Start with the big problems—exposure, color, and contrast—and then move onto repairing problems, such as dust, mold, and scratches, or removing lines, wrinkles, or blemishes. Make notes on paper or on the file, as described in Chapter 10, "Glamour and Fashion Retouching." The structure of this book reflects my retouching strategy—it starts with the big problems and then moves into ever-finer nuances of restoration and retouching.

4. **Retouch:** Do the planned retouch. As mentioned, work on a duplicate of the original scan and use layers to build up your work.

5. **Output and deliver:** Make a print and deliver the file to the client.

6. **Archive:** Make a backup of all files involved in a project. Burning a CD is an inexpensive and reliable method to make back ups. I recommend burning two identical disks and storing them separately. Use an asset management program, such as Canto Cumulus or Extensis Portfolio, to organize your files and backups.

Tip

The invisible step 7 is to collect payment from the client in exchange for the completed work. Professional retoucher Wayne Palmer says, "I keep all originals until the client has paid for the job. That way I have something of value, which often motivates the client to pay more quickly."

The Retoucher's Workplace

Your retouching studio or work area is a place you'll be spending a lot of time, so it makes sense to invest the time and money to make it as comfortable and productive as possible. You do not need to remodel your home or build an addition; I'm just suggesting you consider a few improvements that can make your workplace a nicer and more efficient place to be.

Environment and Lighting

The retouching environment should be a quiet area away from distractions and foot traffic. Paint the walls a neutral gray and set up the lighting so that there aren't any reflections showing in the monitor. In **figure 1.19** you see a retouching work area that is built into a corner. The L-shaped configuration enables the retoucher to get a lot of work done without having to get up and down to make a scan or print. As you can see in **figure 1.20**, the daylight balanced GTI Graphic Technology lightbox (www.gtilite.com) and 5,000° Kelvin task lamp provides an area to study originals. To make the retouching area more focused, keep your bookkeeping, paperwork, and business phone on a separate desk.

figure 1.19

My retouching area, with both Macintosh and Windows equipment.

figure 1.20

Controlled lighting is essential when evaluating prints and slides.

Furniture

It always amazes me that people will spend thousands of dollars on computer equipment and then put it all on a cheap folding table that wobbles and bows in the center under all the weight. Even worse than those are some of the rickety chairs people sit in to work on the computer. After a few hours they wonder why their neck or lower back is so sore.

A good table without harsh edges, preferably one that angles down to where your arm rests on the table, and a chair with lower-back and arm support is essential retouching equipment. Just think of it; over the course of a few years you'll probably replace your computer a few times. How often do you need to replace a good working table and professional chair? Not very often, so making the investment in good furniture will pay off in health and well being for years to come.

Computer Equipment

Adobe has done a fantastic job in developing and releasing Photoshop for both Macintosh and Windows. So does it matter which computer platform you work on? Yes, it does. It should be the operating system that you're most comfortable with. My first computer experience was on a Macintosh, and since then I've come to appreciate its interface, operating system, and how easy it is to maintain. On the other hand, for every one person who prefers a Macintosh, I'm sure there are many, many people who swear by Windows. Photoshop is Photoshop is Photoshop. The few differences in Photoshop on a Mac or Windows are not going to alter the skills and techniques you need to know to do retouching magic.

Spending money on computer equipment requires research and planning. If you are about to build a workstation for Photoshop work, consider these variables:

- **CPU speed:** The higher the speed, the faster the computer. Be careful to watch the internal bus speed as well; the fastest CPU will not produce the performance increases you expect if the internal bus speed is slow.

- **RAM:** Photoshop is a RAM-hungry program, and the more you have allocated to Photoshop the better it will run. How much RAM do you need? As much as you can afford! Photoshop prefers 3–5 times the amount of RAM as the

image file size that you're working on. Take into account that often you'll have more than one image open and that as you add layers and use History, your RAM requirements will increase. So how much is enough? Take your average image size and multiply it times five, and then use that figure as your starting point. Adding more RAM to a machine is the easiest way to increase Photoshop performance.

Tip

You can see how efficiently your computer system is running by selecting Efficiency from the status bar found at the bottom of the document window. A reading of less than 100% tells you whether the functions you are performing are being done in RAM or are being written to the scratch disk.

- **Hard drive space:** This is a classic "bigger is better" proposition as long as you are choosing from the highest-performance drives. Photoshop wants fast hard drives to write data to when it runs out of RAM, so given the choice, go with speed over excessive gigabytes.

- **Scratch Disk:** The scratch disk is free hard drive space that Photoshop uses as temporary memory after it fills the RAM with image processing. The scratch disk needs to be at least twice the size of the RAM allocated to Photoshop and, more importantly, the space needs to be contiguous—that is, a scratch disk needs to be unfragmented and free of clutter. You can set up partitions on your drive to keep certain areas from being unfragmented, or you can use additional software to optimize your drive over time.

- **Monitor:** This is the visual component of your system, and no matter how fast or sexy your CPU is, if you are not happy with the image your monitor produces, you will not be happy with your workstation. A good monitor will outlast one to two upgrades of your CPU. The only limitation on the effective life of a monitor is the accuracy of the color it produces—something which is usually in the three to five year range.

If you choose a traditional CRT display, 17 inches is minimum and 21 inches is desired. Be careful to match the size of monitor to the amount of video RAM installed in your computer. You must work with millions of colors. Flat-panel LCD displays are much easier on your eyes but harder on your pocketbook. LCD's are smaller, more expensive, and have fewer color-calibration options.

You may consider using an older, smaller monitor as a secondary monitor on which you can keep palettes, dialog boxes, and color swatches, as seen in **figure 1.21**. Since you won't be doing any critical color correction or retouching on the second monitor, it can be less expensive or even a used piece of equipment.

figure 1.21

Using a second monitor (on the left) for Photoshop palettes keeps the primary monitor (on the right) uncluttered.

- **CD or DVD-ROM:** This is a usability and compatibility issue. In either case make sure you have a writeable, not a read-only, CD or DVD drive. In most instances, a writeable CD will be the most practical and usable media to make backups and create disks for your clients.
- **Pressure Sensitive Tablet:** An absolute must. A pressure sensitive tablet lets you work with a stylus, and it feels just like working with a pencil or brush. The harder you push, the thicker the stroke. Wacom is the leader in this technology, and their progressive improvements with these devices continue to be impressive. Wacom tablets range in size from miniature (4×5 inch) to huge (12×12 and larger). Most photographers work best with the smaller (6×8 inch tablets).

 T i p

To decrease reflections and distractions, build a monitor hood with black quarter-inch foam-core board, as shown in **figure 1.22**.

figure 1.22

A homemade monitor hood cuts down on reflections.

- **Back-up or Archive System:** Another critical issue as you take on more and more work. You should always back up your work as well as your system settings. This is a personal discipline that will make you feel very smart when you need the backup or very stupid if you did not back up your files. Temporary backup of your work is best accomplished to an external (or additional) hard drive. Firewire drives can be an extremely fast media for backups. Archiving is best done with removable media, such as CD-R's or Orb disks.
- **Scanners:** Look at the originals you will be scanning—if most of them are prints, then purchasing a good flatbed scanner makes sense. If the majority of your work stems from film originals, then a film scanner would be a better choice.

  It is difficult to make a general recommendation on scanners, as they vary from very poor to very good and cheap to expensive. Most retouchers have a mid-level flatbed scanner that is capable of scanning 11×17 inch prints. Look for a scanner that captures at least 10 bits of data and keep an eye on the optical resolution of the scanner—it should be 400 pixels per inch or higher.

〽️ *Alternative Input Options*

Having a service bureau or professional photo lab do scanning and printing for you can be a good alternative—especially when you're just starting out and need to stagger your equipment expenses. Working with a service bureau also gives you access to high-end equipment and services that you may need only once in a while.

- **Copy Work:** In many cases, antique originals are too large, too fragile, or three-dimensional to scan with a standard film or flatbed scanner. In **figure 1.23** you see medium-format and 35 mm black-and-white copy negatives that will be scanned in for the retoucher to clean up. An additional example in **figure 1.24** shows how Wayne Palmer needed to restore a series of antique photographic images that were mounted inside convex, glass bowl frames. Because the originals were three-dimensional, he couldn't just lay them on a flatbed scanner, so he made copy slides and scanned those.

- **Digital Cameras:** As digital cameras get better and cheaper, they are becoming a good input option. Numerous professional museums and historical collections are working with high-resolution scanning cameras, such as the Better Light 6000 or 8000, to digitize their sensitive artwork and archives. **Figures 1.26** and **1.27** show an example from the Dallas Museum of Fine Art, which is using the Better Light 6000 to catalog their fine art collection.

figure 1.26

Professional digital cameras offer incredible resolution and color fidelity when inputting artwork.

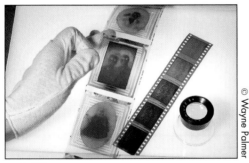

figure 1.23

Working with copy negatives can be a high-quality and cost-effective way to input sensitive originals.

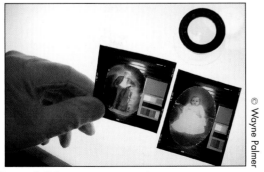

figure 1.24

It's the unique challenges that make the job interesting. The originals were mounted inside convex glass bowls.

figure 1.27

Close-up view of painting.

- **Printers:** The quality of inkjet printers is sky-rocketing while the costs are nosediving. Issues to consider before buying a printer include the size of the prints you need and how long the prints will last once you've printed them. Henry Wilhelm does extensive research on inkjets printers, and you can read the latest up-to-date information at www.wilhelm-research.com. Also visit www.inkjetmall.com and www.piezography.com to see the technology and inks that Jon Cone is developing to make absolutely stunning black and white prints that rival the traditional black-and-white, silver-gelatin darkroom print.

- **Additional Software:** As you do more and more retouching you may want to consider investing in software that can help you file, track, organize, and most importantly find your files (such as Canto Cumulus or Extensis Portfolio). Other purchases to consider include color management packages and production and special effects filters. For color management information visit Andrew Rodney's Web site at www.digitaldog.net and www.adobe.com.

BEFORE YOU BEGIN: A WORD TO THE WISE

Photoshop is a powerful tool that can either work wondrous magic or wreak havoc on image data. To ensure the best results in your restoration, always start with the best image data possible:

- Professional photographers always shoot more than one exposure of an image. Although the exposure difference may seem minimal—believe me, starting with a properly exposed piece of film or digital file will minimize many a headache.

- Start with the best digital data possible. Spend some time with your scanner interface to adjust the incoming data prior to scanning. If your scanner captures high-bit data, take advantage of it.

- Always work on a copy of your original scan.

- Use Adjustment Layers as described throughout the book. (You'll find a concentration of them in Chapters 2, 3, and 4.) Because you can double-click an Adjustment Layer to open it for further finessing, you have much more control and freedom with your tonal, contrast, and color changes.

CLOSING THOUGHTS

The one thing that no computer, book, or class can give you is the passion to practice, learn, and experiment with the skills and techniques it takes to be a good retoucher. Retouching is more than removing dust or covering up a wrinkle here or there. Retouching enables you to give someone cherished memories that have faded with the print. Retouching and restoration is a fantastic hobby and a challenging profession, so let's dive in and get to work.

II

Correcting Tone, Exposure, and Color

2

IMPROVING TONE AND CONTRAST

If you had a choice of walking into two unfamiliar rooms—one with the lights on and one without lights—which one would you choose? Unless you're a horror film aficionado, I imagine you'd choose the room with the lights. Working with the tonality and contrast of an image is similar to lighting a room to influence the atmosphere. Finessing the lights and darks of an image can transform a flat, uninteresting photograph into an image that pops off the page and is a pleasure to look at.

Adjusting an image's tone and contrast is a very important step to bringing an image back to life. Although it may not be as sexy or dramatic as replacing a person's head or removing a bothersome telephone pole, adjusting an image's tone and contrast with Levels and Curves is an essential skill.

In this chapter you'll work with grayscale images and learn to

- Evaluate an image's tonality
- Use Levels to improve highlights and shadows
- Use Curves to adjust image contrast
- Use Blending Modes to save time
- Share Adjustment Layers to save effort
- Apply selective tonal improvements to specific image areas

EVALUATING IMAGE TONE AND PREVISUALIZING THE FINAL IMAGE

Taking a moment to evaluate the tone of an image is tremendously important. In that moment, you should identify the tonal character of the image and imagine what the image should look like after you're finished editing it. This technique, called *pre-visualization*, was developed by the black-and-white photographers Ansel Adams and Edward Westen. By imagining the final image, you create a goal to work toward. For example, you open a dark photograph. Your previsualization would be, "I want the image to be lighter." Having a visual goal in mind helps you stay focused and not get distracted with the many options that Photoshop offers.

An image's tonal character can be light, dark, or average—also called *high-key*, *low-key*, or *medium-key*. Subject matter and how much light was in the original scene determine the tonal character of the image. If you're not sure which tonal-type image you're looking at, viewing the image histogram (Image > Histogram) or a levels histogram can be a helpful aid.

A *histogram* is a graphical representation of the pixels in the image, plotting them from black (on the left) to white (on the right). The greater the number of pixels in the image at a specific level, the taller the histogram is at that point. Knowing this, we can look at the histogram of any image and can tell where the majority of the pixel information falls.

As seen in **figure 2.1**, the high-key image histogram is bunched to the right because the image is primarily made up of lighter pixels. The low-key histogram falls more to the left because the image is primarily made up of darker pixels (see **figure 2.2**). The medium-key histogram is spread out, with most of the information falling in the middle (see **figure 2.3**). Of course, there are images that defy labels as illustrated in **figure 2.4**, in which the histogram's two clumps reveal an image with a split tonal personality.

When editing the tones, it is helpful to recognize which tonal type of image you're working with so that you don't apply extreme tonal corrections. For example, if you are working with a high-key image

in which the histogram is biased to the right, it wouldn't make any sense to try to force the tonal character of the image into the shadows (the left side of the histogram). By becoming familiar with what the tonal values represent—the shadows, midtones, or highlights of an image—you'll learn which areas of the histogram need to be adjusted to either lighten or darken the image.

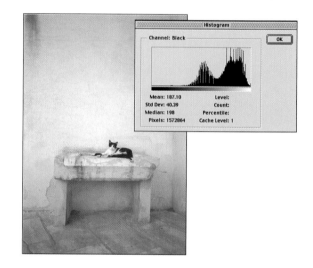

figure 2.1

Although the cat has dark markings, the majority of the image is very light, making this a high-key image.

figure 2.2

The dark chapel alcove is a good example of a low-key image because of all the dark tones in the shadows.

I'm often asked whether there is an ideal histogram shape, and the answer is "No." The image's tonality and character determine the ideal histogram shape. So don't worry if a histogram seems biased to one side or the other—just keep an eye on the histogram as an aid when editing the tonal values.

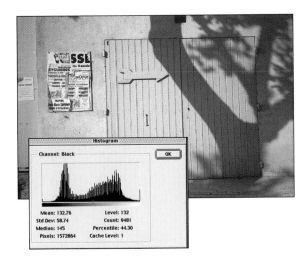

figure 2.3

This image has a full tonal range, from the dark shadows to the light areas of the poster.

figure 2.4

Photographed in the early evening, the lower part of the image is in shadow and the upper part is in sunlight. This image has both low- and medium-key areas.

Note

When working with grayscale images, the Image > Histogram and the Levels dialog box will be identical. When working with color images, the two dialog boxes will show different histograms. With color images the Image > Histogram is showing either the luminance or the individual R, G, B information, while the Levels dialog box is showing the RGB channel composite and the individual R, G, B channels.

Assessing Tone with the Measuring Tools

Evaluating the image on a calibrated monitor in a controlled viewing environment (see Chapter 1, "The Tools and Essential Navigation," for recommendations on setting up a studio) is essential when retouching. If you are unsure about your monitor or your visual assessment of an image, rely on the Eyedropper tool and the Info palette when working on a file to evaluate and measure image tone and to track changes as you work. The Eyedropper is a digital *densitometer* (fancy word for measuring tool) that you can move throughout the image to measure tonal and color values. It is a good habit to keep your eye on the Info palette while editing tone, contrast, and color.

Double-click the Eyedropper tool and set the sample option to 3 by 3 Average. In the Info palette, set the first read-out options to reflect the actual image data and the second read out either to suit your own personal preferences or to reflect your final output. For example, if you are going to use offset printing, your second readout would be CMYK. Photographers that are familiar with the Zone System prefer to use grayscale (K) to read the black tonal-output values.

Tracking Tonal Changes with Color Samplers

In Photoshop 5.0, Adobe introduced Color Samplers—four lockable probes you can tack onto an image, enabling you to keep your eye on specific areas during the image editing process. These four Color Samplers can be used to measure and track shadows, midtones, highlights, and a fourth tone of your choice. In **figure 2.5** I'm using three samplers to track image highlights, shadows, and midtones, but Color Samplers can do something even better. While you're adjusting tonal values, the Color Samplers together with the Info palette provide a before and after read out (see **figure 2.6**).

Color Samplers automatically disappear when you select other tools and reappear when the Eyedropper tool is activated again.

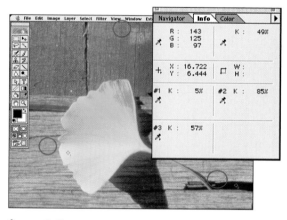

figure 2.5

Using the Color Samplers to track tonal values is a good habit to develop.

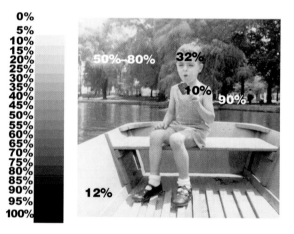

figure 2.6

The Color Sampler readout shows you the value before a tonal adjustment on the left and the value after the tonal adjustment on the right.

> **Note**
>
> To remove Color Samplers, (Option+click) [Alt+click] them with the Eyedropper tool or drag them off the image area. In Photoshop 6, you can click the clear button in the Options bar.

Using a Stepwedge

To help understand how specific tonalities will look on the print, I use a digital stepwedge, as seen on the left side of **figure 2.7**. A *stepwedge* is a target that goes from black to white in exact increments. Photographers and printers have been using them for years as an objective reference to see and measure how tones are captured, displayed, and reproduced.

The numbers on the little boy are the points at which I measured the values in the image. By keeping my eye on the Info palette set to grayscale, I can envision how dark or light the print will be. The highlight on the shoulder will print at 10% (a very light gray), his forehead will be a medium light gray, the trees in the background form a tonal frame around the boy at 50%–80% (medium to dark gray), and the dark tree trunks will have a 90% value.

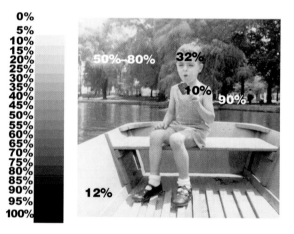

figure 2.7

Using a 21-step stepwedge to see how light and dark tonal values are helps visualize the tonality of a print.

 ch2_stepwedge.jpg

THE IMPORTANCE OF ADJUSTMENT LAYERS

Whether you work with Levels or Curves or any of the other supported image-adjustment features, I insist (yes—insist) that you use Adjustment Layers, one of the very best features in Photoshop. Introduced with Photoshop 4.0, Adjustment Layers are nondestructive layers that enable you to make, change, and refine tonal and color adjustments as many times as needed without altering the underlying layer's original data until you choose to apply them by flattening the image. Adjustment Layers apply the adjustment math on top of the pixel information—making them a fantastic tool to experiment, refine, redo, and learn from tonal and color adjustments.

Use Adjustment Layers when working with Levels, Curves, Color Balance, Hue/Saturation, Selective Color, Channel Mixer, Invert, Threshold, and Posterize. I don't recommend using Brightness/ Contrast because working with Levels and Curves offers better control and uses more sophisticated mathematics to apply the tonal changes. The benefits that working with Adjustment Layers offer include the following:

- They allow you to make tonal corrections without changing or degrading the source image data until you flatten the image.

- They support opacity. By lowering the Adjustment Layer's opacity, you reduce the strength of the tonal or color correction.

- They support Blending Modes. Blending Modes mathematically change how layers interact with the layer below them. They are a great aid for the retoucher to quickly improve image tonality.

- They are resolution independent, allowing you to drag and drop them between disparately sized and scaled images.

- They include layer masks with which you can hide and reveal a tonal correction with the use of any painting tool.

- They are especially helpful when making local tonal, contrast, and color adjustments to parts or smaller areas of an image.

- If you don't like an adjustment, just throw the offending Adjustment Layer into the Layers palette trash and start over.

MASTER TONALITY WITH LEVELS

Working with Levels enables you to influence three tonal areas of an image—the shadows, midtones, and highlights. You can use the sliders and the black-point or white-point eyedroppers to place or reset black or white points (see **figure 2.8**). The gray eyedropper is not available when working with black-and-white images and is used to find neutral points in color images. Often, you can make an image pop right off the page just by setting new white and black points and moving the midtone gamma slider (to the left to lighten or to the right to darken the image).

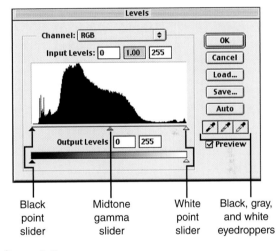

figure 2.8

The Levels Interface.

The most important Level controls to enhance image tone are

- Eyedroppers: Use the eyedroppers to set white and black points for both black-and-white and color images and the neutral gray eyedropper to define a neutral tone in color images.

- Sliders: Use the highlight and black sliders to remap the black and white points. You prompt Photoshop to remap the points by moving the relevant slider to the area of the image that contains the majority of the light or dark information.

- Auto button: Use the Auto button to prompt Photoshop to look at the file and set the lightest point to white and the darkest point to black. This method doesn't give you very fine-tuned results, and, for the most part, I don't recommend it.

To get the most out of Levels you will need to set the black and white target values before beginning. This tells Photoshop which values to use for black and white.

1. Open the Levels dialog box and double-click the white eyedropper. A Select white target color label appears above the color picker (see **figure 2.9**).

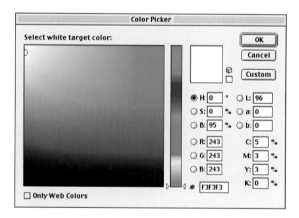

figure 2.9

Setting the white target color to 95% ensures that you retain a slight tonality in the whitest part of your image.

2. Use the HSB scale and set the white target color to 95% brightness, or RGB 243, 243, 243, and click OK.

3. Double-click the black eyedropper and set the black target color to 5% on the HSB scale, or 12, 12, 12 RGB, as seen in **figure 2.10**; click OK.

By setting the white target color to 95% you will hold slight tonality in your whitest whites, and the black target color 5% will hold shadow information in the darkest parts of the image.

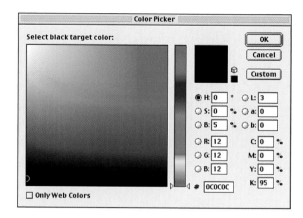

figure 2.10

The 5% black target color setting maintains shadow information in even the darkest areas of the image.

The generic 95% highlight and 5% shadow values are a safe place to start to avoid printing highlights without tone (paper white) or shadows that are so dark with ink that you can't see any detail in them.

IMPROVING IMAGE TONE WITH LEVELS

In the following exercises, we will use Levels to rescue muddy or low-contrast originals to transform them into black-and-white images that are a pleasure to look at because the tones extend across the entire dynamic range from black to white. These exercises will use single-channel monochrome (black-and-white) images. You can use the following techniques on color images only if you work on the composite channel (the primary histogram) and don't venture into tweaking the individual color channels. Color correction is best done by working with individual channels, as you'll learn in Chapter 4, "Working with Color."

Working with the Black and White Point Sliders

This original image, from 1906, is badly faded, as you can see in **figure 2.11**. The areas which should be white have gotten darker, which reduces the contrast and makes the print tonally flat and unattractive. After scanning it on a flatbed scanner, I used the following technique to darken the shadows and clean up the highlights. The corrected image (**figure 2.12**) has snap to it.

figure 2.11

figure 2.12

 ch2_faded.jpg

1. Add a Levels Adjustment Layer by clicking the Add Adjustment Layer icon at the bottom of the Layers palette and selecting Levels from the desired type from the menu.

2. Move the white point slider just to the inside of where the lightest image information begins, as shown on the right side of the histogram (see **figure 2.13**).

3. Move the black point slider until it falls just inside the area of darkest image information, as seen on the left side of the histogram in **figure 2.13**.

figure 2.13

Moving the white and black sliders to improve image contrast.

4. Click OK to accept these changes.

When working on your own images, after adjusting the tonal range with Levels, you may want to continue the retouching process.

Caution

Dragging the white or black sliders too far into the white or black area of the histogram may clip important information to pure white or pure black. Evaluate the image and the image histogram to see where the image information falls, and take care not to clip it with extreme moves of the Levels sliders.

Working with the Midtone Slider

The image in **figure 2.14** was taken in Shanghai in 1906. In addition to using the white and black point sliders, as in the preceding technique, here we'll also use the midtone gamma slider to lighten the image. When working with faded images, using the black and white point sliders to add contrast is a good starting point. If, after using them, the image is too dark, adjust the midtone slider to the left to lighten the image, or if the image is too light move the midtone slider to the right.

figure 2.14

figure 2.15

 ch2_faded2.jpg

1. Add a Levels Adjustment Layer.

2. Move the highlight slider to the area of lightest image information, as seen on the right side of the histogram in **figure 2.16**.

3. Move the black point slider to the area of the darkest image information, as seen on the left side of the histogram in **figure 2.16**.

4. Now, move the midtone gamma slider to the left to lighten the image. The amount you move the midtone gamma slider depends on the original image and how much lighter you want the image to be.

Note

There isn't a magic formula when adjusting tonal information. How much lighter or darker you make an image depends on the condition of the original image and your subjective interpretation of how the final image should look. In some cases, a darker image may better reflect the original scene, and in other cases, a tonally lighter approach may be more appropriate.

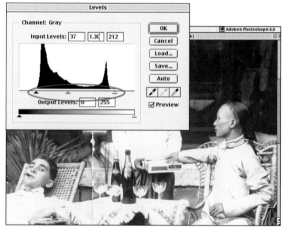

figure 2.16

After adjusting the white and black points, move the midtone gamma slider to the left to lighten the image.

Finding the White and Black Points

The image shown in **figure 2.17** is from the early 1900s. The little girl in the picture is my grandmother. The image is flat, faded, and its corners are missing. After using the black and white eyedroppers and the midtone gamma slider in Levels, I've added contrast and snap to the image, as seen in **figure 2.18**.

There are many instances where you might not be sure where the black or white point of an image is. You can use a temporary Threshold Adjustment Layer to find the white and black points and use Color Samplers to pinpoint those exact spots for reference while adjusting tone.

figure 2.17

figure 2.19

The Threshold Adjustment Layer splits the image into black or white.

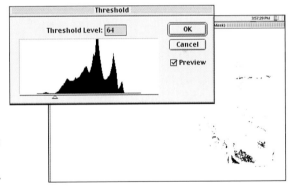

figure 2.20

To find the black point, drag the slider to the left side of the Threshold histogram.

figure 2.18

⊕▷⌐ **ch2_girl.jpg**

1. Add a Threshold Adjustment Layer.

2. The image is now reduced to two tones—black and white—as seen in **figure 2.19**.

3. To find the black point, move the slider all the way to the left and then slowly move it to the right until you see black clumps as seen in **figure 2.20**. Ignore the two bottom corners because they are just the lid of the scanner and are not true image information.

4. Click OK and use a Color Sampler to tack a marker right on top of the black clump.

5. To find the white point, double-click the Threshold Adjustment Layer icon on the layer palette to reopen the threshold layer. Move the slider all the way to the right. Then move the slider to the left until you see white clumps, as illustrated in **figure 2.21**. As with the black point location, ignore areas that are not part of the image, such as the edge of the print.

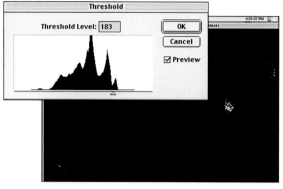

figure 2.21

To find the white point, drag the slider to the right side of the Threshold histogram.

6. Click OK and use a Color Sampler as a tack right on top of the clump of white.

7. Turn off or throw away the Threshold Adjustment Layer and you'll see that the image hasn't been affected but that the samplers are showing you exactly where the black and white points should be placed, as shown in **figure 2.22**.

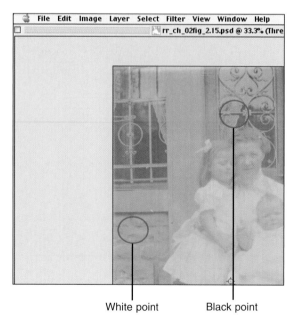

White point   Black point

figure 2.22

After turning off the Threshold Adjustment Layer, the Color Samplers show you exactly where the black and white points should be placed in the image.

8. Now add a Levels Adjustment Layer and use the Color Sampler tacks as reference points in setting the true black and white points.

Working with Levels Eyedroppers

When working with historical images or photographs in which you don't have personal knowlegdge of the tones or color, you can use your visual memory to improve tone. **Figure 2.23** shows a formal portrait that lacks the needed contrast. My estimations of the black and white prints resulted in the much improved image seen in **figure 2.24**.

BEFORE

figure 2.23

AFTER

figure 2.24

 ch2_profile.jpg

1. Add a Levels Adjustment Layer.

2. Click the white eyedropper, then click an area that needs to be reset to white. In **figure 2.25**, I'm resetting the shoulder of the woman's dress. By clicking the area that should be white, Photoshop will remap and redefine the tonal information to change the dingy gray to pure white.

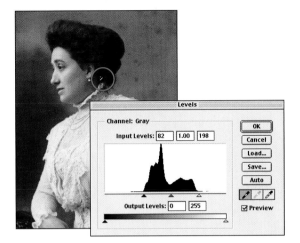

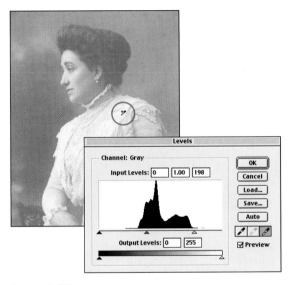

figure 2.25

Use the white eyedropper to identify where the new white point should be.

3. Click the black eyedropper, then click an area that needs to be reset to black. In **figure 2.26**, I'm darkening the area in the woman's hair. Just as the white eyedropper remaps white, the black eyedropper defines and remaps the darkest tones. Using the eyedropper approach is both effective and simple—a winning combination.

4. If setting the black or white point made the image too contrasty, use the black or white point sliders to lessen the contrast. In this example, by moving the black point slider to the left from 82 to 68 the shadows are lightened, as seen in **figure 2.27**.

5. If the image is still too light or too dark, adjust the midtone gamma slider. To lighten an image, move the midtone gamma slider to the left. To darken a light image, move the midtone gamma slider to the right.

figure 2.26

Use the black eyedropper to deepen the dark areas of the image.

Note

If you click an area that isn't representative of white in your image, then other, lighter tones will be forced to white and you could end up losing information that may be important. In case you click an area with any Levels or Curves eyedropper and don't like the results, press (Option) [Alt] to change the Cancel button to Reset. This will return the file to its initial state.

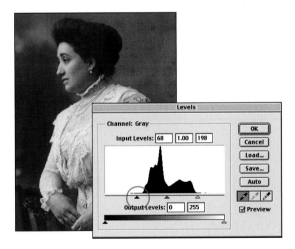

figure 2.27

Moving the slider to 68 produces lighter shadows.

CURVES AND CONTRAST

After you're comfortable working with Levels, Curves is the next tool to add to your Photoshop repertoire. The advantage of Curves is that it gives you sixteen points to influence the tonal values of an image, whereas Levels allows you just three (highlight, midtone, and shadow points).

The Curves dialog box allows you to work with either 0–100 dot percentages or 0–255 tonal values. Click the small triangles circled in **figure 2.28** to toggle between the two. From my experience, people with prepress experience prefer the 0%–100% scale, while photographers prefer the 0–255 scale—the same values used in Levels. The 0–255 scale places the highlights on the shoulder (upper part) of the curve and the shadows on the toe (lower part) of the curve. This is how a photographer reads film curves and why I prefer to use the 0–255 scale. The 0%–100% values are mapped exactly the opposite, with the highlights at the bottom left and the shadows at the upper right.

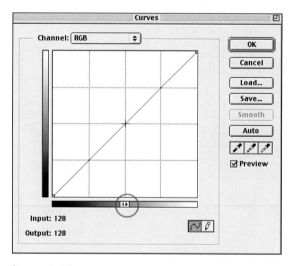

figure 2.28

You can choose to work in dot percentages or digital values by clicking the small triangles.

When you add a point to the curve and move it, you are changing the relationship between a pixel's input to output value. For example, if you move the midpoint 128 value up, you're telling Photoshop to remap the 128 values to a higher value, and the image will get lighter. If you are working with the 0–100% scale, moving the 50% point down will also lighten the image.

The best aspect of Curves is the control you have over the many points of tonal information. With Curves you can quickly enhance image contrast by

applying a classic S-Curve (described in the next section), or you can spend more time with the interface and use bump points to bring out selective tonal details, as we'll do in "Bringing Out Detail with Curves."

Increasing Contrast with Curves

Figure 2.29 shows another family heirloom that has aged significantly. The image lacks contrast, and the highlights, such as in the father's shirt and baby's jumper, are too gray. I used Curves to deepen the shadows and lighten the lighter areas. Applying an S-curve enabled me to quickly add the pop needed, as shown in **figure 2.30**.

figure 2.29

figure 2.30

 ch2_BWfamily.jpg

1. Add a Curves Image Adjustment Layer (see **figure 2.31**).

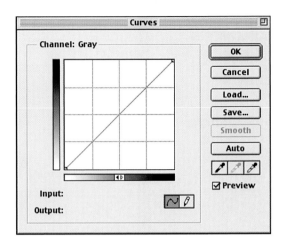

figure 2.31

The Curves dialog box always starts with a straight line, from shadows at the bottom to highlights at the top.

2. (Cmd + click) [Ctrl + click] a light area of the image that needs to be made lighter. This automatically adds a handle on the Curves graph. In this example, I selected the infant's white jumper, as seen in **figure 2.32**.

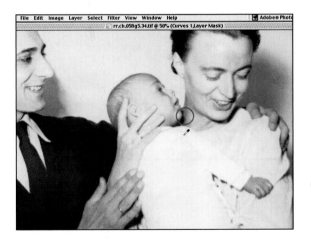

figure 2.32

While in the Curves dialog box, pinpoint a light area of the image that needs to be made lighter.

3. In the Curves dialog box, click the point and move it up to lighten the image highlights.

4. (Cmd + click) [Ctrl + click] on a dark area that needed to be darker. This automatically added a handle on the Curves graph. I used the gentleman's dark sweater as my shadow point.

5. Click the point and move it down to darken the shadows. **Figure 2.33** shows the Curves dialog box after my adjustments.

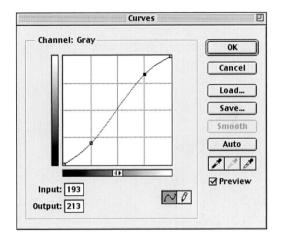

figure 2.33

The Curves highlight and shadow points control image contrast.

When using Curves, keep an eye on the Info palette while you are adjusting contrast and tonal values. You don't want to force the dark areas so far down that they become pure black. Conversely, try to keep some details in your highlights, so don't force whites to 0%. The only values that should be completely white are specular highlights, such as reflections on chrome bumpers.

Caution

When using Curves to increase contrast there is always a trade off. Adding contrast in one area takes contrast and tonal information away from another. Therefore, making adjustments that are too radical can lead to posterization in the flat areas of the curve.

Bringing Out Detail with Curves

The original image shown in **figure 2.34** is faded, but still salvageable. I used Curves to open up the midtones and highlights, deepen the shadows, and target the blacks and whites for printing, as seen in **figure 2.35**. Lightening both the highlights and midtones accentuates the sunny day and focuses attention on the little boy. By darkening the darker tones, such as the trees (visually less important image areas), I am framing the little boy, which draws the viewer's eye to him.

figure 2.34

figure 2.35

 ch2_icecream.jpg

1. Add a Curves Adjustment Layer.

2. (Cmd + click) [Ctrl + click] an area that needs to be made lighter or to which you want to draw attention. In this instance, I used the boy's forehead to lighten the skintones. As you can see in **figure 2.36**, the entire image became lighter.

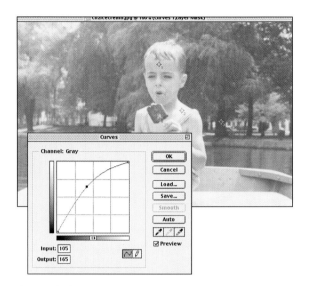

figure 2.36

Starting with the boy's face—the most important image area—I lightened the image to reduce the muddiness and darkness and to draw the viewer's eye to the face.

3. (Cmd + click) [Ctrl + click] a dark tree trunk in the image background to add a handle on the Curves graph. Lower the values of the trees as shown in **figure 2.37**.

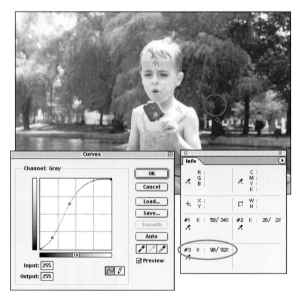

figure 2.37

Darkening the background adds pleasing contrast and tonally frames the boy with trees.

4. Notice the Info palette readout—the high-lights on the boy's collarbone are now at 2%, a value that will print as paper white, without any tonal detail. To reduce the brightness of the highlights while maintaining the effect of the increased contrast, (Cmd + click) [Ctrl + click] the brightest highlight near the collar-bone and lower the highlight value to drop the brightest highlight back to 7%, as seen in **figure 2.38**.

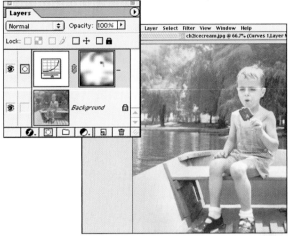

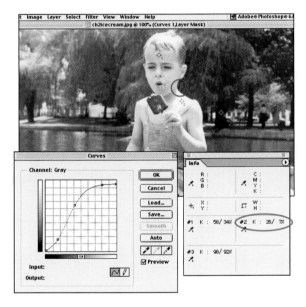

figure 2.38

Reducing the brightness of the highlights ensures that the lightest areas will print with tonality and detail.

5. After adjusting the image contrast, take a moment to look at the image with a fresh eye. Notice where your eye goes in the image. In this case, my eye kept falling to the side of the boat, in the lower-left corner. To selectively reduce the changes made, paint onto the mask of the Adjustment Layer with a 20%–25% black Airbrush, as shown in **figure 2.39**. Wherever you paint with black on the Image Adjustment layer mask, you are hiding the adjustment.

figure 2.39

Airbrushing onto the Curves Adjustment Layer layer mask reduces the contrast and brightness in unimportant or distracting image areas.

WORKING WITH BLENDING MODES

Every Photoshop layer, including Adjustment Layers, supports Blending Modes, which influence how a layer interacts with the layers below it. For retouching work, Blending Modes simplify and speed up tonal correction, spotting, and blemish removal. With the following exercises, you'll work with the most important Blending Modes to solve tonal problems:

- Multiply darkens the entire image and is useful to add density to highlights and midtones. It is especially useful for overexposed or very light images.

- Screen lightens the entire image—use it to open up/lighten dark image areas and to bring out tonal information in underexposed images.

- Overlay, Soft Light, and Hard Light Blending Modes lighten the lights and darken the darks, as they are a mixture of Multiply and Screen, and all three are useful to boost image contrast. Hard Light adds the most contrast, Soft Light adds the least contrast, and Overlay is the average of the three. They are all useful, and I usually try all three when adding contrast to see which one is the most effective Blending Mode for the task at hand.

The best thing about working with Blending Modes is that they are completely reversible, allowing you to experiment to achieve the desired result. To access the Blending Modes, use the pull-down menu in the Layers palette, as seen in **figure 2.40**.

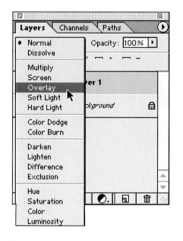

figure 2.40

Accessing the layer's Blending Modes.

Using Multiply to Build Density

As soon as you see a very light or very faded image, you should be thinking *Multiply*. The Multiply Blending Mode works as if you are sandwiching two slides over one another. Imagine you're standing in front of a window and have a slide in each hand. Now place the two slides over one another—the results will always be darker. By using the Multiply Blending Mode on the Levels Adjustment Layer, you are doubling the tonal density of the image. **Figure 2.41** shows a print from 1909 that has not fared well over the years. To restore it to the image you see in **figure 2.42**, we need to build up overall density to strengthen the image.

© Eismann family archive

figure 2.41

figure 2.42

🌐⤵ **ch2_nodensity.jpg**

1. Add a Levels Adjustment Layer and, without changing any settings in Levels, click OK.

2. In the Layers palette, change the Blending Mode to Multiply. **Figure 2.43** shows how the image becomes darker.

figure 2.43

Setting an Adjustment Layer to Multiply automatically adds density.

3. In many cases, adding a Multiply Levels Adjustment Layer is enough to build up enough image density to create a pleasing image. In extreme examples such as this one, you can continue improving the image tone by either

   • Duplicate the Levels Adjustment Layer as shown in **figure 2.44** to increase density even more.

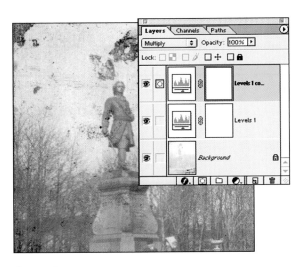

figure 2.44

Increase the image density by duplicating the Adjustment Layer.

OR • Double-click the Levels thumbnail icon in the Layers palette and adjust the sliders by bringing in the black and white point sliders to where the tonal information begins, as seen in **figure 2.45**.

figure 2.45

Adjust the black or white points on the Levels Adjustment Layer to control the contrast of the image.

Note

Deciding which method to use—duplicating the Adjustment Layer, finessing the Levels sliders, or in some cases duplicating the Adjustment Layer and changing its Blending Mode to Soft Light—to add contrast and lighten the highlights is a matter of experimentation and experience. No one can look at an image and say, "I need to do A, B, and C and use these exact values." Keep in mind that the more you experiment with these techniques, the more experience you will gain and the more options you'll have to improve images.

Adding Contrast with Hard Light

Overlay, Soft Light, and Hard Light are great Blending Modes to add contrast to an image. In **figure 2.46**, the original image is from 1897 and is so badly faded that the people are barely recognizable. By using the Hard Light Blending Mode with a standard Levels adjustment, I can see that the image is of four men sitting in a garden enjoying cool glasses of beer (see **figure 2.47**).

figure 2.46

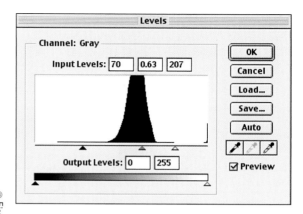

figure 2.48

Adjusting the Levels sliders in addition to using the Hard Light Blending Mode.

TRICKS FOR MAXIMIZING ADJUSTMENT LAYERS

Adjustment Layers can be moved and shared between documents by using the Move tool to drag them from one open document to another. The files don't have to be the same size or dimension— meaning you can make a tonal correction on one file and just drag it over to another file, and Photoshop will apply the same improvement to the second file. Use this drag-and-drop technique when you have a number of similar corrections to make to similar originals.

One project I worked on was to retouch a series of images that were taken at the same time and stored together and, consequently, they all had faded in a similar manner. After scanning in the originals, I opened up one representative image and used a Curves Adjustment Layer to improve the contrast. Then I opened the other files and just dragged the initial Adjustment Layer over to them, which applied that correction to all the subsequent files. Of course I looked at each image and tweaked the corrections where needed, but by using this technique, I was done with the job in no time flat.

Sharing Adjustment Layers

I shot a series of these statues in an outdoor museum in the Black Forest and, although I've returned to the spot a few times, the weather has always been the

figure 2.47

 ch2_biergarden.jpg

1. Add a Levels Adjustment Layer. In case you're not sure which Blending Mode to use, click OK in the Levels dialog box without changing any settings. In the Layers palette, change the Blending Mode to Overlay, then Soft Light, and then Hard Light to see for yourself which one adds the most contrast.

2. I set the Blending Mode to Hard Light and then double-clicked the Levels Adjustment Layer and adjusted the shadow, midtone, and highlight sliders, as seen in **figure 2.48**.

same—gray, cloudy, and damp. So instead of waiting for the weather to improve, I decided to use a shared Curves Adjustment Layer to improve the images. As you can see in **figure 2.49**, the originals are flat and dark, and in **figure 2.50**, they have snap to them.

figure 2.49

figure 2.50

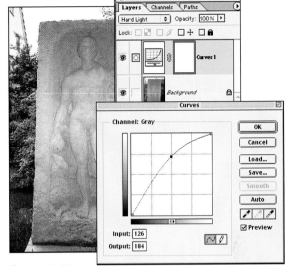

figure 2.51

A Curves Adjustment Layer set to Hard Light Blending Mode.

3. Open up the second image that needs to be corrected.

4. Use the Move tool to drag the Adjustment Layer from the Layers palette or the image area over to the second image as illustrated in **figure 2.52**.

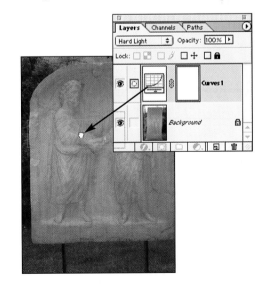

figure 2.52

Drag and share Adjustment Layers between files that need similar tonal corrections.

⊕⊳✕ **ch2_statue1.jpg**

⊕⊳✕ **ch2_statue2.jpg**

1. Open up a representative image and make the tonal adjustments with an Adjustment Layer. In this case, I started with Curves Adjustment Layer set to Hard Light.

2. Hard Light strengthens the dark and light areas of the image and ignores the middle grays. In many cases you will want to lighten the midtones by pulling the midtone Curve up as seen in **figure 2.51**.

© Katrin Eismann

Saving and Loading Adjustment Settings

If you need to correct a large number of images with similar tonal problems, saving and loading the Adjustment Layer settings can really speed up your work. Additionally, if you use Actions to automate your workflow, you can open and adjust many images without breaking into a sweat.

1. Create the appropriate Adjustment Layer and click Save (see **figure 2.53**).

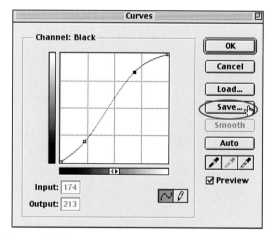

figure 2.53

Clicking the Save button saves the setting so you can use it again.

2. Save the settings into a folder.
3. With the second image active, add a Curves Adjustment Layer and click the Load button.
4. Navigate to find the saved settings and click Open to apply the change. As you can see in **figure 2.54**, all three images were quickly corrected by loading the Curves correction file.

figure 2.54

Three identically corrected images.

Saving Adjustment Layers

The only problem with saving the settings of Adjustment Layers is that any Blending Modes and Opacity settings used are not saved with the adjustment settings file. This is, of course, a drawback to a Blending Mode aficionado like me. In the following example, I boosted the contrast of the image with a Curves Adjustment Layer set to Soft Light at 50% opacity, as shown in **figure 2.55**. To use these settings later, I saved the Adjustment Layer in a separate, empty Photoshop file from which I can drag and drop the Adjustment Layer whenever I need it.

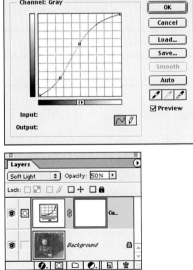

figure 2.55

Saving the Curves Adjustment Layer would not have saved the other layer options that I used to fine tune this image.

1. To save the adjustment settings with the Blending Mode, select the Adjustment Layer and select Duplicate Layer from the Layers palette menu.

2. Make sure to set the destination to a new document, name the file, and click OK (see **figure 2.56**).

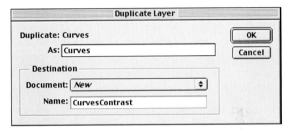

figure 2.56

Setting the destination.

3. This creates a Photoshop document, as shown in **figure 2.57**. As you can see from the Layers palette, the Blending Mode and Opacity settings have been preserved.

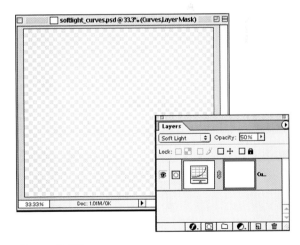

figure 2.57

The resulting file saves layer settings that would otherwise be lost.

4. Save this file into a folder just as you would any Photoshop document.

5. After opening the file, use the drag-and-drop method to add this Adjustment Layer, complete with Blending Mode, Opacity values, and adjustments to any file.

BASING TONAL CORRECTIONS ON SELECTIONS

Until now, we have applied tonal changes to the entire image (global changes), but many times you just want to improve a specific part or area of a file (local changes). That is when you need to start thinking and working selectively. In this section, we'll use Photoshop's selection and painting tools to control where the changes take place. Selective changes can start with either an active selection or with a global Adjustment Layer.

The shadow areas in **figure 2.58** are too dark. When I make a selection and then add an Adjustment Layer, Photoshop knows to change only the actively selected area, as seen in **figure 2.59**. Even better than that—after you've clicked OK to the tonal correction, the image Adjustment Layer is a small black-and-white version of the selection. Photoshop has created a mask—wherever it is black, the adjustment doesn't take place, while the effect shows through the white areas. The best thing about this technique is that you can use any type of selection tool that you are comfortable with—from the Magic Wand tool to the Color Range command—to create the initial selection.

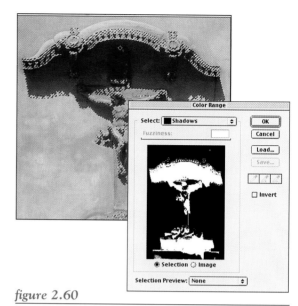

figure 2.60

Using Color Range to select the shadows.

2. Add a Curves Adjustment Layer. Notice in **figure 2.61** that Photoshop automatically creates a mask for the Adjustment Layer using the selection (look at the thumbnail in the Layers palette). Where the mask is black, no tonal correction will take place. Where the mask is white, the tonal adjustments you make will take place.

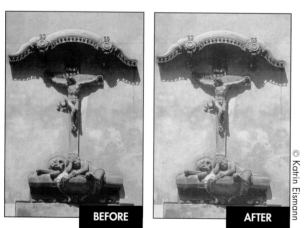

figure 2.58   *figure 2.59*

 ch2_crucifix.jpg

1. Make a selection of the tonal areas that you want to enhance. In this example, I used Color Range set to Shadows shown in **figure 2.60** to create the active selection.

© Katrin Eismann

figure 2.61

Adding a Curves Adjustment Layer when a selection is active creates a mask to control where the tonal adjustments are made.

3. Adjust the Curve to open the shadows, as seen in **figure 2.62**. In some situations, you may want to experiment with Blending Modes to accentuate the adjustments.

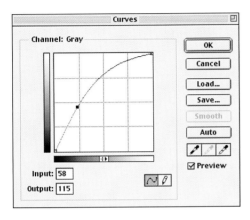

figure 2.62

The edited Curve.

4. If you notice sharp edges along the adjustment after applying the curve, use the Gaussian Blur filter on the layer mask to soften the Adjustment.

THE BENEFITS OF HIGH-BIT DATA

The only problem with my love affair with Adjustment Layers is that Photoshop does not support working with Adjustment Layers on 16-bit per channel images—also referred to as *high-bit* or *high-bit depth* files.

The highest possible number of shades of gray that a standard 8-bit grayscale file can contain is 256. An RGB image uses three channels and is a 24-bit image. A CMYK image uses four channels and is often referred to as a 32-bit image. Oddly enough, this doesn't mean that the CMYK file contains more shades of gray—because each channel is still made up of a maximum of 256 shades of gray.

For very critical, high-quality tonal and color correction, 256 shades of gray per channel does not offer you a lot of room to change tone and color. Working with high-bit data—files that contain more than 256 shades of gray per channel (see **table 2.1**)—gives you more tonal room to change the tonal interpretation of an image.

table 2.1

Bit-Depth per Channel	Shades of Gray
8-bit	*256*
10-bit	*1,024*
12-bit	*4,096*
16-bit	*16,384*

If you work with scanners or digital cameras that capture high-bit data, I recommend you take advantage of the additional tonal information high-bit data provides. Perform the tonal and color corrections and cleaning up dust on the high-bit file before converting to 8-bit data.

Figure 2.63 shows you the histograms for two images. The image on the top was scanned at 8-bit, and the image on the bottom was scanned at 16-bit; otherwise, the two scans are identical.

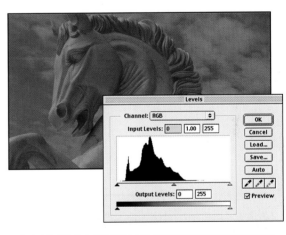

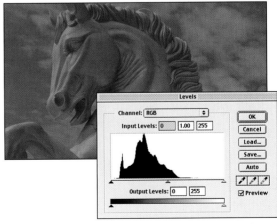

figure 2.63

Before tonal changes, the 8- and 16-bit histograms are identical.

After bringing the files into Photoshop, I made the identical Levels adjustment to apply the same tonal and color correction to both files. The top histogram in **figure 2.64** reveals the tonal decimation to the 8-bit file. Where the white spikes occur in the image, tonal information is missing. In the high-bit file at the bottom of **figure 2.64**, the same changes improve the file, and the histogram shows that I still have plenty of data to work with. Ideally, you want to avoid leaving white gaps in the histogram because image areas with white gaps may band or posterize when printing.

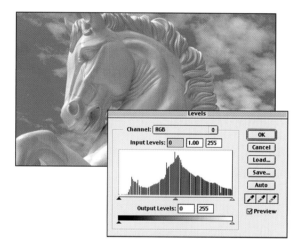

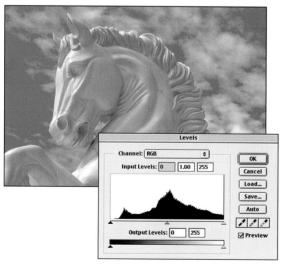

figure 2.64

After tonal changes, the histograms show that the 16-bit image withstood the adjustment far better than the 8-bit image.

Don't Try to Trick Photoshop

Trying to trick Photoshop into thinking it is working with a high-bit file by converting an 8-bit scan to 16-bit, applying changes, and then converting back to 8-bit doesn't work. This voodoo maneuver is as worthless as rotating a file a few degrees, then rotating it back to fool Photoshop into yielding a smoother histogram. This misdirected technique does nothing but produce a file that's a bit softer because of the blurring caused by rotation. Don't waste time on tricks like these that don't improve the actual image information. Remember, your goal isn't to print attractive histograms, but to produce good images.

CLOSING THOUGHTS

Even after years of working with Photoshop, it still amazes me to see how improving image tone can turn a so-so image into an absolutely wonderful one. Rely on your visual intuition to access an image and use Adjustment Layers to bring out tonal detail and information. Working with Adjustment Layers gives you the opportunity to experiment and learn from the process—you may not get the image just right the very first time you try a technique, but believe me, every time you try something new you're learning for the next image challenge. So download the exercise files from www.digitalretouch.org, practice with them, and then apply the techniques to your own images. Although some of the specific values may differ, the concepts of working with Adjustment Layers, Blending Modes, and selections will hold true.

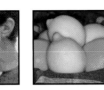

3

EXPOSURE CORRECTION

Who hasn't gone to the photo store to pick up photos, and with bated breath opened the envelope only to be disappointed by pictures that are too light, too dark, or messed up because the flash didn't go off? All these problems can be traced back to incorrect exposure. Although modern cameras have sophisticated light meters and exposure controls, strong back light or well-intentioned but incorrect camera settings can fool these modern wonders into making the wrong exposure.

Additionally, the ravages of time, displaying the photo in strong sunlight, improper storage conditions, poor chemical processing, and the transient nature of most color photographic substrates can wreak havoc on your fondest memories. When pictures fade, they don't contain any rich blacks or pure whites, and often odd color shifts are introduced.

Of course, making the appropriate exposure and protecting your photos by storing them correctly is always better than trying to apply a Photoshop fix; however, sometimes you have to rescue the pictures that fall by the wayside.

In this chapter, you'll work with grayscale and color images to

- Build up density in underexposed images
- Accentuate information in overexposed images
- Add fill-flash to open up backlit portraits
- Selectively paint light back into the picture

The worst aspect of an extreme exposure *faux pas* is that the original image information is missing. No amount of Photoshop finesse can rescue information that wasn't there to begin with. Exposure-challenged images might not be transformed from a croaking frog to a royal prince, but hopefully the techniques in this chapter will salvage your memories well enough to frame and share them with family and friends.

Note

When you have the choice between scanning a print or the original film, working with the original film will most often yield better results. Even extremely over- or underexposed film contains more information than a print made from a poor film exposure does. If possible, try to find the original film or ask your client if they have it for you to scan.

WORKING WITH UNDEREXPOSED IMAGES

Images that are underexposed are usually dark or dull without a true rich-black or clean-white. Shadows that don't have any useful information and white areas that look medium gray are also tell-tale signs that the camera meter was fooled into calculating the wrong exposure. Images that have faded over time can also be symptomatic of underexposure, and these same techniques can be used to rescue them.

Using the Screen Blending Mode

There is nothing worse than trying to rescue drastically underexposed images. **Figure 3.1** shows the original, in which the manual light meter of the camera was fooled by the light center column causing the entire image to be under-exposed by about three f-stops. I used the Screen Blending Mode on a Curves Adjustment Layer to open the image up to get the results seen in **figure 3.2**.

figure 3.1

figure 3.2

 ch3_underexpose.jpg

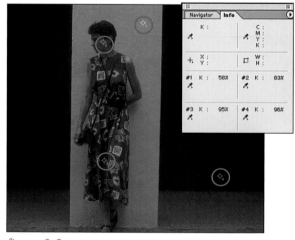

figure 3.3

Color Samplers enable you to measure and track tonal changes. I have added four samplers to track the highlights and shadows of this image.

1. Add Color Samplers to track important tonal information as shown in figure 3.3. In this example, I added four to the various points of the image to track the wall, skin tones, shadow in the dress, and the background.

2. Add a Curves Adjustment Layer and change the Blending Mode to Screen.

Tip

Hold down (Option) [Alt] and click the New Fill or New Adjustment Layer icon to select the Adjustment Layers blend mode.

Notice that, even though the Curve itself has not been changed (yet), the Info palette shows that the Screen Blending Mode is lightening the image (see **figure 3.4**).

- Sampler 1: The wall went from 58% to 34%.
- Sampler 2: The cheek went from 83% to 69%.
- Sampler 3: The dress went from 95% to 90%.
- Sampler 4: The background shadow went from 96% to 91%.

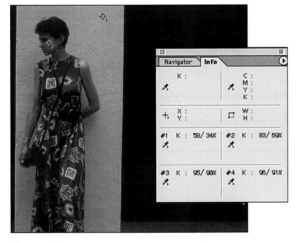

figure 3.4

Watching the Info palette is crucial in understanding how the Blending Modes affect the image data. The first number (on the left) is the original value of the sampler, and the second number (on the right) shows the value after editing.

3. (Cmd + click)[Ctrl + click] the tonal area you want to work with to add a handle to the Curve. Start with the most important tones—in this case, the wall and the skin tones—and adjust the Curve to bring those tones into the desired range, as seen in **figure 3.5**.

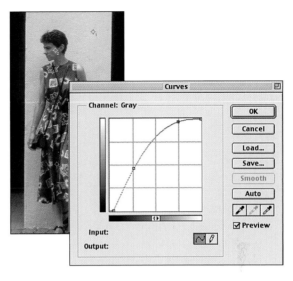

figure 3.5

By working with Curves to lighten the midtones, I darkened the deepest shadows to black by moving the black point (the point in the lower left) in Curves to the right to suppress the noise that the underexposure caused.

Caution

Adding excessive contrast with Blending Modes or tonal changes results in image posterization (as illustrated in **figure 3.6**) that might cause banding when printing. To avoid posterization, be careful how much pushing and pulling (lightening and darkening) of tonal values you do.

figure 3.6

Image posterization can result in banding when printing.

Transitioning a Tonal Correction

Sometimes one side of an image is much lighter or darker than the other side. You can use the Gradient tool on an Adjustment Layer to protect the good part of the image while the Adjustment Layer corrects the bad part of the image. In this example, the camera meter was fooled by the light morning sky, underexposing the lower half of the picture, as shown in **figure 3.7**. As you can see in **figure 3.8**, the final image is tonally balanced and memories of that early morning walk have been saved.

figure 3.7

figure 3.8

I used a Curves Adjustment Layer with the Blending Mode set to Screen to lighten the bottom of the image; however, that blew out the sky. To isolate the Curves Adjustment Layer to the bottom portion of the image, I took advantage of an Adjustment Layer layer mask. Where I wanted the adjustment to affect the image, I made sure the mask was white; where I wanted to hide the adjustment, I made sure the mask was black. Because I wanted an even transition from black to white, I used the Gradient tool to create this transition. When using masks, I think of the Gradient tool as a big paintbrush that allows you to draw over the entire surface from black to white with a smooth, gray transition.

ch3_sky.jpg

1. Add a Curves Adjustment Layer. If the image is too dark (as in this case), select Screen as the Blending Mode. If the image was too light, select Multiply to help darken down image areas.

2. Make your tonal adjustments and focus on the areas that need fixing (see **figure 3.9**). In this case, don't worry about the sky getting too light.

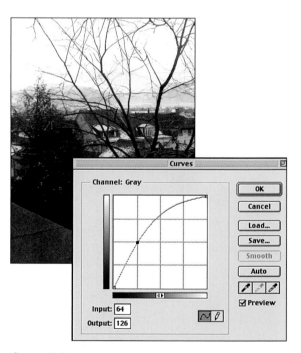

figure 3.9

Using Curves and the Screen Blending Mode will open up or lighten the underexposed areas quickly.

3. Choose the Linear Gradient tool and select the black to white opaque gradient.

4. Activate the Curves Adjustment Layer layer mask. Start the blend where you want the tonal protection to start (just above the horizon) and draw down to where the image adjustment is to your liking (see **figure 3.10**). If you don't draw the blend perfectly the first time, use the Gradient tool to drag gradients until you get the transition you want. Wherever the blend is black, the tonal correction will be hidden, and wherever you leave white, the tonal correction will be revealed.

BEFORE

figure 3.11

figure 3.10

Drawing the blend on the Adjustment Layer layer mask controls where the effect is taking place.

Painting with Adjustment Layers

Of course, not all image imperfections fall on a straight line as the previous example did. When I need to enhance irregular areas I prefer to use Photoshop's Brush tools and a Wacom pressure-sensitive tablet to hide and show image adjustments by painting in their masks. In the picture of the beauty queen (see **figure 3.11**), the main subject is too dark. By lightening her face, the viewer's eye is drawn to her, as seen in **figure 3.12**.

AFTER

figure 3.12

1. Add a Curves Adjustment Layer set to Screen to lighten the image. **Figure 3.13** shows that the entire image is affected by the Adjustment Layer, which makes the image look better but also takes away tonal focus from the primary figure.

figure 3.13

Lighten the entire file.

2. I find it easier to hide the entire tonal correction by inverting the Adjustment Layer layer mask (Cmd + I)[Ctrl + I] or filling it with 100% black. Then you will selectively paint in the correction.

3. Select the Airbrush, set white as the foreground color, and decrease the opacity to 10%–20%. Begin painting on the Adjustment Layer's mask. Decreasing the opacity allows a gradual build up of white paint in the mask, slowly revealing the adjustment in the image, as **figure 3.14** illustrates.

figure 3.14

Painting in the Curves Adjustment Layer layer mask carefully lightens only the areas that require it.

This technique gives you the ability to decide where and to what extent the tonal changes take place. The soft-edged airbrush will yield a soft-edged tonal transition that is difficult to detect.

SALVAGING OVEREXPOSED IMAGES

Slide positive originals or digital camera files are images that are most likely to be overexposed. Slide films, such as Kodak Ektachrome and AgfaChrome, and consumer digital cameras do not have the exposure latitude that color negative film has, which makes them more sensitive to overexposure. As with underexposure, a severely overexposed image might not give you much (if any) image information to work with. If the overexposed areas are clear, blownout to white, or if the Info palette reads 255, 255, 255, there is no amount of Photoshop magic that can recreate image information that wasn't captured to begin with. In the following exercises, we will work with very light and faded images to learn techniques to bring out subtle information to create images that are saturated and rich.

Correcting Overexposed Images from Digital Cameras

In the following example, the original image was captured with a consumer-level digital camera, and it is overexposed (see **figure 3.15**). After adding density to the file, the image is richer and more saturated (see **figure 3.16**).

figure 3.15

figure 3.16

⊕↗≺ **ch3_coneroad.jpg**

1. Start by loading the image's luminosity by pressing (Cmd + Option + ~)[Ctrl + Alt + ~] to create the active selection (see **figure 3.17**). Loading the luminosity uses the overall image brightness to make the selection.

figure 3.17

Load the image's luminosity.

2. Select Layer > New > Layer Via Copy or press (Cmd + J)[Ctrl + J] to create a new layer based on the selection.

3. By turning off the Background layer, you can see the subtle nature of the added layer (see figure 3.18).

> **N o t e**
>
> You can also load image luminosity by (Command) [Control] clicking on the composite channel icon (RGB, CMYK, LAB, or Grayscale) in the Channels palette.

figure 3.18

Just for curiosity's sake, view the resulting layer.

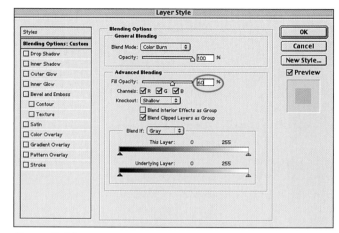

figure 3.20

The Layer Style dialog box controls how layers interact with one another.

4. Make the Background layer visible again. Make the new layer active, and change the Blending Mode to Color Burn. The image will most likely look muddy, as seen in **figure 3.19**.

6. To strengthen the effect, duplicate the Color Burn layer and lower the duplicated layer's opacity to create the desired effect, as seen in **figure 3.21**.

figure 3.19

Duplicating the layer and changing the Blending Mode to Color Burn.

5. Double-click the Color Burn layer and change the Advanced Blending Fill Opacity to 60%, as seen in **figure 3.20**.

figure 3.21

Duplicating the layer and adjusting opacity fine-tunes the correction.

Correcting Slight Overexposure and Reducing Specular Highlights

In this example, the studio still life of the citrus fruit is slightly overexposed and flat, as seen in the original file in **figure 3.22**. By correcting the shadow point and toning down the specular highlights on the fruit, the final image as seen in **figure 3.23** could (almost) pass for a correctly exposed image. I say *almost* because it is always better to work with the correct exposure rather than trying to fix a mistake.

BEFORE

figure 3.22

AFTER

figure 3.23

⊕▷꞊ **ch3_lemons.jpg**

1. The lack of information on the left side of the Levels histogram is symptomatic of an overexposed image (see **figure 3.24**). Move the shadow slider to the right to where the darkest information starts. In this case, ignore the few pixels that occur before the majority of the histogram.

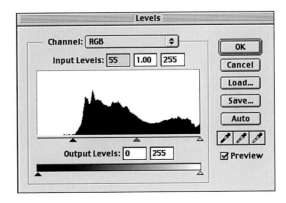

figure 3.24

Moving the shadow slider to where the tonal information begins deepens the shadow and makes the image look richer.

2. One of the problems with overexposed images is that the highlights have a tendency to blowout to pure white. After measuring the highlights on the fruit and getting an RGB reading of 255, 251, 251 (see **figure 3.25**), you can see that the highlights need to be toned down individually.

© Katrin Eismann

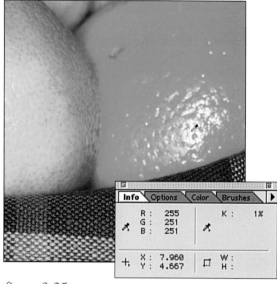

figure 3.25

Measure highlights with the Eyedropper.

3. Add a new layer and name it hotspots. Use a soft-edged brush and the Clone Stamp tool to clone over the highlights. I lowered the opacity of the hotspot layer to bring back a hint of the highlights, as shown in **figure 3.26**. (For more detail on these spotting and Clone Stamp techniques, see Chapters 5, "Dust and Mold Removal," and 6, "Damage Control and Repair.")

4. Finally, fine-tune the image contrast with a subtle S-Curve. **Figure 3.27** shows the Curves adjustment and the final image.

figure 3.26

After cloning over the hotspots, experiment with the opacity of the layer to bring back some of the visual interest by letting the highlights shimmer through.

figure 3.27

The gentle S-Curve boosts the contrast just a bit and allows the color of the fruit to shine through beautifully.

Balancing Exposure and Fading

The original image in **figure 3.28** is faded and flat, whereas the corrected rendition in **figure 3.29** balances the exposure between the center figures and the windows. In this example, the light coming through the windows over-powered the center of the image. To balance the exposure, we'll use a combination of an Overlay Adjustment Layer and the Gradient tool.

figure 3.28

figure 3.29

 ch3_xmas.jpg

1. Add a Curves Adjustment Layer with the Blending Mode set to Overlay to enhance the contrast.

2. The Curves Overlay Adjustment Layer helped the center of the image, but to add even more density, duplicate the Curves Adjustment Layer. This improves the center of the image but makes the window light too bright.

3. Select the Gradient tool and choose the black to transparent gradient. Drag the gradient from each upper corner toward the center of the image, as seen in the Layers palette in **figure 3.30**. The secret here is to set the Gradient tool to work from foreground (black) to transparent—this allows you to combine gradient blends with one another.

figure 3.30

Protect the corners of the image with two gradients.

ADDING FILL-FLASH

Have you ever noticed how photographs taken in the middle of the day have really dark shadows, or when portraits are taken in front of a window that the people seem silhouetted? In these situations, the exposure problems are caused by the extreme difference between the strong light and the deep shadows, which can fool even the best camera exposure meter. When you're taking pictures, you can avoid these problems by taking your pictures in the morning or late afternoon when the sun is lower and softer or by adding light with a flash or a white fill-card. Of course, knowing those photographic tidbits after the fact doesn't help you one bit, but knowing how to add a bit of light with Photoshop is a great technique to rescue those portraits from darkness.

When working outdoors on sunny days or in high-contrast lighting situations, it is recommended to use flash or fill-flash to reduce lighting ratios and fill in the shadows. In **figure 3.31**, that obviously didn't happen, and now we need to use Photoshop to open up the dark areas without changing the lighting ratio too much to achieve the effect in **figure 3.32**.

figure 3.31

figure 3.32

 ch3_backlit.jpg

1. Duplicate the original image by choosing Image > Duplicate.

2. Select Image > Mode > Grayscale to convert the duplicate file to grayscale.

3. Select Filter > Blur > Gaussian Blur and use a 3–6-pixel Radius setting to soften the details (see **figure 3.33**). Use a lower Gaussian Blur setting for small files under 5MB and higher settings for larger files.

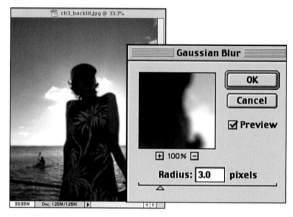

figure 3.33

Apply a Gaussian Blur with a 3–6 radius setting.

4. Invert the tonal values with Image > Adjust > Invert or (Cmd + I)[Ctrl + I] to create a negative image, as seen in **figure 3.34**. This negative image will be used to mask the digital fill-flash.

figure 3.34

Invert the black-and-white file to create a mask that will be light where you need more effect to take place.

5. Return to the original color image and choose Select > Load Selection. Check that your black-and-white mask image is selected in the Document pull-down menu, as seen in figure 3.35.

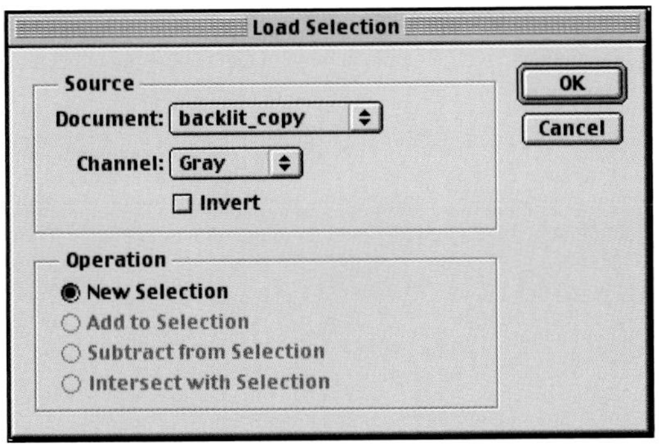

figure 3.35

Load the selection from the inverted document.

6. Select Layer > New > Layer Via Copy (Cmd + J) [Ctrl + J] to create a new layer based on the active selection.

7. Use the Fill dialog box to fill the new layer. For content, select 50% Gray. Change the Blending Mode to Color Dodge and check Preserve Transparency to tell Photoshop to ignore all clear areas of the new layer (see figure 3.36).

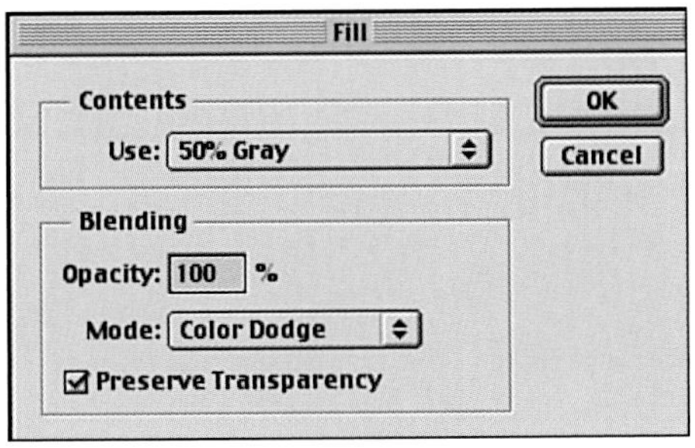

figure 3.36

Fill the active selection with 50% Gray set to Color Dodge with Preserve Transparency checked.

8. Notice how much lighter the image is now. If need be, erase any affected areas in the sky that don't need to be lighter, as shown in figure 3.37.

figure 3.37

You can erase image areas that were affected with the digital fill-flash.

9. If need be, duplicate the layer to increase the effect of the fill-flash and experiment with the layer's opacity to fine-tune the effect to your liking.

PAINTING WITH LIGHT

Good photographers are very sensitive to the light, and I don't mean they get sunburned quickly. Rather, they understand how the sun rakes over a landscape in the early morning or evening and brings out hidden textures and colors or how they can work with light to create a flattering portrait. Photoshop isn't omnipotent (yet), but with a bit of selective lightening and darkening you can make a dull, lifeless photograph pop off the page. If you've ever worked in a traditional darkroom, these techniques will seem similar to dodging and burning techniques used to emphasize the atmosphere of the photograph.

The original image (see **figure 3.38**) doesn't have any drastic exposure problems, but it lacks the dramatic mood that the solo tree and stormy sky should convey. By using Photoshop to accentuate the darks and lights, the viewer's attention is focused on the tree, as seen in **figure 3.39**.

© Katrin Eismann

BEFORE

figure 3.38

figure 3.39   **AFTER**

 ch3_lonetree.jpg

1. Load the image luminosity by (Command + Option) [Control + Alt] and ~ tilde and clicking on the RGB icon in the Channels palette.

2. Select Layer> New>Layer via Copy (Command + J) [Control + J] to create a new layer based on the selection.

3. Change the new layer's Blend Mode to Overlay.

4. Duplicate this layer once or twice to strengthen one saturation as seen in **figure 3.40**.

   Note

   You can also load image luminosity by (Command) [Control] clicking on the composite channel icon (RGB, CMYK, LAB, or Grayscale) in the Channels palette.

figure 3.40

Apply the Overlay Blending Mode to the new layers.

5. Add a new layer, fill it with a 50% gray, and change its Blend Mode to Overlay.

6. To paint in the lighter rays of light, use a large, soft-edged, white Airbrush at 2%-3% opacity and paint on the gray Overlay as shown in **figure 3.41**.

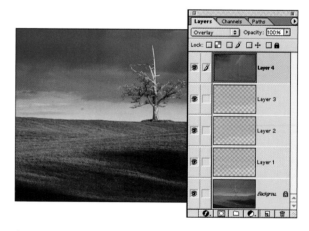

figure 3.41

Use a white Airbrush at 2%-3% Opacity to create a new light.

CLOSING THOUGHTS

All in all, it is always better to start with a well-exposed picture; however, for those times when the light meter is fooled, the batteries run out, or the ravages of time wreak havoc on a beloved photo, turn to these Photoshop techniques to do the image justice.

4

WORKING WITH COLOR

We are very sensitive to color and our eyes are tremendous tools to see and compare color. The emotional and subliminal importance of color in our world cannot be denied. For retouchers, being sensitive to color values can make the difference between a so-so print and a print that looks as vibrant as the memories it represents.

The importance of color challenges us to work with our visual memory in combination with the best that Photoshop has to offer: Adjustment Layers, the Info palette, the Histogram dialog box, Painting and Selection tools, and Blending Modes. In this chapter, you'll work with color images to learn

- Additive and subtractive color correction with image variations and color balance
- Global color correction with Levels and Curves
- Selective and interchannel color correction
- Correcting color temperature problems

Many of the tools and techniques used to improve tone, contrast, and exposure that are discussed in Chapters 2, "Improving Tone and Contrast," and 3, "Exposure Correction," will serve as the foundation for working with color. I highly recommend that you review those two chapters before diving into the wonderful world of color.

COLOR ESSENTIALS

There are two types of color in the world, additive and subtractive. In the *additive* world, a light source is needed to create color. When the primary colors (red, green, and blue) are combined, they create white, as shown in **figure 4.1**. An example of additive light is your monitor.

In the *subtractive* world, color is determined by the absorption of light. When the secondary colors—cyan, magenta, and yellow—are combined, they create black-brown, as seen in **figure 4.2**. Printing ink on paper is an example of subtractive color. In creating inks for print, impurities in the pigments result in a muddy black-brown when cyan, magenta, and yellow are combined. To achieve rich shadows and pure blacks, black is added to the printing process, which also cuts down on the amount of the more expensive color inks used.

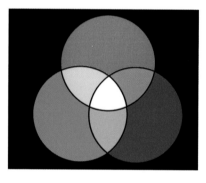

figure 4.1

The additive color space is formed by the red, green, and blue primary colors.

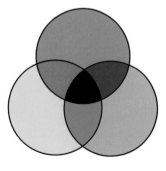

figure 4.2

The subtractive color space is formed by the cyan, yellow, and magenta primary colors.

Combining additive primaries yields the subtractive primaries, and combining the subtractive primaries creates the additive primaries. For the retoucher, understanding this opposite relationship can be very useful when identifying and correcting color problems. For example, if an image is too blue, you have two ways to approach the problem—either increase yellow (which is the opposite of blue to neutralize blue) or decrease the blue in the image. Both yield the same result: an image with less blue.

In digital imaging, the four most prevalent color modes are RGB, CMYK, Lab, and HSB:

- RGB is the additive color space that monitors, scanners, digital cameras, and color slide film originals work or exist in. The advantages to color correcting and retouching in RGB include smaller file sizes, equal values of red, green, and blue will always result in a neutral color, and a larger RGB color space allows the file to be converted into multiple gamuts and repurposed for multiple final output destinations.

- CMYK (cyan, magenta, yellow, and black) is the subtractive color mode. Many people (especially people with prepress or printing experience) prefer doing color correction and retouching in CMYK because they are more comfortable with CMYK color values, and editing colors that are in the same gamut as your printer can help avoid unhappy surprises after the ink hits the paper.

- Lab is a three-channel color mode in which the black and white L (luminosity) channel information has been separated from the color information. The "a" channel carries cyan to magenta and the "b" channel carries blue to yellow information. Lab is a device-independent color space used by color management software and by Photoshop when converting RGB files to CMYK. Color correcting in Lab is a delicate task as the slightest move on the "a" or "b" channels can result in a very strong color shift. On the other hand, Lab is a useful color mode to use when adjusting exposure or to clean up color artifacts from digital camera files, as discussed in Chapter 5, "Dust and Mold Removal."

- HSB stands for hue, saturation, and brightness. Hue refers to the color, brightness refers to the amount of light in the color, and saturation determines the amount of color. You can take advantage of HSB to emphasize or de-emphasize color in portrait retouching, as shown in Chapter 10, "Glamour and Fashion Retouching."

Each color mode has numerous pros and cons, all of which have been described in detail in *Real World Photoshop* by David Blatner and Bruce Fraser and *Professional Photoshop* by Dan Margulis. Rather than reworking information that is well explained by these digital maestros, I propose we learn how to identify and correct color casts.

Are All Color Casts Evil?

There are only two types of color casts in the world: those that accentuate the image and those that detract from the image. Positive color casts include the golden tones of the early morning or late afternoon sunlight, the warm color created by candlelight, and the color tones created when the photographer filters the lens or light to create or accentuate the color atmosphere. Undesired color casts occur if the photographer used the wrong color film to take a picture, the picture has faded over time, light has leaked into the camera, a scanner introduces a color cast, or if an undesired color is being reflected into a photograph.

I'm sure you've seen pictures taken in a stadium or in an office in which the color temperature of the light doesn't match the color balance of the film used. The orange, red, or green color casts introduced by using the wrong color film or not compensating for the light temperature with photographic filters are both what I would categorize as undesired. Another example of an undesired color cast occurs when sunlight is filtered through green tree leaves and the people in the picture look slightly Martian-like.

IDENTIFYING A COLOR CAST

The color correction process always starts by identifying the color cast—you have to know what the problem is before you can apply a solution. The tools used to identify a color cast are your visual memory, the Info palette, reading the individual image channels, and practice. Color casts that are similar, such as blue and cyan or magenta and red, take a bit of practice to identify correctly.

Tip

Color casts are easier to identify in image highlights such as a white shirt or in a neutral area such as a sidewalk. Interestingly enough, clearing up the color cast in the lighter and neutral areas usually takes care of most of the required color correction work throughout the entire image.

Start the color cast correction process by thinking globally. Look at the entire photo and take care of the worst problems first. Correcting the big problem usually takes care of many of the smaller problems along the way.

UNDERSTANDING COLOR CORRECTION WITH IMAGE VARIATIONS

If all this talk about identifying color casts is making your head spin—don't worry. Photoshop Variations (Image > Adjust > Variations) is a very useful tool if you're just starting out or need a refresher on color correction. Variations is similar to the color ring-around chart that photographic printers have been using for years to see which way to move color when making a color print. The color correction part of Variations shows you six pictures, each representing one of the primary colors (red, green, blue, cyan, magenta, and yellow) opposite its counterpart (red to cyan, green to magenta, and blue to yellow) as seen in **figure 4.3**.

Next to the OK and Cancel buttons are radio buttons that you click to control the image feature that you want to base your adjustments on: Shadows, Midtones, Highlights, or Saturation. When using Variations to do color correction, I recommend that you start with the midtones and then refine the highlights. The only problem with Variations is that it is not an Adjustment Layer, so your color correction is applied directly to the image pixels. To insure that you don't alter original image data, always work either on a duplicate file or duplicate the Background layer.

figure 4.3

The Variations dialog box is a useful tool to identify color casts and offers you many options for color correction.

The original image shown in **figure 4.4** was taken indoors in fluorescent light with a digital camera that was set to daylight color balance, turning the image yellow-green. With a few clicks in Variations, the image is neutral and much more pleasing (see **figure 4.5**).

© Katrin Eismann

figure 4.4

figure 4.5

⊕⊳⊱ ch4_greenjohn.jpg

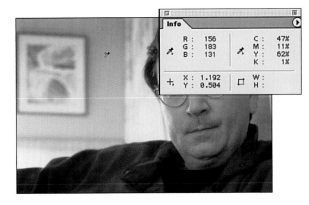

1. Use the Eyedropper tool and the Info palette to measure an area in the image that should be neutral. Because you haven't seen this room, how can you know what the real color is? Use your visual memory of a similar scene and you can guess that the wall in the background could be white or at least a very light neutral color. **Figure 4.6** shows the readout of 156 Red, 183 Green, 131 Blue.

   In relationship to the other colors, the much higher green readout in this example is a dead give away of a strong green color cast, and the low blue readout tells you that this image also has a yellow color cast. Properly adjusted, all three colors will be within one to two points of one another.

2. Duplicate the Background layer. This will protect the original pixels while you experiment with the color correction.

figure 4.6

Start by sampling an area you believe should be neutral and examining the color readout in the Info palette.

3. Select Image > Adjust > Variations and click the Midtones radio button. To see how Variations applies the opposite color principle, move the strength slider under the Saturation radio button to the right. **Figure 4.7** shows the six color variations very nicely. Notice how the lower two—More Blue and More Magenta—look the best.

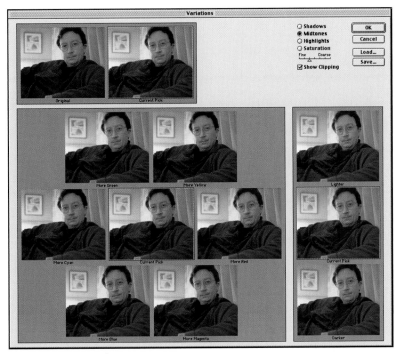

figure 4.7

Start your Variations color correction with the midtones.

4. To work subtly, move the strength slider one notch toward Fine to reduce the strength of each change and click More Blue to reduce the yellow, and then click More Magenta to reduce the green component. Variations updates the center image to reflect the image you just clicked. To strengthen any changes, just click any image again.

5. Adding the blue and magenta into the midtones might be making the image darker. You can offset this by clicking the Lighter image.

6. Finally, click the Highlight radio button and click More Magenta once or twice to take out the last vestige of the green color cast.

7. Click OK and compare the before and after images using (Cmd + Z) [Ctrl + Z] to undo and redo the Variations. Or toggle the visibility of the duplicated background layer on and off to reveal the original background layer.

8. You can also check the results with the Info palette as seen in **figure 4.8**, where the RGB readout is now 160, 160, 156, which is a perfectly acceptable neutral for a snapshot like this one.

figure 4.8

Check the neutral image areas with the Eyedropper and Info palette to double-check that the color cast has been removed.

Tip

When using Variations, you can undo all changes by clicking the original image in the upper left-hand corner.

MIMICKING THE COLOR DARKROOM WITH COLOR BALANCE

If you've ever done any photographic color printing, using Photoshop's Color Balance Adjustment Layers will seem familiar to you. Like Variations, it also works on the principle of increasing or decreasing opposite colors to color balance an image.

Figure 4.9 shows a class photo that was taken in the middle of the summer on a very bright day. To soften the light, the group was positioned under a tree. The combination of shooting at high noon (when the light has a high color temperature with a high blue component) and the light coming through the leaves added a blue-green color cast to the image. This made the people's skin tones too cool. **Figure 4.10** shows the same image after I applied a Color Balance Adjustment Layer. People's skin tones are now less green and more red, and white shirts are actually white. Also notice that the grass in the picture isn't as green anymore. Because the subject of the image is the people and not the grass, it's okay to let the unimportant image areas (the grass) be less attractive. Concentrate on the essential, which, in this case, is the people's skin tones.

BEFORE

© Katrin Eismann

figure 4.9

figure 4.10

1. Check the image with the Eyedropper tool and the Info palette. Notice how the white shirts have a high blue value and the skin tones are also too green and blue (see **figure 4.11**). The white shirts show more blue because white with detail (white that is not overexposed) has a higher reflectance and will show the color cast much more readily.

figure 4.11

Checking the image with the Eyedropper and Info palette reveals the green and blue color cast.

2. Add a Color Balance Adjustment layer.

3. Always start the color-correction process with the most important image areas. In this case, the group's skin tones are more important than the shirts. Select Midtones for the Tone Balance and increase magenta (to decrease green in the image) by moving the Magenta-Green slider to the left (see **figure 4.12**). A green color cast might also have a cyan component in it, so I added 5 points of red to warm up the skin tones a touch.

figure 4.12

Work on the image midtones to remove the green color cast.

Note

Red and magenta color casts can look very similar, as can blue and cyan, and green and yellow, and working on the similar color of the color cast can help clear up color problems. In this example, adding magenta reduced the green and the addition of red removed any traces of cyan.

4. Select the Highlights Tone Balance, increase the red by 10 points, and decrease the blue with a 30-point move toward the yellow, as seen in **figure 4.13**.

figure 4.13

Work on the image highlights to remove the blue color cast.

GLOBAL COLOR CORRECTION

As you know by now, Photoshop often gives you three or more ways of reaching the same end result. Some people don't like this and believe that their way is the only way. Puh-leeze...! Color correction is an art form that relies on your perception, experience, and interpretation of the image. With the following exercises, we'll use Levels and Curves to rescue some pretty sad photos from color cast fates worse than death.

Subtle Color Correction with Levels

Working with the Levels or Curves eyedroppers to define the one, two, or three neutral areas of white, gray, or black will often remove a bothersome color cast. Figure 4.14 shows a scene not many of us have seen in real life, but we all can look at the picture and see snow and soldiers in snow-camouflage suits. I would bet that many of you have seen snow or at least know that it should be a light neutral to white color. In this image, it certainly isn't—it's green. With a few clicks in Levels, we can clean up the snow and add some contrast back into the shadows, as seen in figure 4.15.

figure 4.14   *figure 4.15*

1. The first step is to identify the color cast. If you're working with a well-calibrated monitor and have a good sense for color, you'll see that the original is green. If you're not sure about color or your monitor, use the Info palette to look at the color of the sky or snow. The higher Green value reveals that there is a green color cast (see **figure 4.16**).

figure 4.16

The values in the Info palette help you identify the color cast.

2. I added a Levels Adjustment Layer and selected the white eyedropper. I clicked a light part of the snow to define a new white point. Clicking with the eyedropper not only redefines the pixels clicked to white, it also neutralizes them. In the Info palette, I noted that the values of Red, Green, and Blue are equal, proving that I removed the color cast.

3. I selected the black eyedropper and used the dark area under the truck between the left soldier's boots, as seen in **figure 4.17**, to set the new black point.

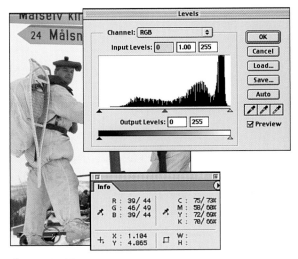

figure 4.17

Using the Levels black eyedropper to define a new black point to improve image density.

4. After defining the white and black points, take a second look at the image. If the image looks too dark or too light, use the midtone slider to lighten (by moving the midtone slider to the left) or darken (by moving the slider to the right). In this example, I moved the midtone slider to the left slightly to lighten up the midtones.

Extreme Color Correction with Levels

I sincerely hope you never have to work with an image that is as bad as **figure 4.18**. The original film was poorly stored and processed, resulting in a very dark image with a dominant green cast. In a case like this, the goal is to take the pathetic and create the acceptable, as shown in **figure 4.19**.

figure 4.18

figure 4.19

As discussed, identifying the color cast is always the first step in the color correction process. In this case, your eyes would have to be closed not to see the green problem, but take a moment to really look at the image. What is it a picture of? It's a woman standing by a wall. Look again—read the image more closely—look for clues that will help you make the best color decisions. The straw hat and open midriff hint that it's a picture of a woman on a summer day. With that clue, you can imagine that the dress could have been white. Keeping this scenario in mind will guide your color correction. Use your visual memory and color perception to develop a scenario to guide your color correction.

ch4_greenwoman.jpg

1. Add a Levels Adjustment Layer. The strong color contamination and tonal problems pushes the histogram severely to the left (see figure 4.20).

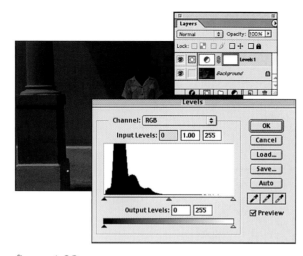

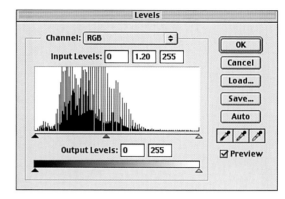

figure 4.22

Moving the midtone slider to the left lightens the image overall.

figure 4.20

The Levels histogram is strongly biased to the left—a dead giveaway for a dark or underexposed image.

2. Look for a point in her dress that could be pure white. See how the sun is coming down from the upper left and hitting the edge of her skirt that is in the breeze? Click that with the Levels white eyedropper to remove the color cast, as shown in **figure 4.21**.

Tip

You can zoom and pan while the Levels and Curves windows are open with the following command keys:

-   **Pan in the image**—Hold down the space bar to access the Hand tool.
-   **Zoom up**—Press (Cmd + Space + click) [Ctrl + Space + click].
-   **Zoom out**—Press (Cmd + Option + Space + click)[Ctrl + Alt + Space + click].

Tip

Sometimes it's just easier to start over. When working with Adjustment Layers, if you don't like where the color correction is going, you can get back to the original image by pressing (Option)[Alt] to change the Cancel button to Reset. Click and the image will revert to its original settings.

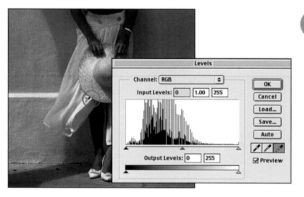

figure 4.21

After clicking with the white eyedropper, the color cast is eliminated.

3. If need be, open up the midtones of the image by sliding the gray midtone triangle carefully to the left (see **figure 4.22**). In this example, don't worry that her face is still too dark—that is a selective problem and shouldn't be treated while working on the global problem.

Improving Color and Contrast with Curves

With older images, it is often difficult to decide whether you need to fix a tonal problem or a color problem. In this example, the original slide was either slightly underexposed or the forty years since the picture was taken have taken their toll (see **figure 4.23**). In this instance, I decided to set a new black point in the child's eyes and improve the midtones with a Curves Adjustment layer to create the image seen in **figure 4.24**.

figure 4.23

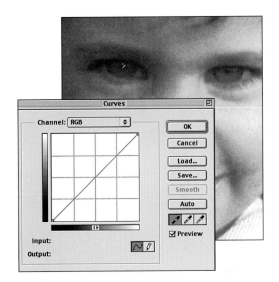

figure 4.25

Use the black eyedropper in Curves to define a new black point.

2. Boost the shadows and midtones by dragging the curve upward to add the sparkle back (see **figure 4.26**). Be careful to monitor the highlights in the girl's dress and cheeks in the Info palette so they are not forced to pure white.

figure 4.24

🌐▷ **ch4_ballgirl.jpg**

1. Add a Curves Adjustment Layer. Both Curves and Levels offer the same eyedropper tools to define white, black, and gray balance. Use the black eyedropper to carefully define a new black in the little girl's pupil, as seen in **figure 4.25**.

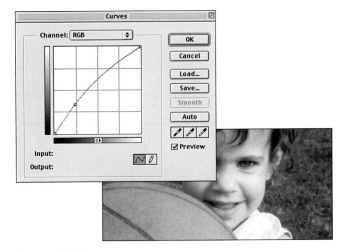

figure 4.26

Lighten the image with Curves.

Rescuing Extremely Faded Images

Over time, color slides fade and may change color. To protect your film from this fate, work with qualified professional photo labs when processing your film and store the processed film in a cool, dark, humidity-controlled environment.

The original photograph in **figure 4.27** was taken in Berlin in the early 1960s, and the slide is faded, has a cyan cast, and is covered with mold and dust damage. Not a pretty picture. The final image in **figure 4.28** has better density, color balance, and with some effective clean-up techniques, looks acceptable. (All the spotting, dust, and mold removal techniques are illustrated with this same image in Chapter 5 "Dust and Mold Removal.")

BEFORE

figure 4.27

AFTER

figure 4.28

© Eismann family archive

🌐 ⤳ **ch4_berlin.jpg**

1. In this case, the problem is two-fold. The image has both a density and a green color cast problem, which can be addressed at the same time. Add a Levels Adjustment Layer with the Blending Mode set to Multiply (which will add density), as shown in **figure 4.29**.

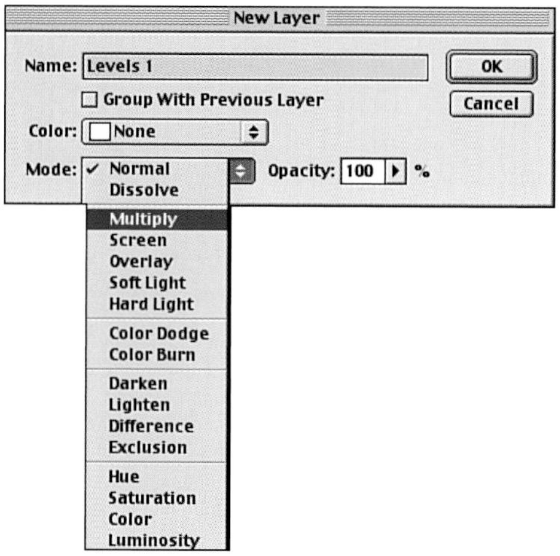

figure 4.29

(Option + click) [Alt + click] the New Adjustment Layer icon and select Levels to open the New Layer dialog box.

2. Using the gray balance eyedropper, click the sidewalk to define a neutral tone, as seen in **figure 4.30**. As with the black and white point eyedroppers, the gray balance eyedropper shifts the colors in the image to a neutral tone.

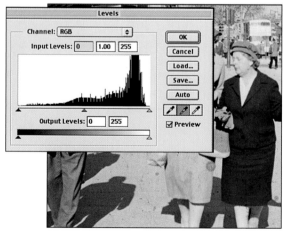

figure 4.30

Use the gray balance eyedropper to define a new midpoint value.

In this instance, the combination of the Multiply Blending Mode—needed to build up density—interfered with the neutral eyedropper and the midtones still contain too much green as seen in the Info palette (see **figure 4.31**).

3. To finesse the sidewalk to gray, change the channel in the Levels dialog box to Green and lower the green midtone slider so that the Green readout matches the Red and Blue readouts (see **figure 4.32**). For additional information on color correction by the numbers see the next section, "The Numbers Don't Lie."

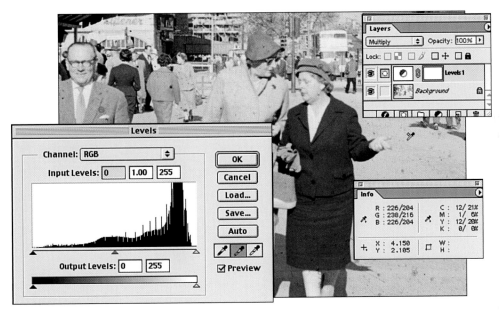

figure 4.31

Sometimes building image density with the Multiply Blending Modes exaggerates the color cast.

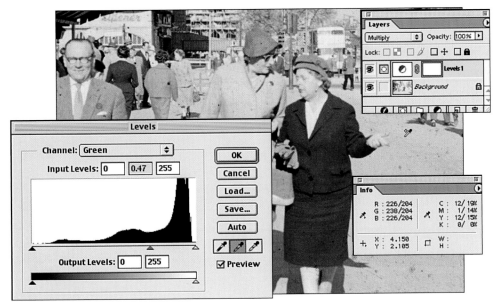

figure 4.32

Balancing the RGB values in the Info palette ensures that the color cast in the midtones has been corrected.

THE NUMBERS DON'T LIE

You're tired, had a fight with the dog, the kids played with the monitor dials, and you're just not sure what the original image really looked like. Many factors, including your mood, age, gender, and the second drink last night, can influence your color vision. So what are you supposed to do if the files are piling up and you have to get them done before going home tonight? When in doubt, do your color correction by the numbers to balance images with a mathematician's precision.

Working by the numbers entails monitoring the values in the shadows, midtones, highlights, and skin tones while you adjust individual color channels with Levels or Curves. When the highlight, midtone, and shadow RGB values are equal, your color cast problems will disappear. Working with skin tones (also called flesh tones) takes a bit more interpretation as people's skin varies with age, race, and sun exposure and will be addressed in a later section, "Balancing Skin Tones with Curves."

Tip

Here are some specifics for color correcting by the numbers with RGB files:

- **To balance highlights**—Use the highest value as read in the Info palette as the target and match the lower values to the higher.

- **To balance midtones**—Use the middle value as the target (as read in the Info palette) and match the higher and lower values to the middle one.

- **To balance shadows**—Use the lowest value as the target (as read in the Info palette) and match the higher values to the lower.

Here are some specifics for color correcting by the numbers on skin tones in CMYK files:

- In light-skinned babies, yellow and magenta are equal.

- In adults, yellow is up to 35% greater than magenta.

- Cyan makes people look tanner and darker.

- Only people with very dark skin should have noticeable amounts of black ink in their skin tones.

Balancing Neutral Tones with Levels

Color correction by the numbers always begins by identifying reference points. Look for a white, a neutral, and a shadow point to reference. I used the light clothing for the highlight reference point, the gray stone as the midtone reference, and the shadows in the background as a dark reference point. In the example seen in **figure 4.33**, the image is green and flat. After a color correction, the kids look almost as if they might be enjoying themselves, as seen in **figure 4.34**.

© Corel Corporation

BEFORE

figure 4.33

AFTER

figure 4.34

1. I added Color Samplers to the highlight (white jacket), midtone (gray rock), and shadow (dark background) reference areas, as shown in **figure 4.35**.

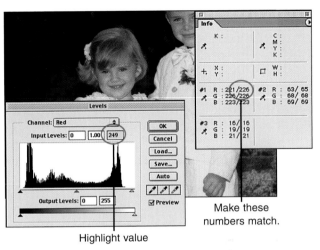

Make these
numbers match.

Highlight value

figure 4.36

Increase the Red channel highlight value to balance the highlights.

figure 4.35

Adding the Color Sampler reference points. The readout of the #1 Color Sampler is measuring and monitoring the image highlights. The higher green value reveals the green color cast and is the target value to match to neutralize the highlights.

2. I created a Levels Adjustment Layer. To eliminate the color cast in the highlights, the three RGB values should all be made equal by matching the two lower values to the higher value. In this example, the 226 readout of the Green channel in the Info palette will be the target number to match.

3. In the Levels dialog box, I selected the channel with the lowest highlight value, in this case the Red channel, and lowered the highlight value (the field farthest to the right) by tapping the down arrow key until it matched the Green channel's target of 226 (see **figure 4.36**). This does not change the Input level in the Levels dialog box to 226, but rather adjusts the Input Level until the number for the Red channel in the Info palette reads 226.

4. I selected the Blue channel and the Input Level and changed the Blue value in the Info palette to match the Green target value of 226, as shown in **figure 4.37**. Again, be sure to look at the numbers in the Info palette and match them.

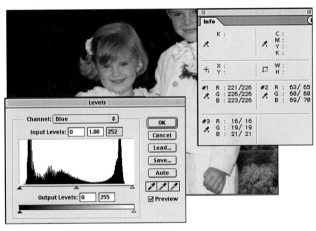

figure 4.37

Increase the blue highlight value to balance the highlights.

5. To balance the neutral areas, I worked with the midtone target values (on the stone sidewalk) by changing the midtone value (marked by Color Sampler #2) to match the median value of 68. In this example, I matched the Red and Blue channels to the 68 value of the Green channel.

6. When balancing shadows (marked by Color Sampler #3), use the lowest number as your target. In this example the Red values are the lowest, and I reduced the Green and Blue values a touch to match the target value of 16.

Balancing Skin Tones with Curves

Most of the recognized color values for reproducing skin tones are based on prepress experience and are therefore expressed in CMYK values. The schematic in **figure 4.38** shows that at one end of the spectrum the skin of a light baby has equal amounts of yellow and magenta without any cyan or black. Moving to the other end, as people mature, the amount of yellow increases in relationship to the magenta. The tanner or darker they are, the higher the amount of cyan ink is. The far end of the spectrum represents people of African descent with the additional black ink needed to accurately represent darker skin.

			C :	0%
R :	244		M :	15%
G :	222		Y :	15%
B :	204		K :	0%
X :	0		W :	
Y :	140		H :	

Light baby skin

			C :	8%
R :	213		M :	35%
G :	172		Y :	45%
B :	129		K :	0%
X :	416		W :	
Y :	126		H :	

Average Caucasian; add yellow for Asian descent

			C :	15%
R :	191		M :	49%
G :	139		Y :	68%
B :	85		K :	0%
X :	710		W :	
Y :	126		H :	

Tanned person; add Cyan to deepen tan or skin tone

			C :	27%
R :	136		M :	50%
G :	105		Y :	63%
B :	75		K :	21%
X :	1022		W :	
Y :	138		H :	

Darker-skinned person

			C :	47%
R :	65		M :	50%
G :	57		Y :	63%
B :	52		K :	55%
X :	1414		W :	
Y :	140		H :	

Very dark person

figure 4.38

CMYK representation of skin tones is shown here.

Tip

These tips will help you when working with portrait color correction and retouching:

- Set the Info palette's second readout to CMYK and watch the relationship between yellow and magenta.

- To get an overall feel for the skin tones of a person, measure an average medium value on the person's face. Avoid dark shadows and extreme highlights.

- A woman's make-up can distort the readout. Try to avoid areas that have a lot of make-up, such as cheeks, lips, and eyes.

- Collect patches of various skin tones (see figure 4.39). Select a color-corrected patch of skin, run the Gaussian Blur on it to destroy any vestige of film grain, copy it, and create a file with various skin tone swatches. Refer to these skin colors when color correcting and during advanced portrait retouching sessions.

figure 4.39

A collection of blurred skin samples can be used as a reference for color correction.

As Dam Margulis explained in the on-line ColorTheory discussion group, "Persons of Hispanic or Asian ancestry tend to share approximately the same range, which is roughly the same as the dark half of the Caucasian population. Persons in these ethnic groups always have significantly more yellow than magenta, normally 10 to 15 points. Cyan plus black tends to be 1/4 to 1/3 of the magenta value, occasionally higher in the case of unusually dark or very tan skin.

The ethnicity loosely known as black or African-American has a much wider range of possiblities than any other. Cyan is usually at least 1/3 of the magenta value, but there is no upper limit and there may also be significant black ink. In the case of someone with light ("coffee-colored") skin, the yellow is significantly higher than the magenta. However, unlike other ethnicities, as the skintone gets darker, the variation between magenta and yellow decreases, so that in the case of a very dark-skinned person, the values would be almost equal.

In **figure 4.40**, the original picture of the bride suffers from a contrast and color problem. The shadows are blue and muddy, whereas the highlights are yellow and flat. After I did some color correction by the numbers to neutralize the highlights and shadows, I targeted her forehead and created the pleasing skin tone of a young, light-skinned woman, as seen in **figure 4.41**.

figure 4.40

figure 4.41

1. I added four Color Samplers to monitor the color changes: the highlight in the wedding dress, the midtone in the mother's dress in the background, the shadow point on the father's tuxedo, and the bride's forehead.

2. I added a Curves Adjustment Layer and used the black, gray, and white eyedroppers in Curves to define the shadow, gray, and white neutral areas.

   Although the three neutral areas are defined, the #4 Color Sampler readout shows that the bride's skin tones are still too cyan and yellow.

3. I selected the Cyan channel in the Curves dialog box and moved the highlight point to the left. This clears up the muddiness and lets her skin begin to shine through, as shown in **figure 4.42**.

4. I selected the Yellow channel and decreased the yellow until it is approximately 25% higher than the magenta ink (see **figure 4.43**).

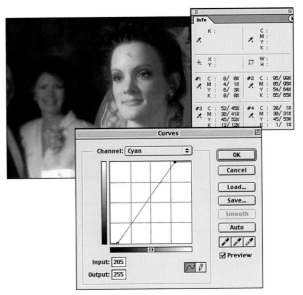

figure 4.42

While watching the #4 Info palette readout, I reduced the Cyan channel's highlight to take out the 20% cyan cast that was in the bride's forehead.

Tip

While in the Curves dialog box, (Cmd + click) [Ctrl + click] the area that you want to change to add a handle to the curve that you can manipulate with the mouse or the arrow keys

Pressing Ctrl + Tab on both platforms will move from point to point on the curve.

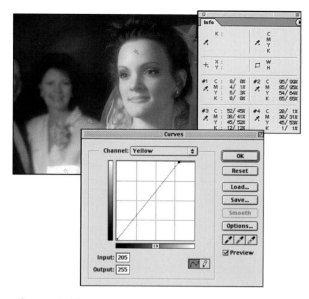

figure 4.43

The yellow ink can be ¼ to ⅓ higher than the magenta.

5. By taking out the tiny bit of black that was still in her skin tones, the overall density was removed, which opened up the tonal rendition of the image, as seen in **figure 4.44**.

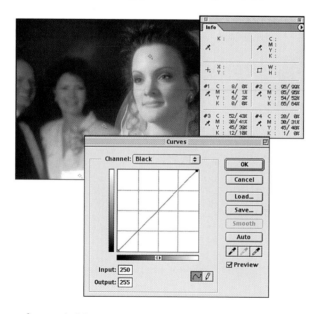

figure 4.44

Reducing any hint of black ink lightens up the overall tone of her face.

SELECTIVE COLOR CORRECTION

Until now, we've worked on global color correction, but images can have different problems in different areas. Sometimes one part of the image will be fine and another area is way off color. Differing color casts can occur due to poor storage conditions, mixed lighting when the photo was originally taken, or misprocessing. Always start with the global color correction, then select the problem areas that remain and apply local color correction.

Combining Global and Selective Color Correction

The image in **figure 4.45** contains a horrid yellow cast throughout the image. After applying a global color correction with Levels to remove the cast, the farmer's face was still much too red and ruddy. After making a selection and applying a local color change with a Selective Color Adjustment Layer, he looks much better, as seen in **figure 4.46**.

figure 4.45

figure 4.46

1. I added Color Samplers to a highlight (window frame), midtone (sidewalk), shadow (inside left window), and skin tone point to monitor the color correction process.

2. I used Levels to apply the color correction by the numbers technique as described previously to balance out the highlights, midtones, and shadows. Often, removing a global Color cast will clean up the entire image, but in this case, the farmer's face is still much too yellow-red, as seen in **figure 4.47**.

figure 4.47

After global color correction, the farmer's face is still too red and yellow.

3. To control where the local color correction takes place, I selected the area—the farmer's face—with the Lasso tool with a 3-pixel feather. As you can see in **figure 4.48**, I wasn't very careful with my selection, and that's okay, because this selection will serve as a basis for the next color-correction step.

Note

The amount of feathering used depends on the file size. Higher resolution images require a higher feather amount.

4. With the selection active, I added a Selective Color Adjustment Layer. As you can see in **figure 4.49**, Photoshop automatically creates a mask displaying the color correction in what was the selected area and is now the white area of the mask. Selective Color enables you to target specific colors as RGB, CMYK, or neutral values. Selective Color lets you work in absolute or relative mode. I prefer absolute because it removes or adds the specified percentage; the relative method

jumps through mathematical hoops to calculate the percentage within a color and I can't predict what it is doing.

figure 4.48

Selecting the face with a feathered Lasso tool.

figure 4.49

I removed red and yellow from his face with a Selective Color Adjustment Layer.

5. Because his face still has a very strong yellow cast to it, I dropped down to the yellow component and removed the yellow. Because he is an older man who has spent a lot of time outdoors, leaving some cyan and black component makes sense for him.

6. After I clicked OK to the Selective Color correction, I zoomed in on the farmer's face to inspect the edges of the color correction.

7. If there are some unaffected areas or areas where color correction took place that I didn't like, I used a white brush on the Adjustment Layer to add color correction or use a black brush to take away (hide) unwanted color correction, as seen in **figure 4.50**. Refining the active area with a brush enabled me to refine edges with much greater ease than trying to make a perfect lasso selection in the first place.

Tip

When making changes to a mask, don't forget that you can change the hardness of any brush to achieve a better match of areas in the mask that are already feathered.

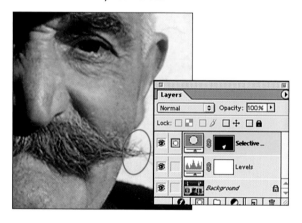

figure 4.50

Painting directly on the Adjustment Layer's layer mask allows you to refine the edges of the color correction.

Targeting the Problem Color

In **figure 4.51**, the color cast is rather subtle, but the higher green readout in the Info palette reveals that the neutral tone of the studio background does have a green cast. Additionally, looking at the individual grayscale channels can be helpful to see a color cast. Because the studio background is supposed to be neutral gray, all three color channels should have the same black density. As you can see in **figure 4.52** the red and blue are balanced with 47% density, but the Green channel is only at 40%. Wherever the channel is lighter, more light is allowed through, creating a color cast.

At first I thought this would be a simple file to color correct; just add either a Curves or Levels adjustment layer and use the gray balance eyedropper tool to click the neutral background to remove the Color cast and I'd be done. But after neutralizing the backdrop, I noticed that the man was still much too yellow, and the challenge remained to select just the yellow as described to achieve a balanced image, as seen in **figure 4.53**.

figure 4.51

Red channel, 47%   Green channel, 40%   Blue channel, 47%

figure 4.52

Checking the balance of individual channels.

figure 4.53

1. I added a Levels Adjustment Layer and clicked the studio backdrop with the gray eyedropper to neutralize the green color cast in the studio backdrop.

2. The man is still too yellow as seen in **figure 4.54**. The yellow problem isn't on the Adjustment Layer but rather the Background layer. Always work on the layer that contains the problem, which in this case is the yellow cast in the man. I made the Background layer active.

figure 4.54

The man's skin tones are still too yellow.

3. To select just the yellow components of the image, I chose Select > Color Range and selected Yellows from the drop-down menu, as seen in **figure 4.55**. The Color Range interface shows how Photoshop is making a selection mask that we can use in combination with any type of Adjustment Layer.

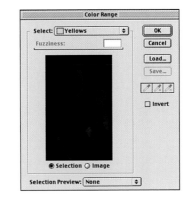

figure 4.55

Select the yellows with Color Range.

4. Photoshop may pop up a warning box that says that no pixels were selected more than 50%. You can ignore this warning, as the selection will still be active. Photoshop just won't display the dancing ants!

5. I added a Curves Adjustment Layer and switched to the Blue channel (because blue is the opposite of yellow). In the Layers palette, a mask is automatically created from the Color Range selection. Wherever the mask is black, no color correction will take place, and wherever it is white or lighter, more color correction will occur.

6. I dragged the curve upward to remove the yellow color cast, as shown in **figure 4.56**.

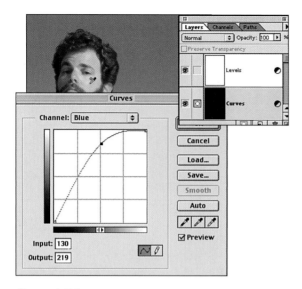

figure 4.56

I raised the Blue curve to remove yellow.

Repairing Color

Color damage can be caused by light leaks in the camera, misprocessing, or time, and it can be among the most challenging things to repair. In this example, the image is too dark and there is a blatant blue-magenta splotch on the bottom right corner of the image (see **figure 4.57**). After improving the tone and repairing the color damage, the final print is acceptable, as seen in **figure 4.58**.

figure 4.57

Tip

Only fix that which is broken or damaged. Don't mess with channels that contain good information.

figure 4.58

Before jumping into the repair process, take a moment to look at the image and, in a case like this, inspect the individual color channels. As you can see in **figure 4.59**, only the Blue channel reveals any significant damage. This tidbit of useful information will guide our repair workflow.

Red channel

Green channel

Blue channel

figure 4.59

Inspect the individual channels to isolate damage.

ch4_patio.jpg

1. Start by improving the overall tonal value of the image with a Curve Adjustment Layer. Set the white point on the edge of the door, the gray point on the concrete of the patio, and lighten the shadows by moving the lower portion of the Curve upward.

2. To fix the splotch, make the damaged Blue channel active. Select the damaged area with either the Magic Wand tool or the Lasso tool as seen in **figure 4.60**.

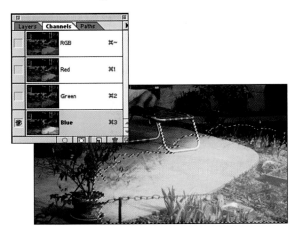

figure 4.60

Select the damaged area.

3. Return to the layers palette and add a Hue/Saturation Adjustment Layer. Because the damage is only on the Blue channel, select Blues from the Edit menu as seen in **figure 4.61**.

figure 4.61

Target the blues.

4. The goal is to match the damaged Blue channel with the intact Red and Green channels. Remove all Saturation from the Blue channel and visually adjust the Lightness setting to tonally balance the splotch area with the rest of the image, as seen in **figure 4.62**. This will yield a neutral area for you to recolor.

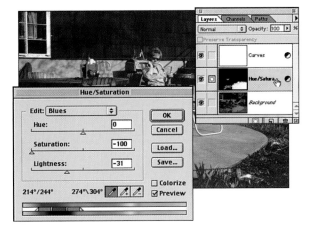

figure 4.62

Pull out saturation and fine-tune the lightness to balance the image.

5. Removing saturation and balancing the tone has created a grayscale splotch as seen in **figure 4.62**. Add a new layer and set its Blending Mode to Color. Use greens and browns to paint on the Color Layer as seen in **figure 4.63**.

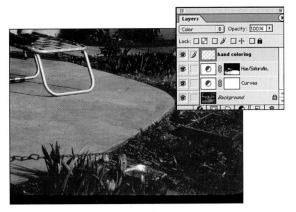

figure 4.63

Color the image to rebuild the illusion of plants.

CORRECTING COLOR TEMPERATURE PROBLEMS

As I mentioned earlier, color casts can happen when you use the wrong color temperature film for the lighting situation at hand. For example, using daylight film indoors can lead to green or orange pictures. Our eyes don't see color temperature while taking the photograph, because they balance out light to white no matter how cool or warm the light really is, but these color casts show up on film.

In the following example, I was photographing in a museum in England. I had only daylight film and the museum was illuminated with fluorescent lighting fixtures—a lethally green combination, as **figure 4.64** shows. With a few Photoshop steps I was able to change the color temperature of the file from fluorescent green to neutral daylight as seen in **figure 4.65**. A useful correction method is to compensate for the undesired color temperature of the light by filtering the image with the opposite color.

figure 4.64

figure 4.65

 Note

It is always better to use either the right color temperature film for the task at hand or to filter the lens or your lights to balance the color temperature. As I've said many times before, if the picture is taken correctly, there will be less work to do on the computer, and a smaller chance of unnatural results. However, this often requires professional equipment, including a color meter, color correction filters, and gels that you might not have on hand.

 ch4_knight.jpg

1. Use the Eyedropper tool to sample an area that is midtone to highlight and contains the offending color cast (see **figure 4.66**).

2. Add a new layer to the image and fill it with the sampled color.

3. Change the layer's Blending Mode to Color.

figure 4.66

Select the offending color with the Eyedropper tool.

4. Invert the color by selecting Image > Adjust > Invert or (Cmd + I)[Ctrl + I] to change the selected offending color into its opposite. This will neutralize the color cast.

5. Lower the opacity of the layer. My experience has taught me that 50% is effective.

6. In some cases, you might need to boost the contrast with Curves, as seen in **figure 4.67**.

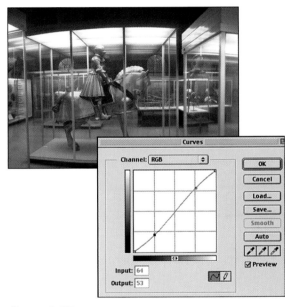

figure 4.67

Fine-tune the image contrast with Curves.

INTERCHANNEL COLOR CORRECTION

Photoshop offers many different perspectives for retouching. For example, my photographic training allows me to work out imaging solutions from a photographic and darkroom perspective, whereas people with a lot of prepress and printing experience will approach Photoshop from a different point of view. As I was working on this book, I had the pleasure of having my Photoshop eyes opened by Chris Tarantino, who comes to Photoshop with 20 years of dot-etching and high-end prepress experience.

When Chris looks at a CMYK file, the first thing he looks at are the flesh tones. As Chris explains, "When the flesh looks good, the viewer will be attracted to the product." His color correction process always starts by evaluating the individual color channels for tone, gradation, and transitions that he can take advantage of to shape the color of an image. Rather than working with Adjustment Layers, Chris does all his color correction through the Apply Image command. The Apply Image command allows you to mix varying amounts of different channels with each other with precise control.

In the following example, Chris color corrected the photograph of the model for a very demanding high-quality import catalogue. As you can see in **figure 4.68**, the model's skin tones are too ruddy and, due to lack of tonal separation, the clothing is disappearing into the background. After applying interchannel color correction, the model's face is clear, and the sweater has been color corrected to match the merchandise, as seen in **figure 4.69**. Chris creates selection masks for each image element.

BEFORE

figure 4.68

figure 4.69

Chris always starts with the skin tones, and upon inspecting the four channels (shown in **figure 4.70**), he saw that the Magenta channel was too dark, blocked up, and lacking in detail. However, the Cyan channel had a full range of gray throughout that he could use to add tone and detail to the Magenta plate.

Chris selected Image > Apply Image and, as seen in **figure 4.71**, he blended 25% of the Cyan channel into the Magenta channel. Interestingly enough, he used the Magenta channel to mask itself out by checking mask and invert. Wherever the Magenta channel had been dark, it would now be light, and the Cyan grayscale information could be added to provide tonal detail for her face.

By using the better channel to replace the weaker one, Chris can simultaneously apply color correction and build up tonal and detail information, as seen in **figure 4.72**.

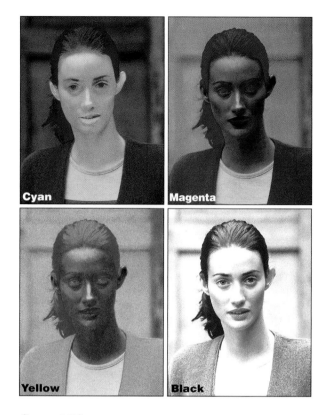

figure 4.70

Chris starts by looking for detail, gradation, and information in each of the individual color channels.

figure 4.71

Chris uses the Apply Image command to add good cyan grayscale information to the weaker magenta plate.

figure 4.72

After improving both the magenta and yellow color plates, the model's skin is much clearer.

CLOSING THOUGHTS

The importance of good color—pleasing color—cannot be underestimated. Trying out the techniques in this chapter on your own images will teach you more than any book. So open up some images and learn to really *see* color, both to remove it and to accentuate it—it's all-important.

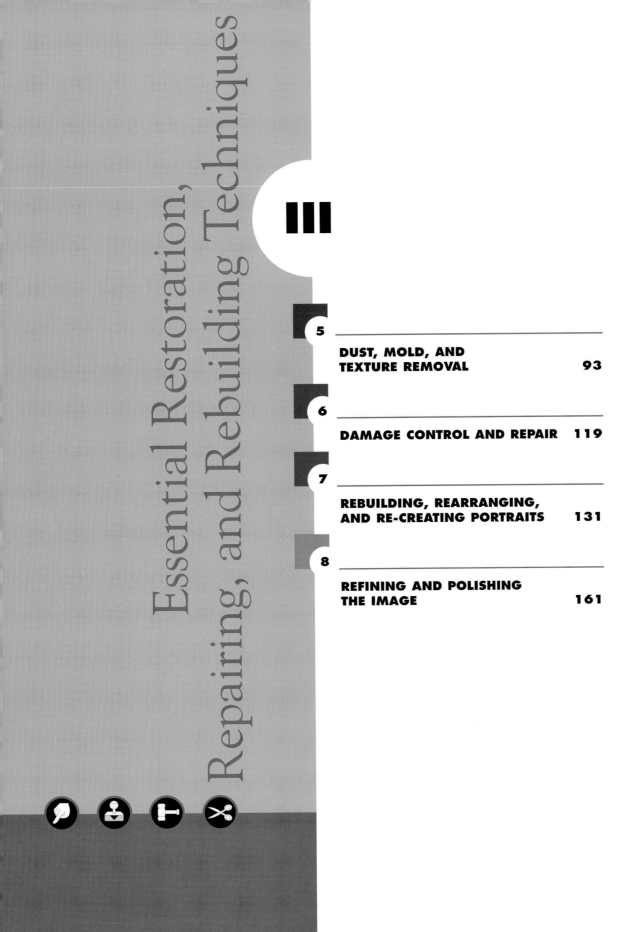

III

Essential Restoration, Repairing, and Rebuilding Techniques

5

DUST, MOLD, AND TEXTURE REMOVAL

Cleanliness is next to godliness, and without starting a religious debate, I am sure you agree with me that the bane of all retouchers is dust, mold, moiré patterns, print texture, and film grain. Removing these problems can be a time-consuming, eye-straining, arm-numbing endeavor, all of which can really take the fun out of digital retouching. In this chapter you'll face the worst problems and learn the best techniques to rescue your images from the evils that lurk in historical negatives, glass plates, prints, contemporary film, and digital images.

The problems tackled in this chapter include

- Removing dust, mold, and scratches
- Minimizing moiré patterns and paper texture
- Reducing, maintaining, and matching film grain

The tools used to conquer these dusty and dirty challenges include

- Layers and Blending Modes
- The Clone Stamp tool
- The Blur tool
- Photoshop filters
- The History palette and History Brush tool

So roll up your mousing sleeve and let's get to work.

Depending on the severity of the problem, there are numerous Photoshop techniques to clean up dust and mold, many of which can be used interchangeably or in combination with one another. My favorite technique is to avoid the problem in the first place by cleaning the negative, print, or scanner before making the scan. By carefully brushing or blowing off loose dust from a negative or print, you're removing the source of the problem. Never rub film, prints, or scanner platens very hard because you can scratch and permanently damage them.

Because there isn't one perfect method to remove dust specks or to reduce mold damage, this chapter includes a variety of methods to tackle these problems. Dust problems are most often seen as very small specs of dark or light pixels, and mold damage looks mottled, patterned, or discolored and affects larger areas. By experimenting with or combining methods, you'll develop techniques to take care of your image's worst problems.

DUSTBUSTING 101

An important concept to recognize is that there is no dust in a digital file. The dust was on or in the original. In the digital file all you really have is lighter or darker pixels in contrast to darker or lighter backgrounds. Taking advantage of this concept can speed up your dustbusting sessions.

Using the Blur Tool

The Blur tool is especially useful on files that have a lot of small, random dust specks on a variety of backgrounds. Over the years dust became embedded in the original image shown in **figure 5.1**. After scanning, the myriad of small, dark specks makes the wall and the image look dirty and unattractive. The Blur tool was used successfully to clean up the image, as seen in **figure 5.2**.

figure 5.1

figure 5.2

 ch_5dust01.jpg

1. Add a new layer to the file.
2. Activate the Blur tool and set its options to 100% Pressure and Use All Layers as seen in **figure 5.3**. To eradicate light specks, set the Blur tool's Blending Mode to Darken; to make dark specks disappear, set the Blending Mode to Lighten.

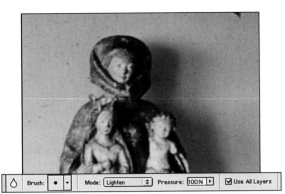

figure 5.3

Set the Blur tool to 100% Pressure and Lighten Mode to remove dark specks.

3. Zoom in to 100% or 200% view.

4. Set the Blur tool's size to approximately match the size of the dust speck.

5. Click and hold the Blur tool over the dust spot (see **figure 5.4**). The longer you hold down the mouse button, the more the dust will be blurred into oblivion.

figure 5.4

Hold down the Blur tool over the speck until it disappears.

 N o t e

Be careful not to overblur the dust because that will soften the image area so much that soft blobs will begin to appear. There is a fine balance between just right and too much blurring—with a bit of practice you'll develop an eye for the right amount of blurring.

T i p

Matching the size of the brush to the size of the dust speck to be removed and using a hard-edged brush ensures that you don't soften the grain of the image surrounding the dust speck. Use the keyboard shortcuts to control the size of the brushes:

Left bracket ([) decreases brush size.

Right bracket (]) increases brush size.

Using the Shift key with either bracket adjusts the brush hardness in 25% increments.

The Float and Move Technique

Use the *float and move* technique on unimportant image areas such as skies or backgrounds to quickly disguise dust on large surfaces. Duplicating a troublesome area with a slight offset and applying a Lighten Blending Mode is a quick and easy way to remove many flaws. I first heard about this technique from Stephen Johnson as he was retouching numerous glass plate negatives for his book, "The Great Central Valley."

Figure 5.5 and **figure 5.6** show before and after detail of the identical file that was cleaned up with the float and move technique. Notice how the dust and mold has been minimized in the sidewalk and the sky. (Because I didn't float and move any important image areas such as the buildings or people, they still have dust and damage that will require individual attention later in the retouching process.)

figure 5.5

figure 5.6

🌐▷⬦ **ch5dust02.jpg**

1. Select the Lasso tool and set the Feather to 2–5 pixels. The amount of feather depends on your file size—a 10MB file needs a larger feather than a 1MB file.

2. Make a very rough, irregular selection around the dusty areas, as seen in **figure 5.7**. Our eyes more easily detect a straight line, so the ragged edges disguise your retouching better.

figure 5.7

Roughly selecting the dusty area helps hide any obvious edges in the sky after retouching.

3. Transfer this selection onto a new layer by selecting Layer > New > Layer via Copy (Cmd + J)[Ctrl + J].

4. Press V to select the Move tool and use the arrow keys to nudge the new layer down and over to the right 2–3 pixels.

5. Change the moved layer's Blending Mode to Lighten to hide the dark spots (see **figure 5.8**).

figure 5.8

After moving the new layer, change the Blending Mode to Lighten to hide dust and mold.

A Professional Float and Move Example

Photographer John Warner used the float and move technique to repair the lawn of a croquet field which had been aerated to promote lawn growth. John needed to photograph the playing surface for a promotional brochure before the grass had a chance to recover, as shown in **figure 5.9**, so he used Photoshop to repair the lawn faster than Mother Nature could have (see **figure 5.10**).

BEFORE

figure 5.9

AFTER

figure 5.10

1. John duplicated the Background layer and set the Blending Mode to Darken, then named the layer Lawn Care.

2. He used the Move tool and the arrow keys to move the Darken layer several pixels down until the white holes disappeared.

3. Duplicating and moving the entire layer also affected the cottages. To bring the cottages back into focus, John added a layer mask by clicking the Add Layer Mask icon on the Layers palette.

4. He used the Gradient tool to draw a black-to-white blend on the layer mask to block the Darken Blending Mode from affecting the cottages and upper part of the lawn, as seen in **figure 5.11**.

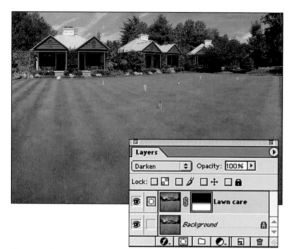

figure 5.11

A gradient will hide areas that you don't want affected with a layer mask.

5. Finally, John cloned over any remaining white marks on the croquet lawn to add the final polish to the image.

Controlling the Dust & Scratches Filter

The float and move technique works very well on unimportant image areas, such as sky and studio backgrounds. As good as this technique is, it may also soften important image texture or film grain. Use the following Dust & Scratches filter technique whenever you need to maintain texture or film grain.

Figure 5.12 and figure 5.13 show a before and after detail of the identical file that was cleaned up with this Dust & Scratches filter technique. Notice how the numerous dust specks and most of the mold has been removed from the sidewalk although the film grain and sidewalk texture is still visible.

figure 5.12

figure 5.13

🌐▷〈 **ch5dust02.jpg**

1. Select the Lasso tool and set the Feather to 2–5 pixels. The amount of feather depends on your file size—a 10MB file needs a larger feather than a 1MB file.

2. Make a very rough, irregular selection around the dusty areas, as seen in **figure 5.14**.

figure 5.14

Roughly selecting the dusty area helps hide any obvious edges in the sidewalk after removing the dust and mold.

3. Transfer this selection onto a new layer by selecting Layer > New > Layer via Copy (Cmd + J)[Ctrl + J].

4. Select Filter > Noise > Dust & Scratches. Move the Radius setting up until the dust is obliterated, as seen in **figure 5.15**.

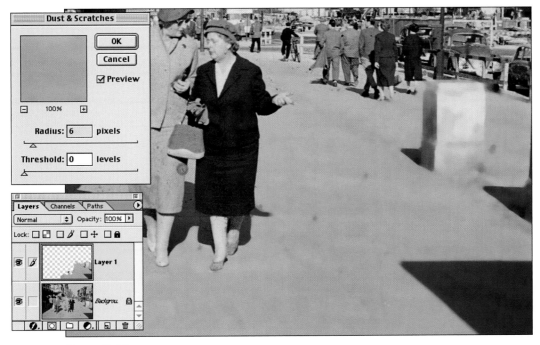

figure 5.15

Adjust the Dust & Scratches filter filter to remove the flaws in the duplicated layer.

5. Increase the Threshold value of the Dust & Scratches filter so that the texture is maintained while the dust remains hidden, as seen in **figure 5.16**.

figure 5.16

Increasing the threshold allows you to maintain texture while hiding the dust and the majority of the mold.

ERADICATING MOLD, MILDEW, AND FUNGUS

The best way to avoid mold, fungus, and mildew problems is to store your photographs in a humidity-controlled environment with a relative humidity of 65% or less. According to Henry Wilhelm's book, *The Permanence and Care of Color Photographs*, the problem lies in the fact that "gelatin, the major component of the emulsion of films and prints, is unfortunately an excellent nutrient for fungi." Couple that fact with the reality that fungal spores are everywhere and can thrive even in the coldest environments (think of the bottom drawer of your refrigerator) and you have a mold-growing time-bomb on your hands. It gets even worse—insects are attracted to fungus, and they're more than happy to munch on your valuable photographs too.

Working with the Clone Stamp Tool

At the first sign of a fungus attack, clean the film with a cotton swab and Kodak Film Cleaner. Then scan in the film and use the following techniques to rid the world of this evil. Removing mold from a print should be done only by a professional photo conservator. Do not try to wash, clean, or treat original prints unless you can live with the consequences that anything you do to the original print might actually damage the paper more than the mold already has. **Figure 5.17** and **figure 5.18** show a before and after that I cleaned with the following Clone Stamp technique. This exercise continues with ch5dust02.jpg from the previous exercise, or you can download ch5mold01.jpg to work along.

BEFORE

figure 5.17

AFTER

figure 5.18

ch5mold01.jpg

1. Create a new layer and name it Mold Removal.

2. Set the Clone Stamp options to work in Normal mode at 100% Opacity and—most importantly—click Use All Layers. This tells the Clone Stamp tool to sample down through all the layers.

3. Working on the dedicated Mold Removal layer use the Clone Stamp tool as you usually would: (Option + click)[Alt + click] to sample good image areas and then clone over the mold. **Figure 5.19** shows the cleaned-up image. In **figure 5.20**, I've turned off all layers except for the Mold Removal layer for you to see what it looks like.

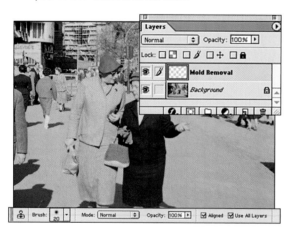

figure 5.19

Working on an empty layer with the Clone Stamp tool set to Use All Layers gives you the ability to add and erase repairs without affecting the background layer.

figure 5.20

The isolated retouch layer.

Working with History

Photoshop's History feature keeps track of your steps and enables you to move backward and foreward in your editing process. By taking snapshots you can take notes of the state of the file at certain points in the retouching process. An additional feature is the History Brush tool that enables you to selectively paint back from History. In the following example, the original image, seen in **figure 5.21**, reveals extensive mold damage, but the retouched file in **figure 5.22** is mold free and pleasing in tone and color.

figure 5.21

figure 5.22

ch5_antiquemold.jpg

1. Start the retouching session by inspecting the three individual channels. As you can see in **figure 5.23**, the mold shows up the worst on the Blue channel.

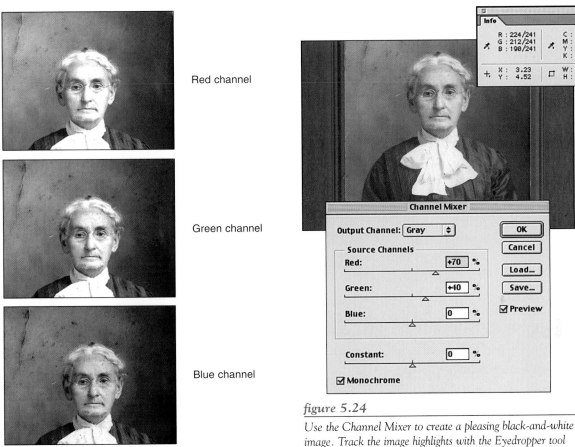

Red channel

Green channel

Blue channel

figure 5.23

Inspect the three channels before retouching to determine which is the best to work with. Often you can make quick work of your job by discarding severely damaged channels.

2. Use a Channel Mixer Adjustment Layer to change the yellow faded original to a pleasing grayscale image, as shown in **figure 5.24**. In this case I only used the Red and Green channel information by checking the Monochrome box to make Photoshop ignore the damaged Blue channel. As a general rule of thumb, when using the Channel Mixer, the total of the three color percentages should equal 100% in order to maintain the original image tonality. However, by adding 10% more green information, I am able to boost the image's contrast.

N o t e

There are no hard and fast numeric values that you can apply to all antique images. Practice your visual judgement to create images with pleasing contrast and tonal detail.

figure 5.24

Use the Channel Mixer to create a pleasing black-and-white image. Track the image highlights with the Eyedropper tool and the Info palette.

3. Take a snapshot of the merged layers by (Option + clicking)[Alt + clicking] the Create a New Snapshot icon on the History palette. Just as with layers, get into the habit of naming the snapshots, as seen in **figure 5.25**.

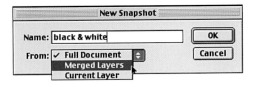

figure 5.25

Creating and naming a History Snapshot.

4. Make the Background layer active and choose Filter > Noise > Median set to a 2- or 3-pixel radius. The careful reader will notice that I am modifying the Background layer, something I rarely do. In my own defense, I have found that working with History gives me wiggle room to experiment and modify layers without losing too much sleep.

5. Take and name a snapshot of the blurred Background layer.

6. Open the History Brush options and set the options to Soft Light at 25%–50% Opacity. Set the History Source to the Black and White snapshot created in Step 3.

7. Paint with a large, soft brush over the figure's face and clothing (see **figure 5.26**). Notice how the face and clothing come through the blur while the mold damage is being ignored. The large tears and cracks in the background will need some refinement with the Clone Stamp in Part 2.

figure 5.27

Working with both the History Brush and the Clone Stamp allows you to quickly touch up an image.

10. One of the nicest aspects of old pictures such as this one is the frame, but the Median filter also blurred the frame. Select the center part of the image with a 2-pixel feather Marquee tool, as seen in **figure 5.28**. It is often easier to select the areas you do not want to affect and then choose Select > Inverse to select the opposite areas.

figure 5.26

Brushing the face back with the History Brush.

figure 5.28

Selecting the inside of the frame.

8. To refine the mold removal and to clean up the areas behind the woman, use the Clone Stamp on an empty layer. Add and name a new retouch layer.

9. Use the Clone Stamp set to Use All Layers to clean up the details on the background and to spot out any remaining specks, as seen in **figure 5.27**.

11. Make the Background layer active.

12. Set the History source to the Black and White snapshot, select Edit > Fill, and set the Contents to History, as seen in **figure 5.29**. Click OK and notice how the frame pops back into focus. Deselect the frame.

figure 5.29

Setting up the History Fill parameters to bring the frame of the old photograph back into focus.

13. To add that old-fashioned, sepia-toned look to the final image, select a color either from the original file, another image, or use the Photoshop Color Picker to select a color of your choice.

14. Add a new layer on top of the retouching layers and fill it with the selected foreground color.

15. Set this layer's Blending Mode to Color and lower the Opacity until the desired tone and color is produced (see **figure 5.30**).

figure 5.30

Changing the Blending Mode to Color and lowering the Opacity to create the desired effect is an easy and quick way to tone an image with any color you like.

MINIMIZING OFFSET MOIRÉ

Sooner rather than later, a client will have only a printed image clipped from a magazine or brochure for you to work with. The entire image in **figure 5.31** is covered with moiré rosette patterns caused by four-color separation offset printing. The following retouching technique, developed by the late Carl Volk, works well for removing moiré problems. In this process, you are throwing the image out of focus a little, then trying to sharpen the contrasty areas without sharpening the dot pattern. **Figure 5.32** shows the improved image after this resizing and blurring process.

Before you start trying to repair the damage, ask the client politely if she might have a photographic original. If not, swallow hard and follow these recommendations to minimize the horrid moiré effect.

figure 5.31

figure 5.32

Note

I am not condoning scanning images from magazines, books, or stock catalogs, as that would be breaking U.S. copyright law. Rather, I am recognizing that sometimes you or a client has only a magazine or brochure image of her factory (for example) for you to work with. Or in the worst case scenario, the original negative or film has been lost or damaged and the only image available is a prescreened one.

ch5_postcard.jpg

1. Scan the printed piece at three to four times higher resolution than you will need for your final print.

2. Start with the following values, which you might need to adjust for your own moiré problem images. Apply a .5-pixel Gaussian Blur to the Red channel, .7 pixels to the Green, and 1 pixel to the Blue.

Tip

Use keyboard shortcuts to quickly access the individual channels in your image. Use (Cmd + 1)[Ctrl + 1] for Red, (Cmd + 2)[Ctrl + 2] for Green, and (Cmd + 3)[Ctrl + 3] for Blue. (Cmd + ~)[Ctrl + ~] will return you to the composite image. When one of the separated channels is active, pressing ~ will keep the color channel active but preview the full-color image in the Photoshop window.

3. To resample the file down 25%, select Image > Image Size (see **figure 5.33**). Change the Width unit of measurement to percent and enter 75. (The other values will change automatically when Constrain Proportions is checked, as it should be.) Be sure to check Resample Image.

4. Repeat the Gaussian Blur procedure on each channel with approximately 25% lower Gaussian Blur amounts. The .7 amount can be dropped down to .5 and the .5 to .3. The 25% lower values are used because the image size has been reduced by 25%.

5. If the moiré pattern is still visible, resample the image down 25% again.

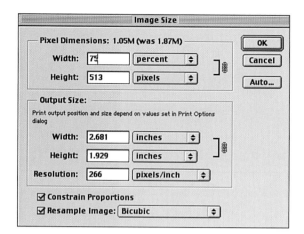

figure 5.33

Resampling the image down by 25%.

6. After it starts looking better, and as you are approaching your final resolution and size, choose Filter > Sharpen > Unsharp Mask. For a 300-dpi file or close, use these settings: Amount, 100; Radius, 1.7; Threshold, 12 to 16. After using the Unsharp Mask filter to offset the softness added with the Gaussian Blur and image resizing, the image details should look acceptably sharp. As described in Chapter 8, "Refining and Polishing the Image," you should use the Unsharp Mask filter carefully as you don't want to create ugly, white-halo artifacts around image edges.

7. Resample the image down to final size. After resizing the image, you might need to run the Unsharp Mask filter again to create a pleasingly crisp image. Use a smaller Radius setting on this final pass of the Unsharp Mask filter.

As you can imagine—going through all these steps is a last resort technique to remove moiré—it would be best to start from the original film.

REDUCING DIGITAL CAMERA NOISE AND MOIRÉ

Digital cameras are based on a variety of technologies, including scanning, peizo, three-shot, and the one-shot cameras. Every digital camera technology has its pros and cons, which have been addressed in *Real World Digital Photography*, which I coauthored with Deke McClelland.

The one-shot cameras work just like your film camera, except that a CCD (Charged Coupled Device) with a color mosaic filter replaces the film. The CCD structure, in combination with the filter, can cause color artifacts that look like little twinkles of colored lights or rainbow-like moiré patterns might be visible in areas of high-frequency, fine-detail information, such as eyelashes, flyaway hair strands, specular highlights, small branches of trees, or woven fabrics, as seen in **figure 5.34**.

Even if you don't use a digital camera, you might pick up moiré patterns when scanning images with fine fabrics, and you can use the following techniques to take care of those problems.

Blurring and Sharpening in Lab Color Mode

Moiré and color artifacts like those in **figure 5.35** show up as problems in the color channels. By separating the color information from the black-and-white image information, you can fix what's broken—the color artifacts—without affecting what's not—the tonal information, as seen in **figure 5.36**.

 Tip

When using any of these techniques to remove moiré or color artifacts, make sure you view your image at 100% monitor view to accurately see what is occurring.

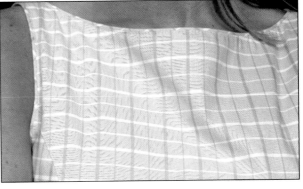

figure 5.34

Extreme rainbow moiré problems might be impossible to eradicate completely.

BEFORE

figure 5.35

AFTER

figure 5.36

© Katrin Eismann

ch5_moire_crop.jpg

1. Choose Image > Mode > Lab Color to convert the RGB file to Lab.

2. Make the "a" channel active and then press ~ to see the full-color image. Run the Gaussian Blur filter with a high-enough radius to soften the artifacts. Don't try to eradicate all artifacts at once because you will be repeating the Gaussian Blur filter on the "b" channel in the following step (see **figure 5.37**).

figure 5.38

Sharpening the Lightness channel to sharpen the black-and-white image information.

Note

It would be unwise to use my values as the right values for all image problems. The Gaussian Blur and Unsharp Mask settings shown here offer good starting points. You might need to increase or reduce values to fine-tune the artifact removal in your images.

figure 5.37

Blurring the a channel to lessen the color artifacts.

3. Select the "b" channel and run the Gaussian Blur filter on the "b" channel. Use a higher radius than you used on the "a" channel as the "b" channel usually has more color artifact problems.

4. Select the Lightness channel and choose Filter > Sharpen > Unsharp Mask to sharpen up the black-and-white information, as seen in **figure 5.38**.

5. Make the composite channel active and inspect the image for any stray color artifacts. Use the Sponge tool set to Desaturate to brush away any artifacts that the global approach might have missed.

6. Using this Lab blur and sharpen technique can sometimes desaturate the entire image, making it look flat and faded. To offset this undesired side effect, use a Hue/Saturation Adjustment Layer to boost the saturation, as seen in **figure 5.39**.

figure 5.39

Boosting overall saturation.

This technique might sound like a lot of steps but, thankfully, the entire procedure and settings are actionable. By making a Photoshop Action, you can batch process an entire folder of digital camera images in a fraction of the time it would take to do this step-by-step. Go to www.digital retouch.org and download the Action moiré_removal.atn. Another practice file, ch5_costume.jpg, is also on the site.

Using Quantum Mechanics Software

If you work with a lot of digital camera files, making a modest investment in Quantum Mechanic™ Lite or Pro (www.camerabits.com) to do all the previously described work for you and do it better makes a lot of sense. Both Quantum Mechanic Lite and Quantum Mechanic Pro are designed to remove color noise and artifacts. They work very well with Kodak's cameras and high-end cameras that don't do any similar kind of filtering in their host software.

Quantum Mechanic Lite (see **figure 5.40**) uses a quick filtering mode with simple controls for busy workflows, such as newspapers. QM Pro (see **figure 5.41**) has complete control over all the parameters of color filtering, and includes a more advanced filtering mode to retain color detail. Best of all, both flavors of the plug-in work in 48-bit mode and the sharpening is much more effective in 48-bit mode, producing less artifacting with smoother results and better shadow noise reduction. After selecting specific areas, use the Quantum Mechanic Moiré Eraser to take care of any stray color artifacts and color moiré, as seen in **figure 5.42**. The Moiré Eraser is a heavy-duty filter and must be used with care.

Both Quantum Mechanic Lite and Quantum Mechanic Pro will remove some color moiré, but only if the moiré pattern waves are close together. As the waves get farther apart, the radii values need to be increased, and you can run the risk of desaturating other color detail in the image. **Figure 5.43** shows an extremely bad example of wide-band moiré. As **figure 5.44** reveals, the moiré problem has contaminated all three color channels, making this a tough, tough job to fix. After separating the red sweater onto its own layer, I was able to minimize the color artifacting of the moiré with repeated use of Quantum Mechanic Pro and selective use of the Quantum Mechanic Moiré Eraser. The results in **figure 5.45** are certainly better.

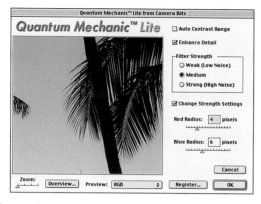

figure 5.40

Quantum Mechanic Lite simplifies the moiré reduction process.

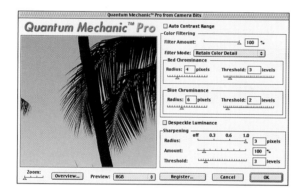

figure 5.41

Quantum Mechanic Pro offers additional controls to reduce moiré.

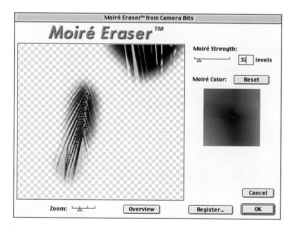

figure 5.42

Quantum Mechanic Moiré Eraser is used to clean up stray color moiré problems.

figure 5.43

An extreme case of color moiré with very wide bands.

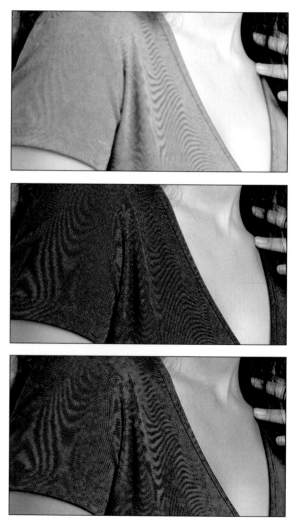

figure 5.44

By inspecting the three color channels you can see that the moiré problem is throughout the entire file. This will make it especially tough to retouch.

figure 5.45

After using Quantum Mechanic Pro and Quantum Mechanic Moiré Eraser, the color moiré has been reduced.

Avoiding Moiré Patterns When Shooting Digital Pictures

If you notice moiré problems while you're taking pictures with digital cameras, you can lessen them with the following tips:

- Move the camera closer or farther away from the subject by just a few inches to change the relationship between the grid of the CCD color filter and the high-frequency information that is causing the problem.

- Open the aperture to use a larger *f*-stop. This decreases the depth of field, which means that less of the subject matter is in focus. The out-of-focus parts have lower spatial frequency content and hence fewer aliasing artifacts. The in-focus areas might still reveal some artifacting.

- Some people recommend defocusing the camera a smidgen and then over-sharpening the file in Photoshop. I'm not a huge fan of that approach, but offer it as a technique you can experiment with.

REDUCING PAPER TEXTURE

In the early to mid twentieth century, photographic supply companies offered dozens of black-and-white papers. Many of these were textured, which looked interesting at the time, but are a nightmare to scan and retouch today.

The secret to minimizing paper texture without getting too many gray hairs is to compromise—let the unimportant image areas blur out and concentrate your efforts on the important image areas. The following technique uses a combination of blurred and masked layers with spotting retouch layers to achieve the final results. Because each image is unique and a large variety of paper textures exists, there are no quick fixes or easy answers to this problem. **Figure 5.46** shows the original scan and **figure 5.47** is the retouched version.

figure 5.46

figure 5.47

 ch5_texture.jpg

1. Duplicate the original layer and apply a Gaussian Blur with a high radius setting to blur the image so that the texture disappears as seen in **figure 5.48**.

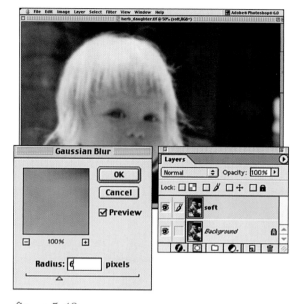

figure 5.48

Blurring the texture.

2. Add a layer mask and use a large, soft black brush set to 50%–75% opacity to paint back the important image areas. In **figure 5.49**, I have painted back the little girl's face and sweater while leaving the unimportant background blurred.

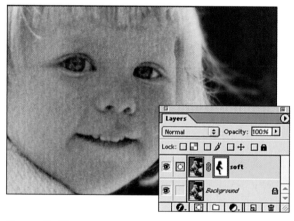

figure 5.49

Painting on the mask to hide the blur effect on the little girl's face.

3. You can move between the textured and the soft version of an image by using a low-opacity white Airbrush on the dark areas of the layer mask. In this example, I used a 20% white Airbrush on the layer mask to paint back some of the softness onto the little girl's skin, as seen in **figure 5.50**.

figure 5.50

The softness of the child's skin can be airbrushed back in by working on the layer mask.

4. Increasing the contrast in the little girl's eyes, mouth, and hair will draw the viewer's eye away from the unimportant image areas. As shown in **figure 5.51**, I increased the image contrast with a Levels Adjustment Layer.

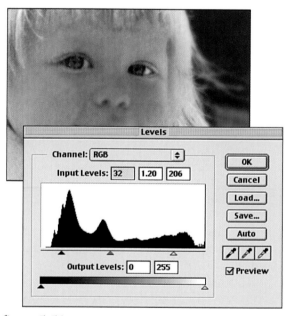

figure 5.51

Bring the viewer's attention to the child's face by selectively increasing the image contrast. Start by applying a global contrast adjustment.

5. Fill the Levels Adjustment Layer layer mask with black and use a small, soft, white brush on the Levels mask to trace over the eye contours, mouth, and a few hair strands. This paints in the added contrast, as shown in **figure 5.52**.

6. To finish the image, use the Clone Stamp tool on an empty layer to clean up remaining texture or damage.

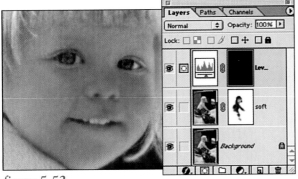

figure 5.52

Painting on the layer mask adds the contrast on the facial features of the little girl.

Reducing Print Texture & Moiré Before Retouching

Experiment with reducing print texture in the input stage with the following techniques. Please note that I used the word *experiment*—each print brings specific challenges in terms of texture, size, warping, how reflective the surface is, and other damage that needs to be de-emphasized. The time you use to experiment, make mistakes, and learn how to do copy work or scan a textured print will be well worth it in saved retouching hours.

- When working with copy negatives, there are three techniques to make it easier to reduce texture and reflections: Make a copy negative or have a copy negative made of the print that you'll then scan in. When doing this copy work, use polarizing filters on the lights and the camera lens and look through the camera viewfinder as you turn the filter to see the effect as the lighter areas of the texture darken and lighten. Take the picture when the texture is least visible. Polarizing the light and lens also cuts down on irritating reflections on the print.
- When making a copy negative, defocus the camera slightly to soften the texture.
- As Wayne Palmer, of Palmer Multimedia Imaging, explains, "A case can be made for a digital-copy negative versus scanning or using film. I have had very good results shooting an image with a Nikon CoolPix 990 and the Nikon SB-24 flash and then retouching the digital file. To light the print with soft diffuse light and avoid any reflections, I rotate the flash head up so that light is bouncing off a large white surface at about a 45° angle to the image. This

method doesn't work with images under glass, in which case I would use my conventional lights, medium format film, and copy stand."

- When you're scanning an image, try either of these methods: Place the print on the flatbed platen on an angle. Experiment with angles and use the scan, in which the light that bounces off of the print makes the texture least visible.
- Use the descreen function in the scanner software to reduce the texture. You'll need to experiment with the best descreen settings for your prints and your scanner software.

REDUCING, MAINTAINING, AND MATCHING FILM GRAIN

All film originals are made up of randomly dispersed film grains that add a structure to every image. The professional slow speed ISO 50 or 100 slide films and color negative materials have very little visible grain structure, while the higher speed amateur films show more grain. The film format the photographer used to take the original picture also plays a role in how much grain is visible. Large format (8 inch by 10 inch, 4 inch by 5 inch, and medium format cameras) use larger pieces of film, allowing you to blow up the print to a greater degree before the film grain becomes visible. On that note, the point-and-shoot and 35-mm photos you might be asked to retouch are often the grainiest and most challenging film formats you'll work with. Files captured with professional digital cameras have absolutely no grain structure whatsoever—often making them smoother and easier to retouch.

One of the problems with doing extensive retouching and image rebuilding is that film grain can get mushy and diffuse, causing the image to have differing textures. Or you'll run into grain problems when obvious grain is not in harmony with the image's subject matter. Reducing, maintaining, and matching film grain and image structure requires a combination of working with layers, blend modes, and floating selections, and building custom brushes that mimic the grain structure.

Reducing Film Grain

In this example, the grain structure detracts from the soft image of the girls at a wedding (**figure 5.53**). After using the Dust & Scratches filter on a duplicate layer in combination with either a layer mask or with the History Brush, the bothersome grain is gone, as seen in **figure 5.54**.

figure 5.53

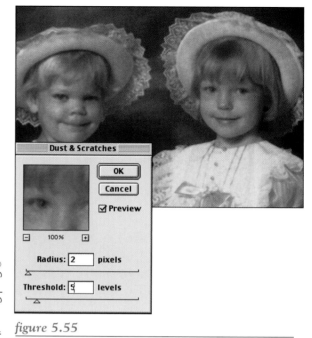

figure 5.55

Working with the Dust & Scratches filter.

3. I added a layer mask and painted over the image areas that should maintain the most detail. In this case, I sketched over the eyes, lips, and a few details in the hair, as seen in **figure 5.56**.

figure 5.56

Controlling where the effect takes place with a layer mask.

figure 5.54

1. I started by duplicating the Background layer.
2. I selected Filter > Noise > Dust & Scratches and finessed the relationship between the Radius and Threshold to minimize the grain without making the image too soft, as seen in **figure 5.55**.

N o t e

A similar effect can be created by using the Dust & Scratches filter on the Background layer and then painting back from History to bring the eyes and lips back into focus.

Maintaining Film Grain

Maintaining film grain is essential to keeping retouching invisible—often, over-eager cloning adds more problems than it solves. To avoid the dreaded patterned Clone Stamp look when hiding blemishes, use a copy-duplicate approach. As you can see in **figure 5.57**, the bride's face has a few freckles and sunspots; in **figure 5.58** they've disappeared while maintaining all film structure.

> **Note**
>
> Before retouching or removing a person's freckles, moles, or wrinkles, always ask if that is desired. In some cases, a person's visual character is based upon a unique mark. Just think of Marilyn Monroe or Cindy Crawford—removing their moles would damage the integrity of their portraits.

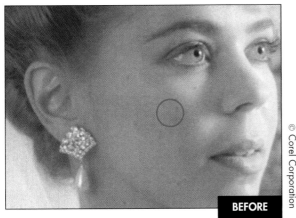

figure 5.57

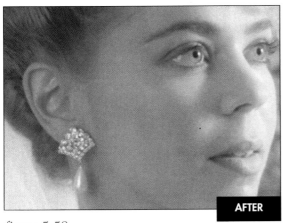

figure 5.58

1. Zoom in on the blemish, spot, or freckle you would like to hide.

2. With the one-pixel, feathered Lasso tool, select an area close to the blemish that has a similar lighting and tone as the blemish to be removed. Don't try to make an even or exact selection, as **figure 5.59** shows.

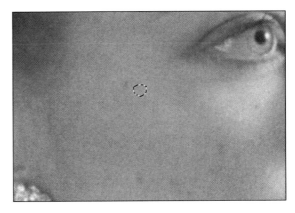

figure 5.59

Selecting blemish-free skin.

3. (Cmd + Option + drag)[Ctrl + Alt + drag] the selection to duplicate the good information. Drag it over the blemish and deselect (Cmd + D)[Ctrl + D]. The results are shown in **figure 5.60**.

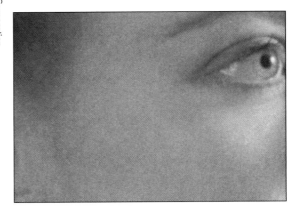

figure 5.60

Dragging good skin over the blemish covers the blemish while maintaining the film structure and skin texture.

Matching Film Grain

Even with the most careful selecting and cloning, you might still have to match film grain to rebuild the image structure. The original image included a necklace that needed to be removed, as seen in **figure 5.61**. After removing the necklace (see **figure 5.62)** the film grain has been smoothed out too much, making the bride's neck blotchy and soft. To match film grain on retouched areas or in composites, use an Overlay neutral layer, filled with monochrome noise, and a quick layer mask to paint grain back into an image wherever needed.

1. I (Option + clicked)[Alt + clicked] the New Layer icon and set the Mode to Overlay and turned on Fill with Overlay-neutral color (50% gray).

2. I selected Filter > Noise > Add Noise and set the filter to Monochromatic to build up texture, as shown in **figure 5.63**.

figure 5.61

figure 5.62

figure 5.63

Adding Monochromatic noise on the neutral layer adds texture to the entire image.

3. I added a layer mask to the Noise layer and filled it with black to hide the noise layer completely.

4. With the Airbrush tool set to white, I painted on the layer mask to paint noise back into the picture wherever needed, as seen in **figure 5.64**. In essence, the black mask hid all the grain, and by painting on it with white I'm revealing the grain only where it's needed.

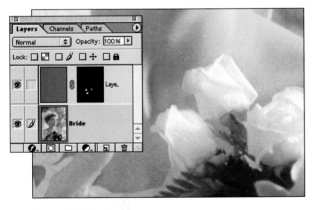

figure 5.64

Using a white airbrush on the black layer mask enables you to carefully reveal the new grain wherever needed.

 Tip

If the size of the faux grain doesn't match the image, transform the noise layer to make the grain as large or small as needed.

Building Custom Noise and Grain Brushes

The Clone Stamp tool can sometimes add softness or cause more problems than it is actually covering up. The problem is not the Clone Stamp tool but the brush and brush settings. To alleviate the mushy edges that cloning can introduce into your image, increase the hardness of the brush by (Control + clicking) [right mouse clicking] and increase the hardness to 50-75% as seen in **figure 5.65**. Increasing the hardness reduces the transition between 100% opacity cloning and the edges of the cloning, which reduces the soft, ghostly edges.

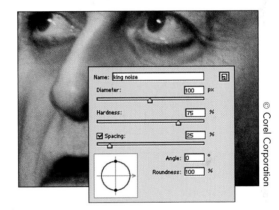

© Corel Corporation

figure 5.65

Increasing the hardness of the brush reduces the softness of the brush edges and minimizes ghostly or soft clone edges.

You can also build your own brushes to match film grain or noise structure by following these steps:

1. Select a part of the image that has even lighting and the film structure you would like to mimic or maintain, as seen in **figure 5.66**.

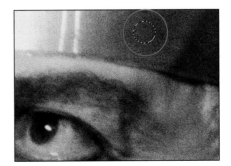

figure 5.66

Select an image area to serve as the foundation of your custom brush.

2. Copy the selection and select File > New. Photoshop will create a new file that is the exact same size as the selected area. Paste.

3. Use Levels to increase the contrast of the grain structure as seen in **figure 5.67**. By moving the shadow and highlight sliders toward the center, I am increasing the contrast and accentuating the structure.

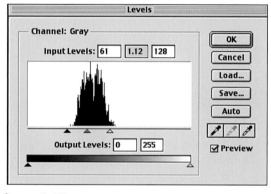

figure 5.67

Use Levels to dramatically increase the brush structure contrast.

4. Since custom brushes do not allow you to adjust the brush hardness and you're trying to mimic grain, roughen the edges of the brush in progress by erasing edges, as seen in **figure 5.68**.

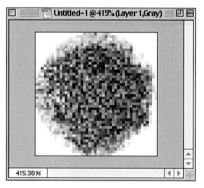

figure 5.68

Roughening the edges of the brush will help to camouflage the cloning later in the process.

5. Select all and then select Edit > Define Brush. Name the brush and click OK.

6. Use the new brush with the Clone Stamp tool set to Use All Layers on an empty layer to clone over grainy blemishes, as shown in figure 5.69 and figure 5.70.

figure 5.69

The blemish on the king's crown needs to be cloned over but that area also needs to retain its grain.

figure 5.70

Using a custom brush retains the grain of the king's crown.

Tip

When using custom brushes, you'll achieve better results if you click-dab on the area to clone over, as opposed to dragging the Clone Stamp tool.

CLOSING THOUGHTS

In most cases, removing dust and mold while maintaining image structure is all that is needed to bring an image back to life. In the worst-case scenario where time, damage, and missing pieces are plaguing your images, you'll need to use the emergency room techniques discussed in Chapters 6 and 7.

6

DAMAGE CONTROL AND REPAIR

The torture we put our old photographs through—storing them in damp basements, carrying them in wallets, folding, tearing, cutting, and pasting them into albums—all leave the telltale cracks, rips, tears, and misshapen corners. So if this is so bad for photographs, why do we put them through the gauntlet of abuse? Because we value, treasure, and cherish them. We like carrying a picture of loved ones in our wallets or purses, we take pleasure in making the family photo album or collage, and sadly we often don't realize that the basement isn't the best place to store a valuable print.

So rather than relegating the damaged to a darker, more forgotten, basement corner—let's get them out, scan them in, and learn to

- Eliminate scratches
- Remove wires and clutter
- Repair tears, rips, and cracks
- Make stains and discoloration disappear

The tools and techniques used to conquer these challenges include

- The Clone Stamp tool
- The Background Eraser tool
- Levels and Layer options

ELIMINATING SCRATCHES

One of the most pedestrian and irritating things you will need to retouch are scratches caused by dirty film processors, coarse handling, or specks of dust on the scanner or digital camera CCD (charged coupled device). But take heart; with the following techniques you'll make those scratches disappear with ease and panache.

Using the Clone Stamp Tool

Old photos and negatives are often plagued with numerous irregular scratches, which can be hidden quickly and easily. **Figure 6.1** shows an original print that curled over time and cracked when it was stored incorrectly and weight was placed on it. **Figure 6.2** shows the repaired file.

figure 6.1

figure 6.2

© Eismann family archive

ch6_scratch.jpg

1. Add an empty layer and name it scratch removal. Select the Clone Stamp tool and set the Mode to Normal, the Opacity to 100%, and check Use All Layers as seen in **figure 6.3**.

figure 6.3

Setting up the scratch removal layer and the Clone Stamp parameters.

2. Select a brush size that is large enough to cover the scratch. Move the mouse 1–2 brush widths to the left or right of the scratch, to an area that has a similar tonal range and (Option + click)[Alt + click] to set the clone source.

3. To spare yourself the trouble of having to draw along the entire scratch, Shift + click the Clone Stamp tool at the top of the scratch.

4. Let go of the mouse button and move the brush about an inch down the scratch, and Shift + click again. The Clone Stamp tool clones in a perfectly straight line (see **figure 6.4**).

figure 6.4

After Shift + clicking along the scratch.

5. Continue Shift + clicking your way along the scratch. The scratch removal layer, shown in **figure 6.5**, shows the cloning that's been applied to the photograph.

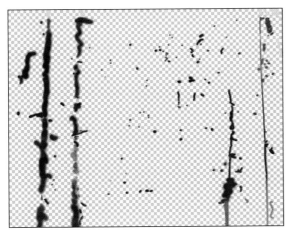

figure 6.5

The isolated scratch removal layer.

T i p

While working with the Clone Stamp or any painting tool, access the context-sensitive menu to change brush size or Blending Modes by (Control + clicking) [right mouse clicking] (see **figure 6.6**).

figure 6.6

Accessing the context-sensitive menu of the Clone Stamp tool for faster brush or Blending Mode changes.

Removing Straight Scratches

Sometimes a speck of dust will land on the scanner CCD, creating a one or two pixel line that runs the entire length of the file, such as the one seen in **figure 6.7**. Don't despair; you can purge the world of that scratch as shown in **figure 6.8** with the outlined steps. To fix a vertical scratch, use the Single Column Marquee tool, and to fix a horizontal scratch, use the Single Row Marquee tool. For this technique to work, the feather must be set to 0 (zero) before you make the selection.

figure 6.7

figure 6.8

ch6_scratch2.jpg

1. Select the Single Column Marquee tool, zoom in on the culprit, and click next to the scratch, as seen in **figure 6.9**. If you didn't land directly next to the scratch, use the arrow keys to nudge the selection into position.

figure 6.9

Selecting good information directly next to the scratch.

2. (Cmd + Option + arrow key) [Ctrl + Alt + arrow key] will duplicate and nudge a single column of pixels over to cover the offending scratch, as shown in **figure 6.10**.

figure 6.10

Nudge to duplicate the good information over the scratch.

REMOVING UNWANTED ELEMENTS

Wires, cables, and clutter only serve to distract the viewer from what is really important in the picture. You can use this technique when preparing real estate photos—by taking out the distracting telephone wires and electric cables, the homes come to the visual foreground and look much more attractive (translation: more sellable).

Dismantling Wires or Cables

To remove telephone wires, cables, or smooth, long, thin scratches, start by tracing the problem with the Pen tool, and then stroke the path with the Clone Stamp tool. In the example seen in **figure 6.11**, the wires detract from the picture of the locomotive, and without the wires the image looks much cleaner, as seen in **figure 6.12**.

figure 6.11

figure 6.12

1. I started by drawing a separate path along each wire (see **figure 6.13**).

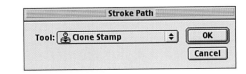

figure 6.13

Creating paths with the Pen tool along each wire.

2. Select the Clone Stamp tool and set the brush to the same width as the wire. Move the mouse 1-2 brush widths from the wire to be removed and (Option + Click) [Alt + Click] to define the clone source.

3. Select Stroke Path from the Paths palette menu (see **figure 6.14**). Select the Clone Stamp (see **figure 6.15**).

figure 6.14

Accessing the Stroke Path command.

figure 6.15

Selecting the Clone Stamp from the Stroke Path menu.

4. Continue drawing and stroking paths until all wires are removed. To hide shorter sections of wire, I prefer to use the Shift + click method I described in the first scratch-removal example in this chapter.

Tip

If the Clone Stamp tool is active, you can just tap the Enter key (not the return key), and Photoshop will stroke the active Path with the Clone Stamp.

Hiding Clutter and Distractions

In the excitement of taking a picture we often forget to look at the entire scene. We might not notice the tree trunk coming out of the skater's head, as seen in **figure 6.16**, or the bits of garbage on the sidewalk or the clutter in the background of a family snapshot. By removing the clutter you can focus the viewer's attention on the picture and clean up the living room without getting out the vacuum.

You can't physically take something out of a digital image, but you can cover it up. You could also take the subject out of the image and put her on a new background (addressed in Chapter 7, "Replacing and Recreating Missing Image Elements."). In the following example, the palm tree that is coming out of the rollerblader's head truly distracts from the picture; with just a few minutes of work, the image seen in **figure 6.17** is much better.

1. Make a generous selection around the clutter to be removed (see **figure 6.18**).

2. Press Q to enter Quick Mask mode and run the Gaussian Blur filter to soften the edge of the mask (see **figure 6.19**). This is identical to applying a feather to a selection, but the advantage is that you can see the effect of the blur.

© Corel Corporation

BEFORE

figure 6.16

AFTER

figure 6.17

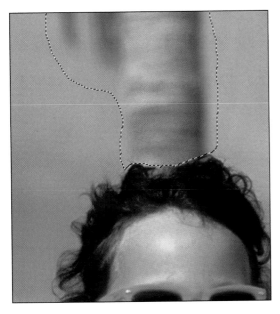

figure 6.18

Roughly selecting the area to be covered up.

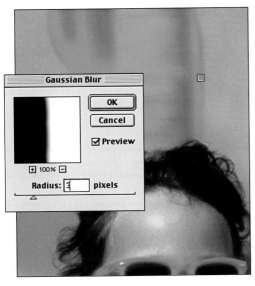

figure 6.19

Blurring the Quick Mask is identical to feathering the selection, except that you have an accurate preview of the effect.

3. If need be, use a painting tool to refine the Quick Mask.

4. Press Q again to exit Quick Mask mode and activate the selection.

5. With any selection tool, move the selection to an area that has uncluttered, good information, as seen in **figure 6.20**.

figure 6.20

Move the selection over to good information.

6. Create a new layer via copy with (Cmd + J) [Ctrl + J]. Use the Move tool to drag the good information over the bad. The result is shown in **figure 6.21**.

figure 6.21

After floating good sky and moving it over the palm tree trunk you might need to do a bit of clean up with the Clone Stamp tool to fine tune the results.

7. Cover up any edge or tone difference with the Clone Stamp tool.

REPAIRING TEARS, RIPS, AND CRACKS

Over the years the photographs that we cherish tend to get folded, cracked, torn, and damaged. If you're lucky, you'll at least have all the pieces to reconstruct the image—if you're not so lucky, you'll have to make up image information to reconstruct the missing pieces. In the following examples the image was torn into pieces, which I was able to scan on a flatbed scanner and then recombine in Photoshop.

As you can see in **figure 6.22**, the original 14.5 inch by 10 inch fiber-based print is torn, cracked, and damaged. With a few repair layers the final image is ready for framing, as seen in **figure 6.23**. Because the print is too large to fit completely on my flatbed scanner, I needed to scan it in sections, as seen in **figure 6.24**. I started the restoration process by opening each individual file to repair the small cracks and large tears, as described in earlier parts of this chapter. When that was finished, I was ready to combine the three pieces and fine-tune the overlapping edges.

 ch6_torn.jpg

Tip

When scanning print pieces, do not change the print orientation by rotating pieces. That will vary the reflectance of the paper texture between the pieces, making them difficult to merge.

© Herb Paynter

BEFORE

figure 6.22

AFTER

figure 6.23

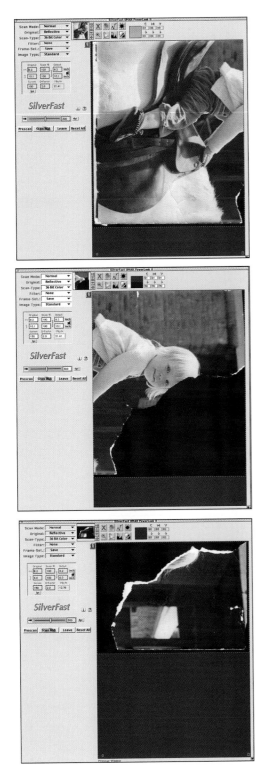

1. Select the Background Eraser and set it to Contiguous with a 20%–50% Tolerance. The lower the Tolerance, the less the eraser will erase, which is very useful when erasing similarly toned areas. In this example, the light areas next to the little girl's light hair required a lower tolerance.

2. Zoom in and keep the Background Eraser crosshair close to the edge of the image as you carefully stroke along the white side of the edge, as shown in **figure 6.25**. Use the Shift + click technique to speed this process up.

figure 6.25

Use the Background Eraser to carefully delete the unwanted white paper fringe caused by the tearing of the print.

3. Select the Lasso tool and draw a complete circle around the corner piece by drawing through the transparent area and circling the entire outside edge of the corner. Then, press (Cmd + J) [Ctrl + J] to move the selected information onto its own layer, as shown in **figure 6.26**.

figure 6.26

Isolating the good information onto its own layer.

figure 6.24

The physical print was larger than my flatbed scanner could handle, so I scanned the pieces in three separate passes.

4. Move the new layer into position making the two pieces meet, and lower the opacity to 50% (see **figure 6.27**). Return the opacity to 100% when the piece is properly placed.

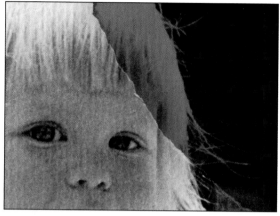

figure 6.27

Lowering the opacity helps you see where to align the pieces with one another.

5. As you can see in **figure 6.28**, there is still a slight line along the tear. Add a new layer and clone over the edges.

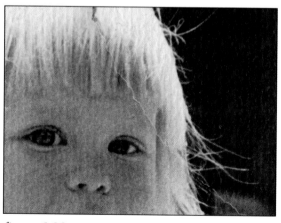

figure 6.28

At 100% opacity, slight image damage is still visible.

6. Of course some fine-tuning Clone Stamping will be required, but the mask method does a lot of the work for you. **Figure 6.29** shows the final layer stack used to retouch this image.

figure 6.29

The final layer stack used to repair this image

MATCHING DENSITY TO MINIMIZE STAINING

The only dirt or stains that you should remove from the physical print original are the ones that brush or blow off easily. A professionally trained conservator should be the only one to treat stains that are embedded in the film or print emulsion. **Figure 6.30** is a fiber-based black-and-white original from 1951 that has survived two transoceanic moves and numerous storage conditions, from the proverbial shoebox to the miscellaneous desk drawer.

After correcting the tone and exposure (as explained in Chapter 2, "Improving Tone and Contrast"), I worked with layers, layer masks, Adjustment Layers, and cloning to hide the staining in the center of the print and on the face of the handsome young man (my father) (see **figure 6.31**). No, the baby isn't me…I'm not that old yet.

To reduce the staining, try covering up the stain with parts of the image that aren't stained, or use the Clone Stamp tool on an empty layer, or work with Levels to balance out the tonal differences. Most of the time you'll need to undertake a combination of these techniques to achieve good results.

🌐▷< **ch6_BWstained.jpg**

1. Select and copy good image information, as seen in **figure 6.32**.

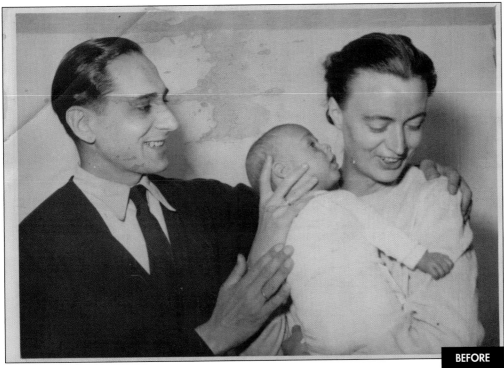

BEFORE

© Eismann family archive

figure 6.30

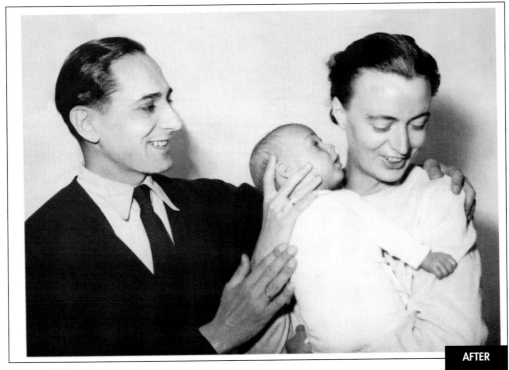

AFTER

figure 6.31

figure 6.32

Selecting replacement information.

2. Loosely select the stain with a feathered Lasso, as shown in **figure 6.33**.

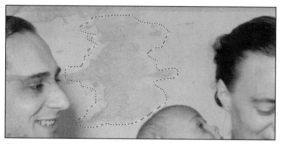

figure 6.33

Selecting the stained area.

3. Select Edit > Paste Into. Photoshop automatically creates a layer with a layer mask based on your Lasso selection.
4. Select Edit > Free Transform and drag the handles to make the new information fit into the stained selection.
5. Select Layer > New Adjustment Layer > Levels. Click Group with Previous Layer as seen in **figure 6.34**. (This is just a time-saver; you can always group layers with one another after the fact with (Cmd + G)[Ctrl + G]).

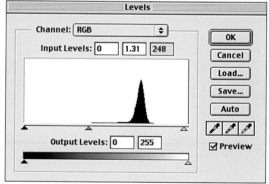

figure 6.34

Adding a grouped Levels Adjustment Layer.

6. Adjust the Levels sliders until the stained area's tone matches the unstained wall, as shown in **figure 6.35**.

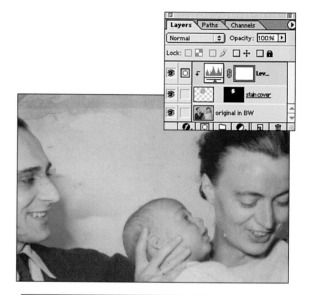

figure 6.35

Working with Levels to match the tones.

CLOSING THOUGHTS

Although repairing tears or removing clutter sounds like a mundane endeavor, I hope that the techniques shown in this chapter have given you some creative approaches to ridding the world of scratches, wires, and clutter. Most importantly, always keep in mind how valuable the photo is that you're working on—the people, the memories, the captured moment might be the only reminder you or your client has of something or someone near and dear to them. By removing those scratches and damage, you're giving them back their memories as clear as the day the picture was taken.

7

REBUILDING, REARRANGING, AND RE-CREATING PORTRAITS

The worst images you will need to repair are the ones that are so damaged by mold, fire, water, and abuse that entire portions of the image are either missing or damaged beyond recognition. In these disaster cases, asking the client for the original negative or a better print is futile because there are none. The secret to replacing, rebuilding, and repairing the beyond-hope images is to beg, borrow, and steal image information from either whatever is left of the original image or to find suitable substitutes to re-create missing backgrounds and body parts.

Although this all may sound like a digital rendition of Stephen Sondheim's *The Little Shop of Horrors*, in which the barber shop was really a butcher shop, rebuilding pictures isn't as gruesome as it seems. So sharpen your digital scalpel and learn to

- Re-create backgrounds
- Build a background collection
- Rebuild a portrait
- Rearrange a portrait
- Reconstruct color

The tools and techniques we'll use include

- Creating and positioning new backgrounds
- Working with Layer Effects and Styles, Adjustment Layers, and Clipping Groups
- Channel swapping and color sampling

> **N o t e**
>
> Many of the techniques used to remove dust and scratches as explained in Chapters 5 and 6 will serve as the foundation for repairing the almost hopeless examples used in this chapter. Keeping this in mind, I've opted to concentrate on explaining the new techniques not addressed up to this point.

RE-CREATING BACKGROUNDS

Re-creating or rebuilding backgrounds can be as straightforward as lifting a person off the original image and placing her onto a blank background or as involved as finding suitable replacement background material. Backgrounds can come from a variety of sources, including other photographs; CD image stock; digital files you've created in Photoshop, Painter, or Deep Paint; and even cloth, textures, or objects you've scanned in with a flatbed scanner. After downloading the tutorial images from www.digitalretouch.org, you'll be able to practice many of the techniques described here.

When replacing or re-creating backgrounds, there are four primary working options to choose from:

- Clone existing background over the damaged area.

- Lift the object or person off the original picture and place onto a new background.

- Paste the new background into the working file, underneath the subject of the photograph.

- Rearrange people or objects to minimize distracting backgrounds.

Your first option of cloning existing background over damaged areas is self-explanatory, and as long as you work on an empty layer you can't get into trouble. The additional approaches are explained in the following sections, giving you a great deal of creative flexibility.

Lifting the Subject off the Photograph

In the example seen in **figure 7.1**, the couple had their photo taken during the wedding reception. Many years later they wished that they had a professional studio portrait, and as you see in **figure 7.2**

the photo now looks as if it was taken in a studio. In an example like this, by Laurie Thompson of Imagination Studios, the background replacement is rather straightforward. Gather the background, in this case a shot of an empty generic studio backdrop as seen in **figure 7.3**, and drop the couple onto the backdrop.

BEFORE

figure 7.1

AFTER

figure 7.2

Retouched by Laurie Thompson, Imagination Studios

figure 7.3

The studio background.

figure 7.4

After making the path into a selection, I saved the selection into an alpha channel.

In a case like this, taking the time to make a good selection around the wedding party is the most important step to creating a realistic composite in which the edges aren't harsh, jagged, or obvious. Believe me, spending a few more minutes at the initial selection stage will save you time later, since you won't have to tediously retouch all the edges to cover up a bad selection.

Photoshop has numerous tools to make a selection, including the Magic Wand, Pen Tool, Color Range, and the Extract command. No matter which one or combination of these tools you choose to use, I recommend saving the selection into an alpha channel as you go, enabling you to return to the channel to refine the edges of the selection with the painting tools.

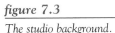 **ch7_BW_wedding.jpg**

 ch7_BW_wedding_backdrop.jpg

1. Make your initial selection by tracing along the edges of the couple with the selection tool you are most comfortable with. Don't worry about getting the selection 100% perfect with your first attempt, as you'll use the alpha channel to refine the selection edges in the next step.

2. I used the Pen tool to outline the couple. After turning the path into a selection, I saved the selection into an alpha channel by clicking the new channel icon at the bottom of the channels palette as seen in **figure 7.4**.

3. With the Alpha 1 channel active, click the Show/Hide icon of the primary channel and use a brush to refine the edges. If you used the Pen tool you would use a hard-edged brush, and if you used a selection tool with a feather to make the initial selection, then you need to use a soft-edged brush to match the quality of the edges.

4. When refining the bottom edge of the bride's wedding dress, keep one finger near the X key. Tapping it toggles between the foreground and background color, in this case black and white, enabling you to quickly switch the color of the brush as you refine the edges.

5. When working with a softer image such as this one, blur the mask with a low-setting Gaussian Blur to soften the selection. As seen in **figure 7.5**, the original alpha channel is active and is being blurred.

Tip

Before applying a filter to an alpha channel, duplicate the alpha channel to make a backup insurance copy. That way you can experiment with blurring the alpha channel mask and still have the backup mask in case you oversoftened the edges.

figure 7.5

Applying a subtle Gaussian Blur softens the edges slightly and makes the resulting image look less like a cutout.

6. Make the grayscale image active (Cmd + 1) [Ctrl + 1]. If you are working with an RGB or CMYK file, use (Cmd + ~)[Ctrl + ~].

7. Load the blurred mask as a selection by dragging it down to the Load Channel as Selection icon on the Channels palette.

8. Select Layer > New > Layer via Copy (Cmd + J)[Ctrl + J] to copy the bride and groom onto their own layer. Name the layer.

9. Open the backdrop file and drag it into the bride and groom file. Position it under the bride and groom layer, as shown in **figure 7.6**. If necessary, use Edit > Transform to scale it to match.

10. Zoom in to a 100% or 200% view and double-check the edges of the bride and groom. Use a small, soft-edged Eraser to erase any remaining edge artifacts that would show up as dark pixels against the lighter backdrop. In the cases where you place a light subject against a dark backdrop, you'd look for telltale light edges.

Tip

When replacing backgrounds it is helpful to use a similarly toned or colored background. Using backgrounds that are very different will make the edges much harder to match.

figure 7.6

Scale the backdrop to fit the wedding couple file.

Creating the Drop Shadow

The detail that makes this composite realistic is the subtle shadow underneath the bride's wedding gown. A slight drop shadow gives the figures the needed visual weight to make them seem as if they're really standing on the new background.

1. Select the bottom part of the dress with the Lasso tool, as shown in **figure 7.7**.

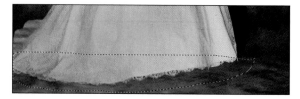

figure 7.7

Selecting just a portion of the area you want to shadow will keep file size down.

2. Select Layer > New > Layer via Copy or (Cmd + J)[Ctrl + J] to float the selected area onto its own layer.

3. Double-click the layer with the hem of the dress to open up the Layer Style palette, as shown in **figure 7.8**. Use the distance, spread, and size to add a subtle drop shadow under the dress. Since the lighting in the original image was diffuse, the shadow should be soft and subtle to match.

4. Photoshop has added a drop-shadow effect around the entire layer, and it looks as if the dress has a dirty tear in it. Move the dress bottom layer to fall under the bride and groom layer, as shown in **figure 7.9**.

🔍 T i p

When creating shadows, mimic the direction and quality of the light in the original photograph. If there are existing shadows in the image, look at them and use them as your reference as you create new digital shadows. You don't want the new shadow to conflict with existing shadow information.

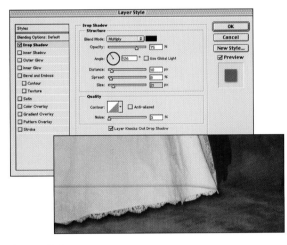

figure 7.8

Use Photoshop Layer Styles to add a slight drop shadow underneath the bride's wedding dress.

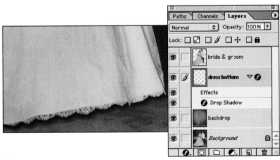

figure 7.9

Position the layer with the shadow underneath the object—in this case, the dress—that is casting the shadow.

To polish the image, Laurie hand colored the couple to finalize the photograph, as seen in **figure 7.10**.

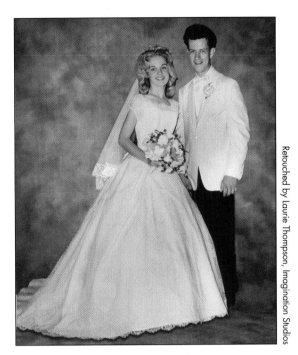

Retouched by Laurie Thompson, Imagination Studios

figure 7.10

The final colorized version is ready for framing.

FINDING SUITABLE REPLACEMENT MATERIALS

The ravages of time often claim entire chunks of photographs, and these more challenging scenarios can be overcome with creative image thinking and image borrowing. In **figure 7.11** the original image is damaged and missing a floor, foot, and backdrop. The final retouched version in **figure 7.12** is an artful repair and replacement job that took advantage of Laurie Thompson's drawing, cloning, and creative borrowing skills. Note that Laurie left the wrinkles in the woman's dress, which gives the retouched version a sense of authenticity.

figure 7.11

figure 7.12

After repairing the couple with the help of cloning image information onto an empty layer, as seen in **figure 7.13**, and substituting a suitable foot for the groom's foot, Laurie still needed to re-create the carpet on which the couple is standing. Upon careful examination, she noticed that the carpet was really a bearskin rug. She couldn't find a picture of a bearskin rug in her collection, but she did have a picture of a live polar bear (shown in **figure 7.14**).

Laurie pasted the live bearskin rug into the picture and used a layer mask to control where the bear showed through, as seen in **figure 7.15**.

figure 7.13

After repairing the background curtain and replacing the groom's foot with an image from Hemera Photo Objects, the next step involves replacing the rug.

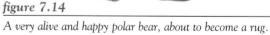

figure 7.14

A very alive and happy polar bear, about to become a rug.

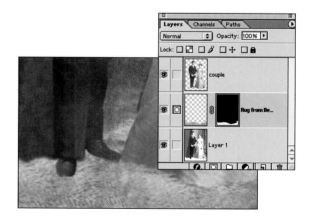

figure 7.15

Working with layers and layer masking to control exactly where the carpet is revealed.

The Beauty Is in the Details

I love catching continuity mistakes in Hollywood productions. The clock that never changes time, the glass that is full, empty, and then full again in the same scene, or the shirts that change color from take to take. You can avoid continuity mistakes in your portrait and background retouching by being aware of the following issues:

- Color and Contrast: Make sure to match the color and contrast of the pieces you are compositing.

- Film Grain and Texture: Double-check to see if the grain and texture match. Use the techniques described in "Reducing, Maintaining, and Matching Film Grain," in Chapter 5.

- Lighting and Shadows: Every image has at least one light source. Sometimes it's the sun, other times a studio light or perhaps even reflected light, illuminating your subjects. Study how the light is falling in an image and use that information when creating shadows. Look for colors that might be reflected into your image from surrounding areas, such as brightly colored walls or trees.

- Edges and Transitions: Mimic the softness or hardness of the edges in the original image to create seamless edges between retouched areas.

- Size Relationships: Match the size of dropped-in objects with the people and objects in the original scene.

- Reflections: If someone has glasses on or there are windows in a scene, double-check that the reflections in these surfaces actually reflect the environment in the picture.

- Hollow Areas: If someone is standing with their hands on their hips or with their legs spread apart, make sure to mask out the hollow triangle so that the new image background can show through.

Picky, picky, picky. When reconstructing images and backgrounds, keep these details in mind to create seamless and invisible retouching.

BUILDING A DIGITAL BACKGROUND COLLECTION

Image elements and backgrounds are everywhere for you to create or take advantage of. The easiest and least expensive replacement backgrounds are the ones you create from scratch with Photoshop. Start with a new file the same size as the image for which you need a background. Fill the image with a Gradient Blend, as seen in **figure 7.16**, and add some monochrome noise. The digital noise will give you additional tooth and texture to work with. (This is exactly what you'll be doing later in the chapter to create a studio background that never existed.)

In this example, I used the Motion Blur filter and then used the Dust & Scratches filter to mottle the background as if it was a studio linen backdrop, as seen in **figure 7.17**. Experimenting with filters and color combinations to create your own backdrops is free, easy, and a great way to doodle away a bit of time. Additionally, you can scan-in pieces of cloth or artistic papers to create your own backgrounds.

figure 7.16

Using similar colors when making the Gradient Blend helps to mimic a photo studio backdrop.

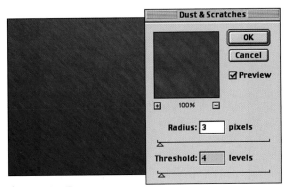

figure 7.17

Combining filters enables you to create unique backgrounds.

Collect your own backgrounds by carrying a camera with you. Whenever you see a pleasant scene or suitable background, take a picture of it—that way you can build your own unique image background library. Very often the image background should be out of focus. It is better to take the picture out of focus rather than using the Blur filters in Photoshop.

In case you can't create, scan, or photograph an optimal background, turn to the Web and CD stock photo collections. Online companies, such as PhotoDisc (www.photodisc.com) and GettyOne (www.gettyone.com), and CD stock companies, such as Hemera Photo Objects (www.hemera.com) and Visual Language (www.visuallanguage.com), offer royalty-free image collections. Always read the usage conditions of the image collection before using the images for commercial purposes. Some collections will not allow you to make calendars or other products for resale nor use the images in a pornographic or offensive manner.

REBUILDING A PORTRAIT

When retouching damaged portraits you might have to finesse a face out of nearly nothing, which requires careful use of the Clone Stamp tool. In extreme situations you might need to "borrow" facial pieces from other photographs to re-create the face. If this all sounds as if you're playing Dr. Frankenstein, just keep in mind how emotionally valuable the retouched photo will be once it is artfully re-created.

Even an image that is as damaged and mold-ridden as **figure 7.18** has enough information and potential to be transformed into the cute portrait in **figure 7.19**. As Laurie explains, "The first place to look for image information to take advantage of is in the image itself." In this example Laurie replaced the damaged background with a digital one, used the right eye and ear to replace the left eye and ear, and repaired the density problems with selective Adjustment Layers and cloning layers. To finish the rebuilding, she then cleaned up the jacket and shirt and straightened out the bow tie.

Replacing the Background

When rebuilding a damaged image like this one, concentrate your time and effort on the essentials—in this case the portrait rather than the unimportant background. By separating the young boy (let's call him Jimmy) from the damaged background and placing him on a faux studio backdrop, Laurie has avoided a lot of tedious repair work.

figure 7.18

figure 7.19

Retouched by Laurie Thompson, Imagination Studios

🌐 ▷ꕷ **ch7_jimmy.jpg**

1. Select the figure with Lasso tool and press Q to enter Quick Mask mode (see **figure 7.20**).

figure 7.20

Using Quick Mask to select the figure.

2. To refine the mask, use a soft brush and paint with black to add to the mask or paint with white to take away masked areas.

3. If the selection edge is too harsh, without a subtle, soft transition between the black and white areas, soften it by selecting Blur > Gaussian Blur. As you increase the amount, the edges become softer (as seen in **figure 7.21**.)

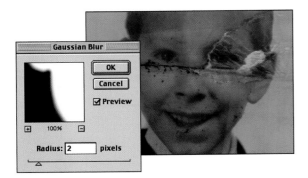

figure 7.21

Using the Gaussian Blur filter to soften mask edges gives you more control as well as visual feedback while softening selections.

4. Press Q to exit Quick Mask mode and activate the selection. Select Layer > New > Layer via Copy to copy the figure onto its own layer.

5. Add a new layer and select the colors you would like the backdrop to be. In this case Laurie selected a gray blue as the foreground

color and a slightly lighter gray blue as the background color. Keeping the foreground and background colors tonally close to one another enables you to use the Gradient tool to mimic a subtle background spotlight on the faux backdrop.

6. Reposition the new layer between the original background and the copy of Jimmy. Make the new layer active.

7. Draw a Radial Gradient from the center of the image to the edge of the image.

8. The faux backdrop is too smooth. To mimic the texture of film grain, select Filter > Noise > Add Noise (see **figure 7.22**). Experiment with the Amount and Distribution settings until the grain in the background more closely matches the grain in the original photograph. The higher the Amount value, the more noise is added. To add noise based on the colors in the image, select Gaussian. To add even amounts of noise throughout the image, select Uniform. Click the Monochrome box to add grayscale rather than color noise.

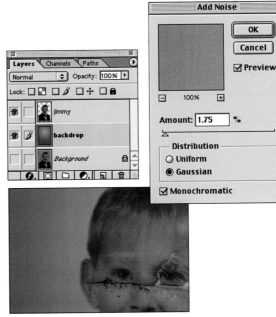

figure 7.22

Adding noise to a digital background mimics film grain and helps it blend into the original photograph.

Eye and Ear Repair

In this example the right side of the print has suffered more damage than the left side. With this in mind, Laurie used the undamaged eye and ear from the right side to replace the damaged eye and ear on the left side. After copying the eye and ear onto their own layers, she had to flip and transform the pieces to match.

1. Use the Lasso tool with a 2–3 pixel feather to select the good eye, as seen in **figure 7.23**. Select Layer > New > Layer via Copy (Cmd + J) [Ctrl + J] to copy the eye onto its own layer.

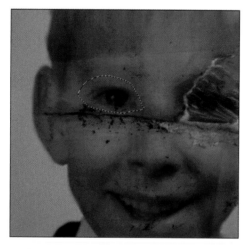

figure 7.23

Making a generous selection gives you more image information to work with.

2. With the Move tool, position the layer with the copied left eye over the right eye. Select Edit > Transform > Flip Horizontally to flip the eye.

3. Select Edit > Free Transform to fine-tune the eye's size and to rotate the eye into position. Lower the opacity of the repair layer to make placement easier.

Tip

To see how layers are fitting together, it is helpful to lower the opacity of the upper layer before selecting Edit > Free Transform. That way you can see through the layer and match it to the underlying layer.

4. As you can see in **figure 7.24**, the eye looks better, but the position and catch lights in the eye need to be adjusted. When we flipped the eye, the direction of the catch lights was reversed. The standard lighting scheme for portraits like this one is one main light and a smaller fill light. The main light created the larger catch light in Jimmy's eye, and the fill light caused a smaller one. The catch lights need to come from the same direction or else poor Jimmy will look very dazed or cross-eyed.

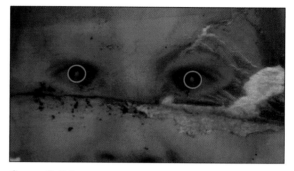

figure 7.24

Reflections from the photographer's lights should appear to have been cast from the same direction. Incongruent catchlights are a sure sign of bad digital work.

5. Make the layer with Jimmy active. Use the Lasso or Elliptical Marquee tool with a feather of 2–3 pixels and select the iris area of the eye (containing the catchlights). The selection is shown in **figure 7.25**. Select Layer > New Layer via Copy. Then, in the Layers palette, reposition this layer to fall on top of the layer with the new eye. Use the Move tool to position it on top of the iris of the new right eye.

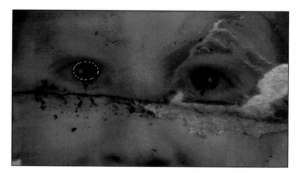

figure 7.25

Copying the good iris and catchlight information is easier than trying to clone or paint faux light sources into eyes.

6. Use the same technique of borrowing with the left ear to replace the extremely damaged right ear. Select the ear with the Lasso tool, copy it onto a new layer, position it, and transform it into place. (Fortunately there are no catch lights in the ear to worry about.)

7. To guarantee that the new ear fits the shape of the original ear, position the new ear layer over the layer with the separate Jimmy on it and select Layer > Group with Previous (Cmd + G) [Ctrl + G] to create a clipping group. This creates a group of two layers where the visibility of the top layer is based on the bottom layer. Wherever there is pixel information on the bottom layer of the group, all other layers grouped with that layer will only be revealed in that area. In this case, the original portrait is on a transparent layer (see **figure 7.26**), and using it to clip the new ear makes the ear fit perfectly, as seen in **figure 7.27**.

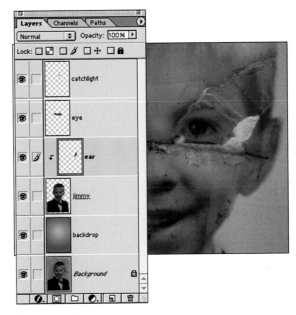

figure 7.27

Taking advantage of clipping groups enables you to reveal layers based on the information in the layer that it is grouped with.

Skin and Eyebrow Repair

Someone taped the torn print with clear tape, and over the years the tape yellowed and stained the print. When you face a stain like this one, matching the stained color to the desired color often alleviates many problems and will reduce the amount of cloning you'll need to do.

🌐⇨✂ **ch7_eyebrows.jpg**

1. Make the layer with the isolated Jimmy on it active and select the stained area with a softly feathered Lasso, as shown in **figure 7.28**. Add a Selective Color Adjustment layer.

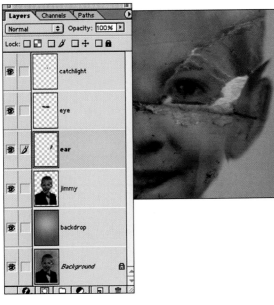

figure 7.26

When first placed, Jimmy's ear doesn't quite fit his head.

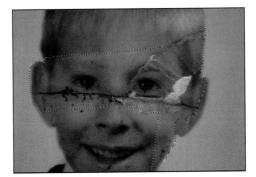

figure 7.28

Selecting the yellowed areas with the Lasso tool.

2. In the Selective Color Options dialog box, choose the offending color from the pull-down menu (in this case, yellow) and reduce the offending color, as shown in **figure 7.29**. As you can see, reducing the yellow allows the skin tones to show through.

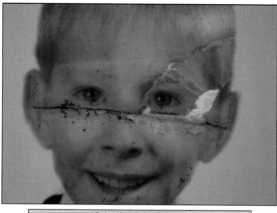

figure 7.29

Using Selective Color to pull out unwanted color casts enables the original color to shine through.

3. The beauty of working with Adjustment Layers is that you can move them up or down through the layer stack and they will affect all underlying layers. The layers with the new eye and ear on them were also yellowed from the tape. By moving the Selective Color Adjustment Layer up, the yellow is removed from all underlying layers.

4. Add a new layer and set the Clone Stamp tool to Use All Layers. Carefully clone over the paper damage. (For more information on this process, see "Working with the Clone Stamp Tool" in Chapter 5, "Dust, Mold, and Texture Removal.") Cloning over such extensive paper damage is a painstaking process, and you might have to erase inexact cloning and try again.

5. As you create more and more layers to build up the retouch, it is very helpful to create a layer set of the working layers to keep them organized. To create a layer set, link the layers that you want in the group, as seen in **figure 7.30**, and select New Set from Linked in the Layers palette menu.

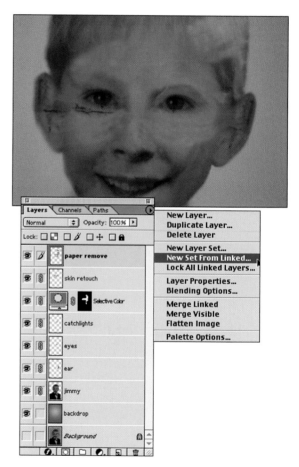

figure 7.30

Photoshop 6's new layer set feature enables you to combine related layers into a group for easier handling.

6. Even with careful cloning, you might lose image information. In this example, Jimmy's eyebrows have practically disappeared. You can borrow eyebrows from another image, like the one shown in **figure 7.31**, to rebuild his features.

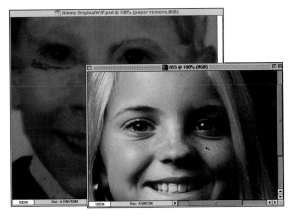

figure 7.31

The picture of the young girl offers similar eyebrows that can be borrowed and positioned into place.

7. For each of the girl's eyebrows, select it with the Lasso tool with a 2–3-pixel feather. Then, use the Move tool to drag each one on to Jimmy's face.

8. Use the Free Transform if necessary to fit the eyebrows to the portrait. Setting the Blending Mode of the new eyebrow layer to Luminosity or changing the opacity of the layer can help blend them seamlessly into the portrait, as seen in **figure 7.32**.

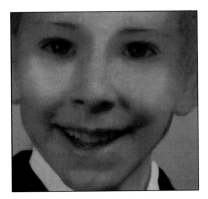

figure 7.32

Working on separate layers and adjusting the eyebrows Blending Mode to Luminosity as well as reducing the opacity blends the eyebrows smoothly into Jimmy's face.

Flattening Your Image

When a retouch is made up of numerous layers it can be less confusing to work on a flattened version. Working on one layer simplifies the process of making selections, applying color correction, and cloning information. There are three ways you can go about creating a flattened image:

- To create a flattened version, save the in-progress file as a PICT file onto your hard drive and then open it to continue working.
- To merge all working layers while keeping the layered document intact, add a new layer on top of the layer stack and, with all layers visible that you want to merge, hold (Option)[Alt] while selecting Merge Visible from the Layers palette menu.
- To merge the layers in a Layer set without merging all the working layers, highlight the set to be merged, and hold down (Option) [Alt] as you select Merge Layer Set from the Layers palette menu. Photoshop will automatically create a new layer with the merged layer set, as seen in figure 7.33.

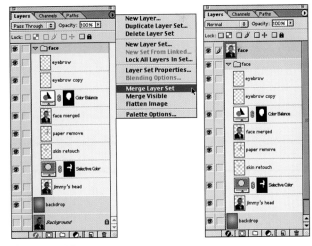

figure 7.33

Merging the layers of a layer set creates a flattened layer on which you can continue your retouching.

Fixing the Clothing

After working with this image for a few hours, I get the feeling that I almost know the little boy. Look at his enthusiastic expression and crooked bow tie in **figure 7.34**. It looks like he just ran in from the playground and can't wait to get back. But I imagine that his mother wished that the shirt and jacket were clean and the bow tie straightened.

figure 7.34

After retouching Jimmy's face, he needs additional work to cleanup the shirt and jacket and straighten out his bow tie.

1. To clean up the jacket, as seen in **figure 7.35,** add a new layer and clone over the scratches and damage with the Clone Stamp tool set to Use All Layers.

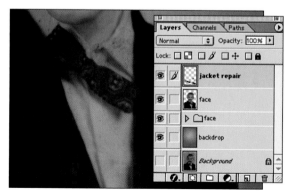

figure 7.35

After merging, the work in progress layers continue working with new layers to build up new areas of the jacket.

2. Although I don't know what color Jimmy's shirt was, I imagine that it was either white or at least much lighter than it is now. To lighten the shirt, select it with either the Lasso tool or Select > Color Range. With the active selection, add a Curves Adjustment Layer and drag the curve upward to lighten the shirt with Photoshop "bleach," as shown in **figure 7.36**.

figure 7.36

After selecting the shirt, use a Curves Adjustment Layer to lighten the shirt and make it more appealing.

3. To clean up the remaining dirt on the shirt, add a new layer and use the Clone Stamp tool set to Use All Layers to remove the last specks of dirt.

Straightening the Bow Tie

To straighten the bow tie, you need to first select it, copy it onto its own layer, and then use the Free Transform to position it. You'll have to return to the shirt layer to replace the missing information with faux shirt information.

1. Make the Jimmy layer active. Select the tie with either the Lasso tool with a slight feather or the Pen Tool (see **figure 7.37**). If you create the selection with the Pen tool, select Make Selection from the Paths palette menu and add a one-pixel feather to the selection.

figure 7.37

Selecting the crooked bow tie is the first step in straightening it.

2. Cut the bow tie onto its own layer by choosing Layer > New > Layer via Cut, and name the newly created layer "bow tie."

3. Select Edit > Free Transform and rotate and move the bow tie into position. As you can see in **figure 7.38**, the cut bow tie goes into position nicely but the empty hole that shows through in the bow tie's original position will need to be cloned over.

figure 7.38

Use the Free Transform to position and rotate the bow tie into place.

4. Replace this missing information by cloning additional shirt onto the jacket repair layer, as seen in **figure 7.39**.

figure 7.39

Since the bow tie was cut onto its own layer, you'll need to reconstruct the shirt.

5. The final touch can be added by double-clicking the bow tie layer and using a Layer Style Drop Shadow to add a subtle shadow, as seen in **figure 7.40**.

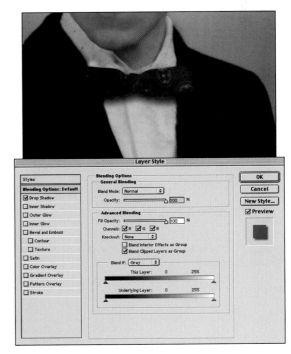

figure 7.40

Adding a drop shadow to the bow tie with Layer Styles adds a touch of realism.

REARRANGING A PORTRAIT

A photo with loved ones can be a cherished treasure—but in some cases the loved one wasn't on hand when the photo was taken. A daughter asked Wayne Palmer to composite her into her father's last portrait, shown in **figure 7.41**. Though she was not present at the time the picture was taken, she now has a lovely portrait (see **figure 7.42**). As Wayne explained, "It was one of those jobs that brought tears to the eyes of the client. I frequently get jobs that involve the last photo of someone."

BEFORE

figure 7.41

AFTER

Retouched by Wayne Palmer, Palmer Multimedia Imaging

figure 7.42

Note

You can use the following masking technique with any image that has fine detail as long as there is a tonal difference between the subject and the background. A dark-haired person standing against a dark wall will be nearly impossible to separate.

Masking Out the Hair of the Daughter's Portrait

The challenge in bringing the daughter into the picture lies in the fact that she has very curly hair, which needs to be masked out to drop her into the photo with her father. There are numerous methods to make a mask in Photoshop—but when I see an image as complex as this one, I use a Difference Mask to select the hair. Making a good mask that maintains image detail is the foundation of rearranging portraits. In the following example, you'll make the mask, add the father, and then refine the details to polish the final portrait.

ch7_daughter.jpg

1. Double-click the Background layer icon of the portrait and name it. It doesn't really matter what the name is, but the default Background layer cannot support a layer mask—something we'll be using in a moment.

2. Use the Eyedropper tool to sample the background color that the person is against—in this case, the blue backdrop.

3. Add a new layer and fill it with the sampled color.

4. Change the colored layer's Blending Mode to Difference to get the results, as seen in **figure 7.43**.

5. Accentuate the difference with a Levels Adjustment Layer to increase the contrast, as seen in **figure 7.44**. Do this carefully, and keep an eye on the dark image areas. You don't want them to start lightening and you don't want to increase the contrast so much that you lose image detail.

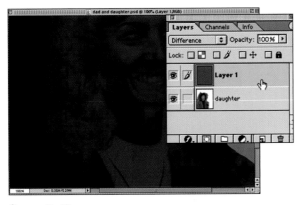

figure 7.43

The Difference Blending Mode shows you everything that is not the same color as the color sampled from the background.

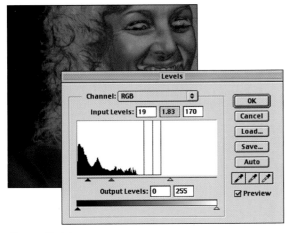

figure 7.44

Use a Levels Adjustment Layer to increase the difference between the light and dark areas.

6. Add another new layer. Select the inside of the figure with the Pen or Lasso tool, being careful not to get too close to the important hair edges, as seen in **figure 7.45**. (If you make a path with the Pen tool, select Make Selection from the Path palette menu and add a slight feather to the selection.)

figure 7.45

Being careful not to go too close to the edges of the hair, select the inside of the figure with the Lasso or Pen tool.

7. Fill the selection with white and deselect.

8. Use a soft brush or Airbrush to paint with white closely to the edge of the hair. Paint with black on the outside edge of the figure, as seen in **figure 7.46**. As you can see, the results look like a mask—black-and-white information with detail.

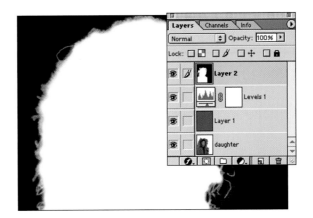

figure 7.46

After filling the selection with white and brushing in some hair information, the mask is more defined.

9. The secret to getting this quasi-mask information into the layer with the daughter's portrait lies in the luminosity. With the topmost layer active, press (Cmd + Option + ~) [Ctrl + Alt + ~] to load the image luminosity.

10. Select the bottom-most layer—the one with the portrait—and click the layer mask icon. (Option + click)[Alt + click] the portrait layer to hide all layers except the portrait layer. You should see the daughter masked onto a transparent checkerboard, as seen in figure 7.47.

11. You can either throw the mask production layers away or just ignore them for the rest of the project.

figure 7.47

Using the luminosity information of the mask on the woman's portrait layer isolates her from the background, while maintaining important image detail.

Bringing the People Together

After separating the father from his background by selecting him with the Pen tool and placing him on his own layer, Wayne created a new digital backdrop. Wayne used the Gradient Blend tool on a new layer to create a soft radial blend, to which he added noise to match the film grain in the original portraits. The remaining steps to move the people into position require care to match proportion, color, and contrast.

🔍 **Tip**

In most cases, match the layer that has more contrast, as it is easier to add contrast than it is to lower contrast.

🌐⇥ **ch7_backdrop.jpg**

🌐⇥ **ch7_father.jpg**

1. Drag the daughter's masked portrait into the picture with the father and position it.

2. Even with the most careful masking methods, you might still see some remnants or artifacts from the original photographs. Color spill from the pink blouse in the original photo are visible in **figure 7.48**. Use the brushes to paint with black and white on the layer mask to finesse which areas are hidden or revealed. Working with a black brush will extend the layer mask and hide more of the daughter, and using a white brush on the layer mask will reveal more of the daughter.

figure 7.48

After positioning the two subjects together, zoom in and check the transitions and edges.

3. After positioning the subjects, take a moment to compare the two. Are the proportions, color, and contrast working with one another? Select Edit > Transform > Scale to fine-tune proportions. Hold down Shift to maintain the aspect ratio as you transform the person.

4. To match color and contrast, use a Curves Adjustment Layer on the daughter's layer to match her to her father. Keep in mind that since the daughter is younger and has had less sun exposure, she doesn't need to be as ruddy or tanned as her father.

5. Adjust the Opacity of the daughter's Adjustment Layer in relationship to her father, as seen in **figure 7.49**.

figure 7.49

Fine-tune the color and contrast of the subjects in relation to one another.

The Beauty Is in the Details

At this point in the portrait construction, you've done most of the hard work. The father and daughter have been reunited and, in most cases, your work would be very close to being done. This is always the point at which I either save and close the file and then come back to it the next day with a fresh eye, or I ask someone I trust and respect to look at the file to double-check any details I might have overlooked. Upon close inspection of **figure 7.50**, you can see a few problems that might give away that this is a photographic moment that never really happened:

- The magenta spill that was reflecting off of the woman's clothing in the original portrait is still visible on the father's shirt.

- The transition along the faces is too harsh and needs to be smoothed and refined.

- His right shoulder is too low and looks awkward.

- The focus of the two people doesn't match.

- The lines on the daughter's face could be lessened to flatter her a bit.

figure 7.50

Several areas still need to be retouched to make this new image appear seamless.

1. When I refine a retouch, I like to work on a flattened back up file. I flatten the original layered file, do a Save As, and continue working, making sure not to overwrite the layered file.

2. To remove the magenta spill, sample the desired color of the blue shirt. Add a new layer and change its Blending Mode to Color. Use a large, soft Airbrush to paint over the magenta spill. As you can see in **figure 7.51**, the blue color layer has removed any trace of the magenta spill that had been reflected onto the father's shirt.

 Tip

When you're matching color and contrast between elements, look away from the monitor every few minutes to clear your visual memory. Then look back at the monitor, and you should be able to see any problems with a fresh eye.

figure 7.51

Painting with the desired color (in this case sampled from the father's shirt) onto a Color layer removes any telltale color spill or contamination.

3. To refine the transition between the daughter's hair and the father's face, select the Clone Stamp tool and set it to Use All Layers. Retouch the edges, as seen in **figure 7.52**.

figure 7.52

Even the most careful mask and compositing will require some additional refinement. By working on a new layer, you have the ability to add and take away information with the Clone Stamp tool without impacting the portraits themselves.

4. To rebuild the father's shoulder, select his right shirt collar, copy it onto its own layer, and move it up, as seen in **figure 7.53**. Keep in mind that most viewers will not stare at the collar, and often the illusion of a collar and shoulder is all that you need to create.

figure 7.53

Selecting and duplicating the collar serves as the foundation to creating the illusion that more shirt and shoulder was in the original image.

5. Merge the work in progress layers, by adding a new layer and holding (Option)[Alt] as you select Merge Visible from the Layer palette menu.

6. Use the Gaussian Blur filter with a setting of 1 to soften the entire file, as seen in **figure 7.54**.

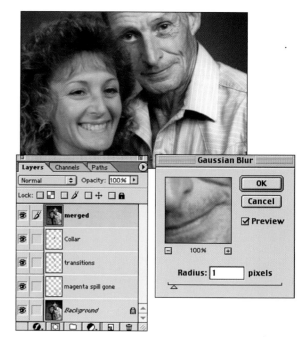

figure 7.54

To match the focus of the two portrait pieces, start by blurring the entire file.

7. Add a layer mask to the merged layer and use a large, soft Airbrush with black to paint over the daughter's face to bring her back into focus. Black will hide the softening effect, and white reveals the softening in the father's image area.

Note

Matching the focus or sharpness of the two people is a challenge. I prefer to soften the sharper image to match the softer image. Sharpening an out-of-focus image is usually a futile undertaking. In this case the daughter's photograph was softer; therefore, I softened the father's image slightly to visually blend the two.

8. Since the eyes of the people in the picture are the most important parts of their faces, I recommend using a 25% opacity black Airbrush on the layer mask to paint over the father's eyes to bring them back into focus (see **figure 7.55**).

figure 7.56

figure 7.55

Double-check that the eyes of the portrait are crisp. By painting on the layer mask with a smaller, lower-opacity Airbrush, you can bring the eyes back into focus.

REARRANGING A PHOTOGRAPH TO MINIMIZE THE BACKGROUND

In the excitement of taking a photograph, many of us either don't look at the entire scene or we're too shy to direct the people in the picture to move closer to one another. In the original photograph, seen in **figure 7.56**, the couple in the photo are standing too far apart and, although the holiday decorations on the door are attractive, the wiring and reflection of the flash certainly distract from the photo. In **figure 7.57**, you can see how Wayne Palmer of Palmer Multimedia Imaging moved the people closer together and rebuilt the shadow caused by the flash behind the woman.

figure 7.57

Moving the Subjects

The distance between the two subjects makes it seem less friendly and warm than the holiday decorations would make it appear. By moving the man and woman together, you create a more central focus for the image so that it has more impact.

1. With the Pen tool, Wayne carefully selected the figure to move. (The advantage of using the Pen tool is that you can go back and refine the path to create a perfect selection.)

2. He selected Make Selection from the Paths palette menu and feathered the selection. Use a zero feather for crisp originals to maintain edge sharpness. Use a one or two feather for older snapshots where the image isn't very sharp, as in this example. Leave the antialias box checked, or the pixels will look too rough around the edges.

3. He used Layer > New > Layer via Copy (Cmd + J)[Ctrl + J] to copy the selected area onto its own layer.

4. With the Move tool, Wayne repositioned the woman, as seen in **figure 7.58**. At this point he was seeing double—the original and the copy.

5. He cropped the image to remove the original woman as well as some of the cluttered background.

6. Often when moving pieces of images, artifacts remain that give away that the person was moved. In this example, the right side of the woman's coat still has pieces of the handrail on it. Wayne cloned over it.

7. To quickly hide small specks of dirt or dust seen on the dark coat, he used the Float and Move technique described in Chapter 5. (In a nutshell: select the coat, (Cmd + J)[Ctrl + J] to copy it onto its own layer, activate the Move tool, and nudge the object down and over 2–3 pixels with the arrow keys. To remove light spots, set the Blending Mode to Darken, or to remove dark spots set the Blending Mode to Lighten.)

8. To force the top coat layer to conform to the shape and size of the left woman layer, Wayne created a clipping group by making the top layer active and selecting Layer > Group with Previous, as seen in **figure 7.59**.

figure 7.58

After selecting, placing, and positioning the person on a new layer, the image will need to be cropped.

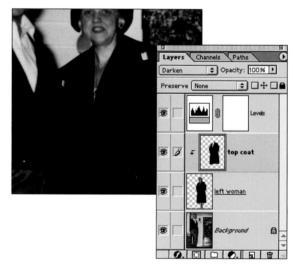

figure 7.59

Clipping the floated and moved top coat layer with the layer of the isolated woman makes the coat conform to the shape of the woman.

9. Moving the top coat layer also covered up or affected some of the woman's hand and details on the coat, as seen in **figure 7.60**. By adding a layer mask and painting with black, Wayne can bring back her hand, neckline, and the decorations on her coat that were affected with the float and move technique.

figure 7.60

Compare the circled areas to figure 7.59 to see how a layer mask can fine-tune how the layers interact to hide any edge artifacts.

10. Moving the woman closer to the man made the photo much friendlier. Cloning over the remaining wires and porch lamp removed the unwanted clutter. Adding the appropriate shadow behind her will finish this part of the job (see **figure 7.61**).

figure 7.61

Now the couple is closer together, and the remaining distractions have been cloned away.

Matching the Shadows

When you combine photographs, always double-check the light sources and the shadows. In this example, the woman needs a shadow to match the shadow cast by the man. Matching the shadow from the flash will require a bit more finesse than Photoshop's Layer Styles offer.

1. Start by hiding all layers that do not contain the image information that needs a shadow. In this case, that's everything but the woman layer and the top coat layer, as seen in **figure 7.62**.

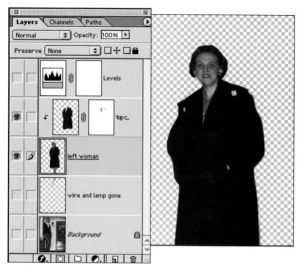

figure 7.62

Hide all layers you do not need to merge before selecting Merge Visible from the Layer Menu.

2. Wayne selected Layer > Merge Visible to combine these layers into one.

3. He (Cmd + clicked)[Ctrl + clicked] the left woman layer thumbnail to load the transparency of the layer as a selection.

4. Wayne used the Eyedropper tool to sample a color from the man's shadow and then added a new layer and filled the selection with that sampled color to create the base for the shadow, as shown in **figure 7.63**.

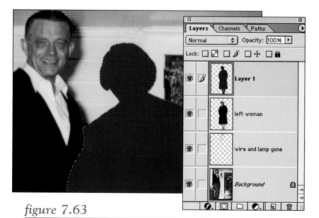

figure 7.63

Use a color from the untouched subject to build the shadow for the moved subject.

Tip

In reality, shadows are not just black. Rather, they pick up color from the environment. Sampling color from the actual image will help your drop shadows to be more realistic.

5. Because the newly filled shadow layer is sitting on top of the subject in the layers palette, Wayne repositioned the shadow by placing it underneath the woman's layer.

6. Compare the new shadow to the shadow behind the man. Wayne used the Move tool to make the woman's shadow fall an equal distance from her as the man's shadow falls from him in the original image. Because the edge of the shadow is too harsh, he used the Gaussian Blur filter to soften the edges of the shadow, as seen in **figure 7.64**.

figure 7.64

Blurring the shadow to match the existing shadow.

7. Shadows are not 100% opaque, and by setting the shadow layer's Blending Mode to Multiply and adjusting the layer opacity, Wayne matched the density of the woman's new shadows with the man's on the porch wall.

8. Often faux shadows look too artificial because they are too smooth. Selecting Filter > Add Noise or Filter > Artistic > Film Grain and adding a touch of monochrome noise as seen in **figure 7.65** can help match the new shadow with the old.

figure 7.65

Adding a touch of monochrome noise to give the shadow some texture helps it to blend into the scene.

As the rebuilt image comes together, it's time to carefully inspect the image for distracting dirt or dust and, more importantly, for unwanted artifacts of the reconstruction. Upon careful inspection, Wayne noticed that the edges of the woman are too sharp in relationship to the man and he used the Blur tool set to 25% pressure to soften the edges where needed.

RECONSTRUCTING COLOR

Photographic color prints and Father Time rarely make a good partnership, and too often colors fade, shift, or disappear altogether. Take a look at the yellow cowboy image in **figure 7.66**. As far as we can tell, the yellow dye couplers broke free from their oil-based encasing molecules and fogged the entire print with a hideous yellow stain. Lloyd Weller, Director of the Photography Program at Everett Community College, was kind to share this image resurrection with me to include in the book. Reconstructing the color in the image as seen in **figure 7.67** involved swapping channels, working with levels, selection, and handcoloring techniques.

BEFORE

figure 7.66

AFTER

Retouched by Lloyd Weller

figure 7.67

Replacing the Damaged Channel

Whenever an image has a blatant color problem like this cowboy image, start by inspecting the individual channels by clicking them in the Channels palette. As shown in **7.68**, the Blue channel doesn't have any useful image information. Because the Blue channel doesn't contain any useful information but is required to reconstruct the color, we'll need to replace it.

figure 7.68

The Blue channel doesn't hold any useable image information and needs to be replaced.

ch7_cowboy.jpg

1. Duplicate the damaged file and select Image > Mode > Lab Color. The Lab Color mode separates the color information from the lightness (also called luminance) information, as seen in **figure 7.69**. You now have the original RGB and duplicated Lab mode files.

2. Activate the Lightness channel as seen in **figure 7.69** and Select>All and Edit>Copy.

figure 7.69

Duplicate the original file and convert it to Lab Color mode to separate the color information from the lightness information.

3. Return to the original RGB file, activate the Blue channel, and Select>All. Use Edit>Paste Into to place the luminance information in the blue channel.

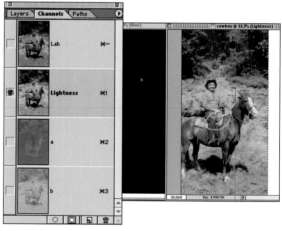

figure 7.70

The Lightness channel contains the information that the original's Blue channel should have had.

4. **Figure 7.71** shows that the ugly yellow cast is gone. Although the resulting image is still off-color, it certainly looks better than the original jaundiced image.

figure 7.71

After replacing the Blue channel, the image might still have a color cast that needs to be corrected.

5. To bring the rest of the color into reasonable balance, use a Levels Adjustment Layer (see **figure 7.72**). Adjust the shadow point slider of the Red channel to where the true Red channel information begins, thus reducing some of the gross overcast. The Levels Input values Lloyd used on the Red channel were 84, 1.00, and 255.

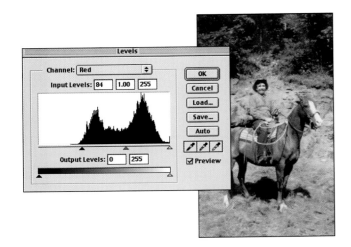

figure 7.72

Adjusting the Red channel in a Levels adjustment layer reduces the magenta color cast.

6. Select the Green channel in the Levels dialog box and adjust the highlight slider to where the majority of the true Green channel information begins (see **figure 7.73**). This will eliminate some of the extreme highlight value information. The midtone gamma slider is also adjusted slightly to assist with the correction. The Levels values Lloyd used on the Green channel were 0, 1.05, 238.

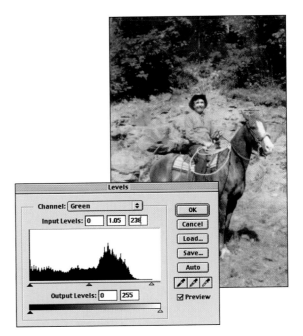

figure 7.73

Adjusting the Green channel in a Levels adjustment layer further corrects the color.

7. Select the Blue channel in the Levels dialog box and bring the shadow slider up to the right to eliminate the blue color cast in the background, as seen in **figure 7.74**. (Try Input Levels settings of 64, 1.00, and 246).

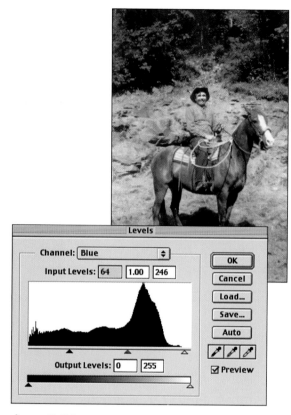

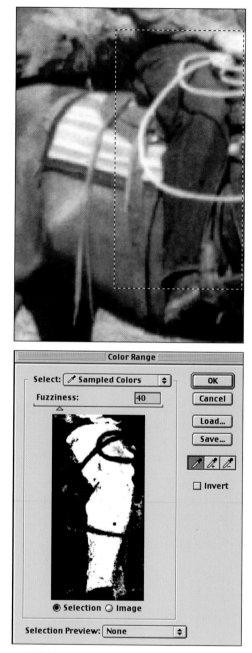

figure 7.74

Adjusting the blue shadow point to the right enables the greens of the background to show through.

Fine-Tuning Individual Color

At this point the image is starting to look believable—a cowboy in (perhaps) a green shirt on a chestnut horse. The handcoloring process involves selecting the area to be colored, adding a new layer, filling the selection with the appropriate color, and changing the layer's Blending Mode to Color. By reducing the opacity of the channel, you can control the color saturation of each image element.

1. Start by making a rough selection around the area to be selected. In **figure 7.75**, I used the Marquee tool to frame the jeans, which will limit the Color Range command to look only inside that selection.

figure 7.75

The Color Range command looks only at specified colors inside the initial selection.

2. When using the Color Range command, you can add colors to the selection with the plus eyedropper or by Shift + clicking the desired colors. In this case, I was careful to select the jeans but not the leather reins or lasso rope.

3. If the selection seems ragged or inexact, press Q to enter Quick Mask mode. Paint in the mask with black (to delete) or white (to add) until the mask is refined, as seen in **figure 7.76**.

5. Changing the layer's Blending Mode to Color changes the color while letting the black-and-white tonal information show through (see **figure 7.77**). Reduce the layer's opacity as needed to avoid an inappropriately oversaturated look. Typically, setting the Blending Mode to Color will lighten the color that you chose. If you don't like the results, try choosing a color that is a bit darker, or try other Blending Modes, such as Multiply, Overlay, or Soft Light.

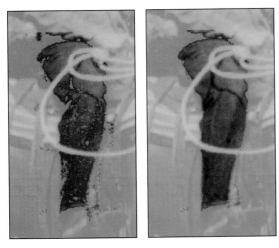

figure 7.76

Check the quality of your selection in Quick Mask mode and refine the mask with the painting tools.

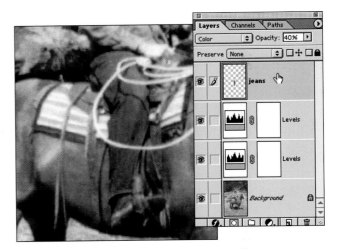

figure 7.77

Adjusting the Blending Mode and Opacity enables the tonal information to show through the color.

4. Press Q again to activate the selection, add a new layer, choose an appropriate blue for the jeans and select Edit > Fill. Set the contents to Foreground Color, the mode to Normal, and the opacity to 100%.

6. **Figure 7.78** shows how Lloyd built up the color of the individual pieces, transforming the seemingly hopeless yellow version to a realistic color photograph that is a pleasure to look at.

figure 7.78

By placing each colorized piece on its own layer, you can control each component independently.

CLOSING THOUGHTS

Replacing, rebuilding, and re-creating missing image elements requires creative problem-solving skills, the willingness to dig around in a file to look for useful material, and the ability to appropriate suitable pieces from other photographs and scenes. The search will result in new images that are much more pleasing and meaningful to display and cherish.

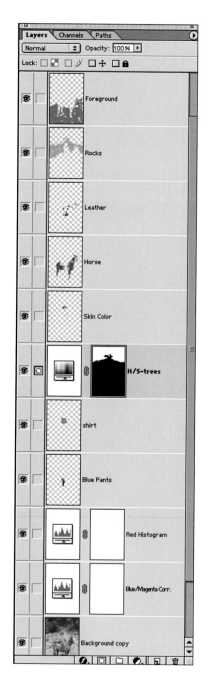

8

REFINING AND POLISHING THE IMAGE

After perfecting an image's color and contrast and repairing the ravages of time, it's time to apply the final polish, the frosting, the cherry on top. Finishing an image can be as simple as converting a so-so color image into a snappy black-and-white photograph, or colorizing a black-and-white photo. You can make the difference between "Ho-hum" and "Wow!" by adding just the right amount of sharpening or a subtle filter effect, or by experimenting with creative exposure and edge techniques to accentuate the image.

All in all, this chapter is about experimenting, dabbling, exploring, and adding a touch of pizzazz to retouched images or forgotten snapshots to make them stand out. You'll learn how to do the following:

- Convert color images to black and white
- Add color to black-and-white images
- Work with soft and selective focus
- Add frames and vignetted edges
- Sharpen images to add snap

CONVERTING COLOR TO BLACK AND WHITE

A fine black-and-white photograph has an abstractness and aura that full-color images often just don't have. They remind us of the rich heritage of the photographic masters—Edward Steichen, Alfred Stieglitz, Ansel Adams, and Edward Weston, to name a few.

If black and white is so attractive, why do most of us use color film? Because we see in color, and therefore it's easier to take a color picture than to figure out how the colors will translate into shades of gray. In fact, I never use black-and-white film anymore, but I do make beautiful black-and-white prints. How, you wonder? I shoot color slides or color negative print film, scan it in, and then use Photoshop to convert the color file into a beautiful black and white image.

As with many techniques in Photoshop, there are numerous methods of converting an RGB file from color to grayscale, ranging from a one-click solution with no control to a multi-step process with infinite control.

Of course, I'd like you to avoid the one-click method because it removes important image information. However, please don't jump to the last, most involved method because you think it must be the best. It may not be the best for the images you're working with. All of the techniques I describe here will work with both RGB and CMYK images. Your numeric values will vary depending on your color and separation setup.

Converting to Grayscale Mode

The fastest (but worst) way to convert a color file to grayscale is to select Image > Mode > Grayscale, which just discards color information without giving you any control over the process. As benign as this process seems, the behind-the-scenes math is rather complicated. Photoshop references your color and ink settings and then takes approximately 30% red, 59% green, and 11% blue to make the single-channel grayscale file. The worst part of this conversion process is that there's no preview and you have no control over the percentages or the final outcome.

To simplify this, Photoshop takes all three channels and smashes them down into a single channel. If one of the channels is damaged or excessively noisy, as shown in **figure 8.1**, those artifacts go into the grayscale file as well. Although this method is fast and easy, I cannot recommend it for either RGB or CMYK files because you can achieve better results with the following methods.

ch8_costume.jpg

figure 8.1

In this digital camera file, the blue channel shows excessive noise that would degrade the quality of the grayscale file if you chose Mode > Grayscale and flattened the three RGB channels into one.

Using a Color Channel

The second way to convert from color to grayscale gives you a chance to choose the best channel before discarding the color information. Inspect the quality and characteristics of each channel and decide which one has the best tonal information. (Remember that combining (Cmd)[Ctrl] with 1, 2, 3, and (for CMYK images) 4 will activate channels individually.)

In most cases it will be the Green channel, but for some pictures, such as creative portraits, the Red channel may offer a pleasingly glowing alternative. In either case, make the best channel active (as shown in **figure 8.2**), and select Image > Mode > Grayscale. Notice the difference in the dialog box. It now says, "Discard Other Channels?" The less-useful channels are thrown away, and the channel you consider the best becomes the grayscale image. Many newspaper productions use this technique to quickly convert a color image to grayscale.

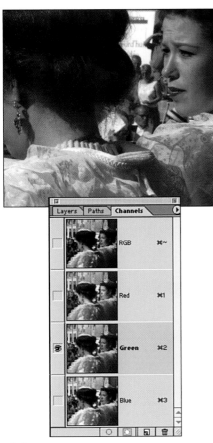

figure 8.2

Converting to grayscale with the best channel active will delete the two (or three) weaker channels.

Using the Luminance Channel

The third method to convert a color image to grayscale starts by converting the RGB or CMYK to Lab, as shown in **figure 8.3**. Then, make the L channel (lightness) active and select Image > Mode > Grayscale. This method maintains the luminance value of the image more closely than using a single channel from an RGB or CMYK file (see **figure 8.4**).

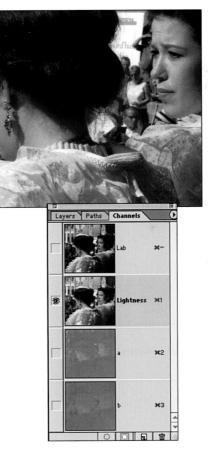

figure 8.3

Converting a color image to Lab color separates the tonal information from the color information.

figure 8.4

The resulting grayscale file doesn't have any of the noise artifacts that the original color image had.

Using the Channel Mixer

One of the best (but unsung) features of Photoshop 5.0 was the addition of the new Adjustment Layer called Channel Mixer. It allows you to add and subtract varying amounts of each color channel to build grayscale files with a wide tonal and interpretive range. This is by far the best balance of ease of use and quality of results for converting color images to grayscale. It's my favorite way to get very good results very quickly, as you can see when you compare **figures 8.5** and **8.6**.

figure 8.5

figure 8.6

1. Add a Channel Mixer Adjustment Layer and make sure that the monochrome (another word for grayscale or single channel) check box is checked.

2. Adjust the color sliders to create a grayscale image that uses tonal attributes from the desired channels. To maintain tonality when converting, the sum total of the numeric values should not exceed 100. However, if your goal is to create the best grayscale image possible, experiment with the sliders until you're satisfied with the results (see **figure 8.7**). (I rarely use the Constant slider because it applies a linear lightening and darkening effect. I'd rather use Levels or Curves to finesse the final tonality of the image after conversion.)

3. Remember to keep an eye on the Info palette, and don't let the highlights get blown out to pure white. Click OK to close the Channel Mixer dialog.

Tip

You can open the Info palette by pressing the F8 key. Press it again to hide the palette. This works even while you're in the Channel Mixer dialog box (or any Adjustment Layer interface).

4. Once you've created the black-and-white image you want, select File >Save as (save it as another filename, to preserve your original color image) and then select Image > Mode > Grayscale. Photoshop will bring up the "Discard Color Information?" warning. All three channels are now equal, so you can click OK without degrading the file.

Tip

When using the Channel Mixer, you can start with 100% Green channel rather than the default 100% Red channel by pressing (Cmd + 2)[Ctrl + 2] before clicking the monochrome button.

Tip

To speed up production when converting similar color files to grayscale, you may either save and load the Channel Mixer settings or drag the Channel Mixer Adjustment Layer between documents. See "Sharing Adjustment Layers" in Chapter 2, "Improving Tone and Contrast," for more information.

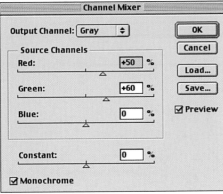

figure 8.7

Using the Channel Mixer to create quality black-and-white images from a color file gives you tremendous control.

⊕▷∻ **ch8_sunflower.jpg**

Channel Mixer allows you to interpret and influence how the color values are translated into black and white. In **figures 8.9**, **8.10**, and **8.11**, I've created three interpretations of the color image shown in **figure 8.8**. Working from left to right, I created subtle-to-dramatic interpretations of the sunflower scene by changing the Channel Mixer settings.

figure 8.8

The original image.

figure 8.9

The Channel Mixer can be used to create a classic black-and-white image…

figure 8.10

…or something a little more dramatic…

figure 8.11

…or something quite stormy.

Using Calculations

The final method of converting an image from color to grayscale is to use the Calculation functions. Besides color management, mastering this feature is the one thing that separates the Photoshop weenies from the meisters. Similar to Channel Mixer, the Calculations command enables you to mix individual channels but with the added benefits of Blending Modes, opacity settings, and masks. Unfortunately, you can only combine two channels at a time. The following technique is especially useful when you're converting a CMYK file to grayscale.

1. Inspect the color channels to see which ones carry the attributes you would like to either accentuate or minimize. Avoid using channels that are too contrasty, noisy, or posterized.
2. Select Image > Calculations.
3. Use the pull-down menus to select the two channels you want to combine, as shown in figure 8.12.

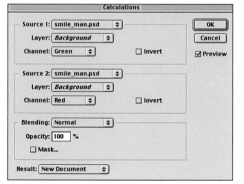

figure 8.12

Start by selecting the channels you want to combine.

4. Change the Blending Mode to influence the interaction between the channels. As you can see in **figure 8.13**, changing the Blending Mode to Soft Light changes the tonal character of the portrait.

figure 8.13

Changing the Blending Mode, opacity, and order of Source 1 and 2 channels influences the final outcome.

5. Adjust the Opacity setting. This controls how strongly the topmost channel (in this case, the Green channel) is used in the calculation.
6. Make sure that Result is set to New Document and click OK.
7. The resulting document is a Photoshop multichannel document. To save the document as a standard grayscale file, select Image > Mode > Grayscale.

© Digital Stock

After you're comfortable with combining individual channels with Calculations to create pleasing and interpretive black-and-white images, experiment with masks to control where the calculation takes place.

1. To use a layer's transparency or an alpha channel mask to control where a calculation takes place, I often create a highlight mask with a Color Range selection. To do this, choose Select > Color Range and choose Highlights. Save the resulting selection as a channel and then use Image > Calculations to recalculate images together to add density to the highlights, as shown in **figure 8.14**.

2. Inverting either the channel or the mask gives you additional control over the resulting image. In this example, I needed to tone down the highlight on the man's forehead. By inverting the Alpha channel, I'm telling Photoshop to affect everything except the highlights. This allows me to create a grayscale image without making the portrait's highlights blow out to pure white.

Caution

When you're calculating with separate images, each image must be exactly the same size, pixel for pixel, or else the Calculations interface won't recognize the file.

COMBINING COLOR AND BLACK AND WHITE

You can draw a viewer's eye to an element by making it the only color object in the picture. This effect is used all the time in advertising campaigns. (For example, a pair of blue jeans are in color and the rest of the picture is in black and white.) Experiment with desaturating an image and painting back a few color elements to create a painterly or nostalgic look.

I was drawn to these tulips because of their color (see **figure 8.15**). Isolating and accentuating the blossoms and leaves, as shown in **figure 8.16**, emphasizes the original character of the bouquet.

ch8_tulips.jpg

1. Add either a Channel Mixer or Hue/Saturation Adjustment Layer to a color image. If you use the Channel Mixer, adjust the channel sliders to create a pleasing black and white image, as described previously. If you use Hue/Saturation, move the saturation slider all the way to the left, as shown in **figure 8.17**.

figure 8.14

Using masks and separate files opens up powerful opportunities when you're working with Image Calculations.

figure 8.15

figure 8.16

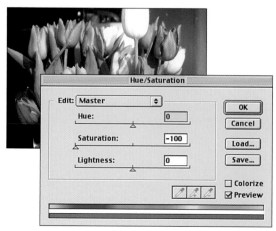

figure 8.17

Use a Hue/Saturation Adjustment Layer to remove all of the color from the image.

2. Make the Background layer active and use any selection tool to select the object you want to be in color. In **figure 8.18**, I used the Pen tool to outline the tulips and then chose Make Selection from the Path palette menu.

figure 8.18

To mask out the tulips, I first drew a path and then converted it to a selection.

3. Click on the mask of the Hue/Saturation Adjustment Layer and fill the selection with black to block out the image adjustment in the selected areas. This fills the selection with the original image's color, as shown in **figure 8.19**.

figure 8.19

Once the mask has been adjusted, the flowers have their beautiful original color.

4. Experiment with using shades of gray to fill the selection in order to maintain a hint of color. Or in this case, I duplicated and inverted the Hue/Saturation layer, double-clicked on it, and saturated the tulips by 20% to accentuate their color even more (see **figure 8.20**).

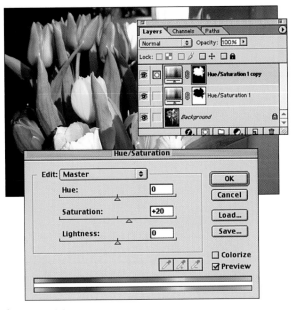

figure 8.20

Duplicating and inverting the original Hue/Saturation layer strengthens the color of the tulips.

TONING IMAGES WITH COLOR

Photographers tone their prints for a number of reasons. Selenium toners add warmth to a print and make it last longer. Ferric oxide toners add a beautiful blue tone, and gold toners add richness that is hard to resist. But toning prints in a traditional darkroom can also pose both health and environmental hazards. Unless you have proper ventilation and chemical disposal options, traditional darkroom toning is not recommended. But with Photoshop, you can tone images to your heart's content without having to clean up messy sinks and smelly trays or dispose of noxious chemicals.

Caution

For any black-and-white image to be colorized or toned, the file must be in either RGB, CMYK, or Lab color mode. Before you begin, convert the file from grayscale to a color mode, preferably RGB or CMYK.

Toning with Variations

The Variations dialog box is the easiest way to experiment with image toning options. The original image is shown, along with a collection of variations (hence the name) created by strengthening

or weakening the colors in the image. It doesn't require a great deal of guesswork on your part because Variations gives you a preview of the finished image. For more details on the Variations dialog box, see "Color Correction with Variations" in Chapter 4, "Working with Color."

Figure 8.21 shows the original image, and **figure 8.22** shows the toned version. To me, the bluer version is much more attractive and fitting to the subject.

figure 8.21

figure 8.22

⊕▷≍ **ch8_buddha.jpg**

1. Select Image > Adjust > Variations.

2. The ring of six color options allows you to experiment by clicking on the color that you want to add to the image. I recommend

reducing the strength of the effect by moving the Fine to Coarse slider to the left, as shown in **figure 8.23**.

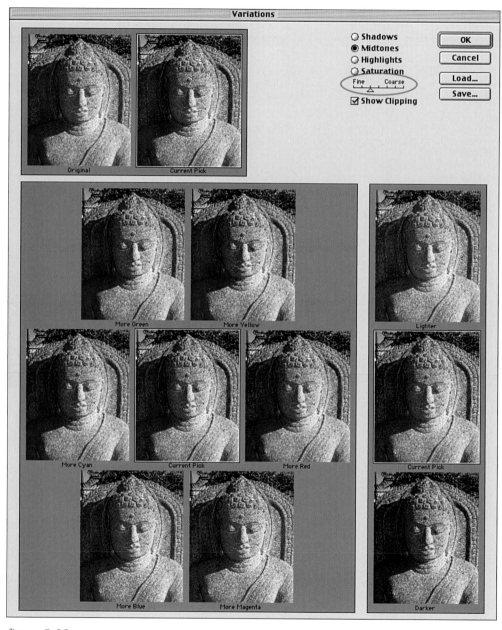

figure 8.23

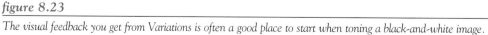

The visual feedback you get from Variations is often a good place to start when toning a black-and-white image.

3. You can click on a color more than once to strengthen the effect, or click on the opposite color to subtract the first color.

 T i p

When working with Variations, you can zero out the effect by clicking the original thumbnail in the upper left of the Variations interface.

Monocolor Toning

Variations is very easy to use, but that simplicity comes with a price because your changes aren't applied to a separate layer or added as an Adjustment Layer. In other words, you're changing the actual image data and not working on a separate layer. To maintain control and flexibility, I prefer to work with separate layers and do my toning with the tools described here and in the next section, "Multicolor Toning." Monocolor toning is a straightforward method of adding one color to an image (as shown in **figures 8.24** and **25**) and can be used to visually tie a group of images together or to add an interpretive mood to an image.

🌐➤⊱ **ch8_ramhead.jpg**

1. Select Layer > New Fill Layer > Solid Color and select a color from the Color Picker.

2. Change the layer's Blending Mode to Color, Overlay, or Soft Light to create the effects shown in **figures 8.26**, **8.27**, and **8.28**.

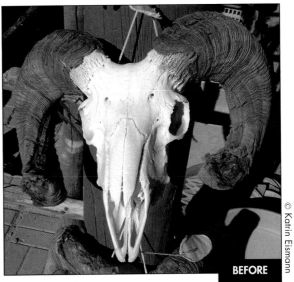

© Katrin Eismann

figure 8.24

figure 8.25

figure 8.26

The Color Blending Mode.

figure 8.27

The Overlay Blending Mode.

figure 8.28

The Soft Light Blending Mode.

3. The advantages to using the Color Fill layer, as shown in **figure 8.29**, are that you can work with the Opacity and Blending Modes to reduce the effect; take advantage of the Layer Mask to control where the effect takes place; and, by double-clicking on the Solid Color layer, select new colors. If you don't like the results, you can just throw the entire layer away and start over again.

figure 8.29

Placing the color on a separate layer enables you to fine-tune the effect with Opacity and Blending Mode settings.

Multicolor Toning

The world is your Photoshop oyster when you work with Adjustment Layers. The Color Balance tool enables you to tone and color highlights, midtones, or shadows separately, just as a fine art photographer would do in a traditional darkroom.

The original parrot photo used in this example is a black-and-white RGB file, as shown in **figure 8.30**. **Figure 8.31** shows how adding complimentary colors into the highlights and shadows makes the image more dimensional and attractive.

figure 8.30

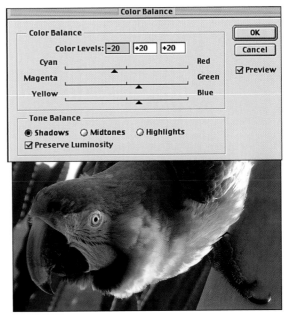

figure 8.32

Adding cyan, green, and blue to the shadows.

figure 8.31

 ch8_parrot.jpg

1. To add subtle colors to the shadows, midtones, and highlights, add a Color Balance Adjustment Layer and click on shadow, midtone, or highlight depending on the area you want to tone.

2. Adjust each area so that it complements and offsets the others. Often, I tone the shadows and highlights and don't alter the midtones. This adds color tension to an image.

3. As shown in **figure 8.32**, I toned the shadows green-cyan. In **figure 8.33**, I chose to contrast the cool tones with warm tones in the highlights.

figure 8.33

Adding red and yellow to the highlights.

The only correct setting for any of these techniques is what looks good to you. So have fun, experiment, and bring those black-and-white images to life.

HAND-COLORING A BLACK-AND-WHITE IMAGE

Since the advent of photography, photographers and artists have hand-colored photographs to add realism. Even in today's era of computers and Photoshop, there are many professional retouchers and photo enthusiasts who still enjoy working with Marshall Oils to add a handcrafted look to their photos. I've never been very good at hand-coloring traditional darkroom prints, which is why I especially like doing it on the computer.

The most straightforward method of hand-coloring an image entails adding an empty layer that has been set to the Color Blending Mode and using any painting tool to color it, as shown in **figure 8.34**.

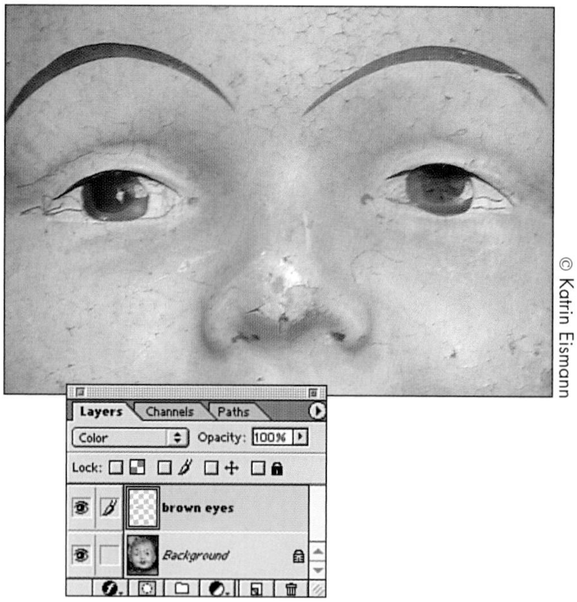

You can also hand-color an image by making selections and using Color Fill Layers, as illustrated by the black-and-white image shown in **figure 8.35**, which Shangara Singh, a London-based multimedia and photography expert, has hand-colored (well, mouse-colored) beautifully, as shown in **figure 8.36**. This coloring method requires a bit more patience, but the flexibility of working with Color Fill Adjustment Layers is well worth the effort.

figure 8.34

By painting on an empty layer that has been set to the Color Blending Mode, you can hand-paint details in the eyes of this window mannequin.

figure 8.35

© Katrin Eismann

© Shangara Singh

BEFORE

figure 8.36

Before you start hand-coloring an image, take a moment to visualize and plan out your color scheme. After scanning in the original photograph of his sister-in-law, Shangara took a moment to decide which basic color palette he would use. Of course, the shrubbery would need to be colored in greens and the road in browns, which made him decide to use magenta (opposite green on the color wheel) for her dress. These opposite colors play off one another and create a more interesting image.

🌐⤷ **ch8_woman_walking.jpg**

1. Select the first element of the image you would like to hand-color. Shangara started by selecting the road with the Lasso tool, as shown in **figure 8.37**.

figure 8.37

The road is the first element to be selected for coloring.

2. Add a Solid Color Layer by clicking on the Adjustment Layer button on the bottom of the Layers palette and selecting Color Fill, or select Layer > New Fill Layer > Solid Color.

3. Use the Photoshop Color Picker to select a color (most likely brown) for the road. The Fill Layer is automatically filled with the color (see **figure 8.38**). Set the layer's Blending Mode to Color to let details from the original image show through.

figure 8.38

The image after the selection has been filled with color and the layer's Blending Mode has been changed to Color.

4. Select the shrubbery on the left, add a new Color Fill layer with green, and set the Blending Mode to Color. Of course, a large patch of shrubbery won't all be an identical shade of green, so make another selection and fill this with a darker shade of green (see **figure 8.39**).

5. In case a color is too strong, as the shrubs are on the left side of this image, you can double-click the Color Fill Adjustment Layer icon and select a new color with the Color Picker. Or, you can reduce the opacity of the layer.

With the patience of a saint, Shangara continued selecting his way up the image, using individual layers for elements as small as his sister-in-law's sandals and bangle bracelets

Since the Color Fill layers are based on selections and have masks with them, you can refine where the coloring takes place by painting with a black or white brush with any painting tool on the layer mask.

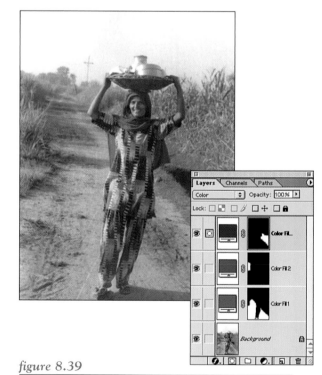

figure 8.39

Using different shades of green makes the shrubbery more realistic.

Hand-Coloring Tips

Hand-coloring can be both tedious and rewarding. Here are a few tips to help you work a little faster and make your results more realistic:

- To speed up hand-coloring work, press (Option)[Alt] while adding a new Solid Color layer from the Layers palette. This brings up the New Layer window where you can change the Blending Mode to Color before selecting the color.

- Use reference photographs to select colors, as shown in figure 8.40.

- When you're sampling skin tones, sample from different parts of a person's face. Each person has numerous skin tones that you can use to make your hand-coloring look more realistic.

- In Photoshop 6.0, save your colors into your color swatches and use the new Preset Manager to name them, as shown in figure 8.41.

figure 8.40

It's very helpful to sample colors from a similar photograph, especially when working on your subject's skin.

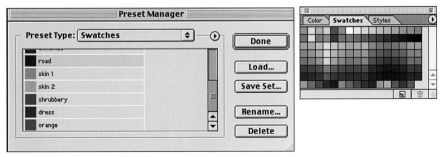

figure 8.41

Photoshop 6.0 has new features for naming and organizing your Swatches palette.

The Beauty Is in the Details

To make the sky realistic, Shangara was smart enough not to use a straightforward light-blue color fill. Rather, he made a rough selection of the sky, added a new layer with a layer mask, and roughly airbrushed in blue at 15% opacity, as shown in **figure 8.42**. I emphasize the word "rough" because leaving some empty areas on the sky layer gives it a realistic hazy look.

figure 8.42

When you're coloring a sky, use a rough airbrushing technique at a low opacity to create a hazy effect.

Being faithful to the original photograph, Shangara added the wires back into the scene.

After coloring the entire image, Shangara added an empty layer to the top of the layer stack. He pressed (Option)[Alt] and selected Layer > Merge Visible to create a complete composite of all the layers in the new layer. On this layer, he can zoom in on and inspect all the details and edges and use the Rubber Stamp tool to clean up any stray artifacts.

 Freehand Hand-Coloring

If you would like to create a softer, less controlled, hand-colored look, experiment with this technique:

1. Add an empty layer and change its Blending Mode to Color.
2. Use the Airbrush or Paint Brush tool with the desired color and paint on the empty layer. Use the Eraser tool to take away unwanted color.
3. Add a new empty color layer for each color used.

WORKING WITH SOFT AND SELECTIVE FOCUS

Photoshop users either love filters or hate them. The haters snub their noses at filters, saying that they're just canned effects that anyone with a mouse could use, as a roomful of chimps with a typewriter would eventually be able to peck out a *Hamlet*. The filter-lovers insist that they use them to apply creative and painterly effects to an image.

Actually, both factions are right—playing around with Photoshop filters doesn't take any talent, but applying them in an intelligent fashion does. By combining filters, layers, and Blending Modes, you can create unique effects and add a special touch to your images. Entire books have been written on Photoshop filters, so I've chosen to concentrate on the photographic filters that control focus.

To control the filter's effect and protect the original image, always duplicate the layer to be manipulated before applying any filters. Working on a duplicate layer lets you experiment with filters and Blending Modes without having to worry about ruining your original image. Best of all, if you really don't like the effect you've created, you can simply delete the layer and start over again.

Soft-Focus Effects

Soft-focus effects can be used to soften a portrait or to add a romantic, atmospheric effect to an image. Photographers use many types of materials to create soft-focus effects, from nylon stockings and Vaseline over the enlarger lens to taking the picture through a screen.

Softening a portrait also minimizes skin imperfections and adds a glow to the person's skin. **Figure 8.43** shows the original portrait for this example, which is rather contrasty. Softening the portrait and then bringing the eyes back into focus makes the new version more attractive and romantic (see **figure 8.44**).

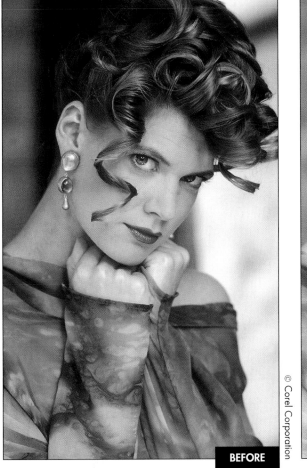

BEFORE

© Corel Corporation

AFTER

figure 8.43

figure 8.44

1. Duplicate the Background layer and set the Blending Mode to Screen. Although the image will look too light, this will let you see the true effect of the next step.

2. Select Filter > Blur > Gaussian Blur and use a very high setting (see **figure 8.45**). Without the Screen Blending Mode, the blur would soften the image into oblivion.

figure 8.46

Painting on a layer mask with a soft-gray-to-black Airbrush lets you control exactly which parts of the image are in focus.

Selective Focus Controls

If you've paged through any fashion magazines recently, you've seen shots in which the model's lower body is thrown out of focus and her face is in focus. In most cases, the photographer has achieved this effect by using a large-format-view camera (4×5" or 8×10") and distorting the plane of focus with the camera's swing and tilt controls.

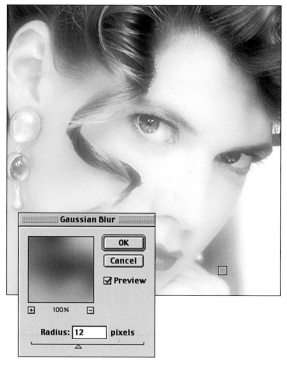

figure 8.45

Duplicating the layer and setting it to Screen allows you to see the true effect of the Gaussian Blur filter.

3. Adjust the soft layer's opacity to blend the two images. I used 70% for this example.

4. To draw the viewer's eye to what's important in the portrait—the eyes, hair curl, and earrings—you need to control the focus. Add a layer mask and use a soft, black Airbrush on the mask to paint at 20%-25% opacity over these features (see **figure 8.46**).

You can achieve a similar effect with the following technique. **Figure 8.47** is the original version, and **figure 8.48** is the selective focus variation.

1. Duplicate the Background layer.

2. Run a very high Gaussian Blur filter (20 pixels is probably a good place to start), as shown in **figure 8.49**.

3. Add a layer mask to the blurred layer and use the Gradient tool to control where the focus is placed. In this example, I wanted her face and neck to be in focus and the lower part of the image to be out of focus, as shown in figure 8.50.

figure 8.47

figure 8.48

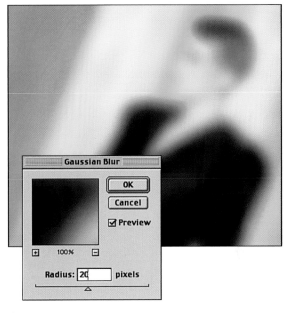

figure 8.49

Duplicating and blurring the original background layer.

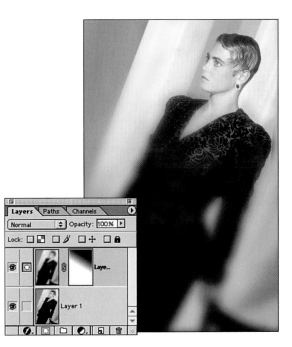

figure 8.50

Use the Gradation Blend tool on the layer mask to control where the image is in focus.

4. If need be, you can strengthen the effect by running the Gaussian Blur filter on the blurred layer again.

Subjective Focus and Exposure

Selective focus can also be used as an interpretive tool to add a hint of mystery or intrigue to an image. As you can see in **figure 8.51**, the color and quality of light give the winter scene an interesting character. But I took the image further, as shown in **figure 8.52**. This is a more fitting interpretation of how I perceived the scene on that winter evening in the Black Forest. The softening effect was created in a similar fashion to what was just described in the Selective Focus Controls section. To accentuate the mood even further, I also darkened and lightened contrasting image areas.

© Katrin Eismann

BEFORE

figure 8.51

AFTER

figure 8.52

🌐▷ **ch8_rest.jpg**

1. Duplicate the Background layer and run the Gaussian Blur filter to soften the image.

🔍 **T i p**

Avoid filters that don't give you control. Use the ones that bring up an interface window for you to adjust settings in. For example, you have a number of options under the Blur filters (see **figure 8.53**). The first two options apply a blur effect over which you have no control. The following four options are followed by ellipses, meaning that an interface will pop up and you'll be able to adjust the settings to suit your image.

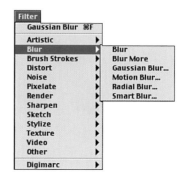

figure 8.53

Selecting the filters that give you more control will produce better results.

2. Add a layer mask and use a large, soft gray Airbrush to paint onto it, as shown in **figure 8.54**. If need be, erase any painted areas on the mask by painting with white.

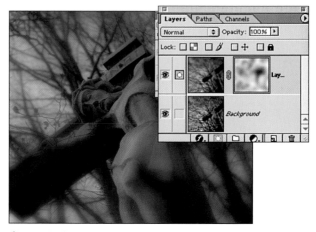

figure 8.54

Painting on the layer mask determines which parts are in focus and which ones aren't.

3. Add a new layer and change the Blending Mode to Soft Light. Choose black as your foreground color. Select the Gradient tool and choose the Foreground to Transparent gradient from the gradient options (see **figure 8.55**).

figure 8.55

Using a black-to-transparent gradient on an empty Soft Light layer will darken the exposure on the edges of the image.

4. Drag the Gradient tool from the edge of the image to the center. You can build up density by using the Gradient tool repeatedly, or by airbrushing with black to add a random, dappled effect.

5. To lighten the figure of Jesus Christ, add a neutral layer. (Option + click)[Alt + click] the New Layer icon. Set Mode to Color Dodge and check the Fill with Color-Dodge-neutral color (black) option, as shown in **figure 8.56**.

6. Paint with a very light-opacity white Airbrush with 2-4% Pressure to selectively lighten image areas, as shown in **figure 8.57**.

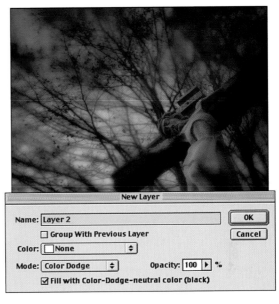

figure 8.56

Adding a Color Dodge layer filled with the neutral color black.

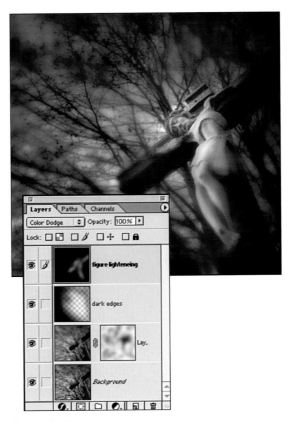

figure 8.57

Carefully lighten the figure to draw the viewer's attention to the crucifix.

Creative Combinations

Throughout the retouching and enhancement process, it's very important to keep in mind the people in the images. Figure 8.58 shows a compelling composite that photographer Mark Beckelman created by combining a picture of his father as a young boy (see figure 8.59) and a more recent photograph of his father looking into a pool of water cupped in his hands.

Mark started by scanning the photograph of the football team. After looking at the scan, he realized that it didn't contain the amount or quality of image information that he required, he made a 4"×5" copy negative of the original print and scanned it (see figure 8.60). Mark then took a photograph of a stream and one of his father's cupped hands, as shown in figures 8.61 and 8.62.

With great skill, Mark composited the images together. Figure 8.63 shows how he employed the many lighting and softening techniques described in this chapter to create a very sensitive portrait of his father looking back through time.

figure 8.58

This image combines old and new images very effectively.

figure 8.59

The original print.

figure 8.62

A contemporary image that was blurred to make it recede into the background.

figure 8.60

A crop of the 4"×5" copy negative.

figure 8.61

A picture of Mark's father's hands holding water.

figure 8.63

You can see how layer-intensive this image creation work can be.

CREATIVE AND VIGNETTE EDGES

The edges of an image are critical visual elements that define the image and ground the composition. In painting, the edge of a composition is defined by the right angles and parallel lines of the frame, which often is a decorative piece of gold-leafed craftsmanship. In other painterly media, such as etching and printmaking, the edges are often defined by the artist's hand; each is unique and as precise or rough as the artist desires. In these instances, the edges are as integral to the final image as any element in the composition.

Photography is a photochemical medium in which the edges of an image are created by the four blades of the easel that holds the paper in place during exposure. Many photographers, desiring to show the entire negative, have been known to file out the negative carriers so they can print a black border around the image. Using the easel, the photographers could create a precise black line around an image. Or, by pulling the easel blades out further along the same black line, they could give the edge a dappled, abstract appearance. Still other photographers who use hand-painted emulsions of platinum and palladium let the brush strokes themselves define the image.

Of all the image-making processes, digital image creation is the most precise. The computer lets us change a single pixel or make radical global changes to the entire image. But the power and precision of the computer can give many images a machine-made feel. Simply put, the perfection of the image-making process eliminates any sense of the human craft; those interesting imperfections and unique qualities that come with handwork. Using creative edges can be an effective way to give computer-generated images a handmade appearance.

Vignetting a Portrait

Using softness or texture to frame an image can often be the finishing touch when you're working with antique images, as shown in **figures 8.64** and **8.65**.

© Eismann family archive

figure 8.64

figure 8.65

 ch8_vignette.jpg

1. Select the center part of the image with the Marquee tool.

2. Press Q to enter Quick Mask mode so you can see the selection, and then add a very large Gaussian Blur (see **figure 8.66**).

figure 8.66

Running the Gaussian Blur filter on the Quick Mask gives you a preview of the softening effect.

3. To avoid banding in the soft transitions, apply Filter > Noise > Add Noise and add a small amount of noise (see **figure 8.67**).

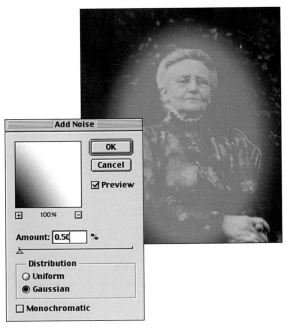

figure 8.67

Adding a hint of noise can offset banding problems.

4. Press Q again to return to Standard mode, and then activate the selection. Choose Select > Inverse.

5. Fill the selection with white and crop as needed.

T i p

If you want added flexibility, build your vignette on a separate layer. This will allow you to reposition it, move it to other documents, or throw it away if you decide you don't like it.

Adding Creative Edges

Working with Quick Mask to break up edges is a quick and easy way to add texture to the edge of any image (see **figures 8.68** and **8.69**). Best of all, everything you need to use this technique is already in Photoshop.

figure 8.68

BEFORE

© Katrin Eismann

figure 8.69

AFTER

ch8_frame.jpg

1. Select the area of the image that you do not want to be affected.

2. Press Q to enter Quick Mask mode.

3. Press (Cmd + I)[Ctrl + I] to invert the mask. Apply a Gaussian Blur of 5 to the mask to soften the edge, as shown in **figure 8.70**. Higher-resolution files might need a larger blur.

figure 8.70

Adding the Gaussian Blur to the initial mask will give the next filter in the process more shades of gray to work with.

4. Experiment with the built-in filters in Photoshop to change the edges of the softened Quick Mask. Good filters to try out include the following:

   • Filter > Brush Strokes > Spatter

   • Filter > Distort > Glass

   • Filter > Sketch > Torn Edges

   • Filter > Texture > Craquelure

5. Run more than one filter on the Quick Mask to create unique edges.

Caution

When you're experimenting with filters, keep an eye on the center part of the Quick Mask. Some filters are so aggressive that they may also affect the area of the image you're trying to frame.

6. When you have the effect you want, press Q again. The Quick Mask becomes an active selection.

7. Add a new layer and fill the active selection with your color of choice.

SHARPENING FILTERS

I wish I had a megabyte of RAM for every time I was asked if Photoshop can focus or sharpen an image that's soft, blurry, or out of focus. Photoshop can't transform poor images into sharp, crisp images that would look as good as well-focused originals. We're working with pixels here, and too many Hollywood spy thrillers have made it look as if a computer can enhance any out-of-focus photograph into a recognizable image.

When to Sharpen

"To sharpen or not to sharpen, that is the question: Whether 'tis better to sharpen during scanning or before printing, or suffer the slings and arrows of outrageous sharpening artifacts…."

Believe me, many a raucous debate has been ignited over the best time to sharpen an image. Rather than joining in, I take my cues from Bruce Fraser and David Blatner, authors of *Real World Photoshop*, and Richard Benson, who is a MacArthur fellow, a brilliant printer, and chair of the Yale School of Art. They say you should sharpen either as the next-to-last step in the printing process, just before converting to CMYK, or the very last step, after converting to CMYK.

If you're outputting your images to inkjet, thermal dye transfer, film recorders, or other direct digital output that accepts RGB data, I recommend sharpening as the very last step. If you're working in or going out to CMYK, do all of your color correction, retouching, and resizing in RGB, convert the file to CMYK, apply sharpening, and then target the black-and-white points for your specific CMYK output.

For a retoucher who's going to RGB output, the sharpening workflow entails the following steps: color correction, retouch, save as, flatten, size image for output, duplicate background layer, sharpen, and save as a flattened version into your Finals folder. Additionally, sharpening on a duplicate layer will enable you to mask out areas that don't require sharpening, such as large surfaces of sky.

Although Photoshop comes with four sharpening filters, all in the Filter > Sharpen menu, you should only use the Unsharp Mask filter (also referred to as USM). In the following section, you'll learn about applying the Unsharp Mask filter, smart sharpening methods, faux sharpening with the Emboss filter, interactive sharpening with the High Pass filter, and working with the Custom filter to sharpen images.

The Unsharp Mask Filter

The worst part of the Unsharp Mask filter is its name. If you haven't worked in a traditional darkroom or prepress shop, you might not realize that something called "Unsharp" is actually excellent for sharpening. In the dark pre-digital days of not too many years ago, a separator would make a pin-registered contact negative of an original. To soften the mask, the repro artist would place a sheet of frosted mylar between the original and the masking film. This soft "unsharp" mask increased edge contrast, making the image look sharper. Similarly, the Unsharp Mask filter looks for edges and differences to accentuate, making the image look sharper. There are three controls you use with the Unsharp Mask filter:

- **Amount:** This is similar to the volume dial on a radio—the higher you crank the knob, the stronger the sharpening becomes. For offset printing, start with a high amount, from 120%–200%, and control the results with the radius and threshold controls. If you're outputting to CMYK offset, you should oversharpen the image by finding visually pleasing settings and then going a bit further. Direct

digital output devices, such as film or photographic paper writers, require a lower amount setting (in the range of 40–80%) and should not be oversharpened. Sharpening for the Web or screen display is the easiest because you can judge the results on your monitor.

- **Radius:** This controls how far out Photoshop looks and determines the width of the edge contrast increase. An accepted rule of thumb for offset printing is to divide the printer's output resolution by 200 and use that as your starting point for the radius setting. This is the most critical setting—pushing it too high will cause ugly dark or light halos to appear along the edges of the image.

- **Threshold:** This scale goes from 0–255. Use it to tell Photoshop to ignore image tones that are very similar. For example, a threshold setting of 5 will ignore all tones that are within 5 level values of each other. Using a setting between 3–6 will protect tonally similar areas from being sharpened. This is especially useful to avoid sharpening image shadows and skin pores, wrinkles, and blemishes (you *really* don't want to sharpen someone's pores), as well as the grain in images that were shot on higher-speed film.

To really understand what the Unsharp Mask filter does, download the sunflower image (shown in **figure 8.71**) from the Web site and apply various amounts of the USM filter to the entire image. Keep an eye on the differentiation between the sunflower seeds, the edges of the petals against the blue sky, and the grayscale on the bottom of the image. The grayscale is a clear indicator of how the USM filter accentuates edge differences. **Figure 8.72** shows the image with the right amount of sharpening, and **figure 8.73** is an example of sharpening gone too far.

ch8_sharpen.jpg

figure 8.71

The original image.

figure 8.72

Just the right amount of sharpening has been applied here.

figure 8.73

The artifacts around the edges indicate that the image is oversharpened.

Before making a lot of prints or sending a service bureau numerous digital files, ask them what they recommend for USM settings. If they don't have any recommendations, run a test by ganging strips of the same image on one page with various USM settings and have it output. The USM filter is a powerful tool that can make your images stand out, either positively (crisp) or negatively (ugly USM halos).

Unsharp Mask Tips

- Always sharpen at 100% view.
- In the USM dialog box, click and hold on the Preview box to see what the image looks like with and without the sharpening effect.
- Experiment with selective sharpening by masking out image areas that don't need to be sharp.
- Print your sharpening tests with the printer and paper that you'll use for the final document.
- Avoid resizing or retouching a sharpened file.
- When you send files to a service bureau, tell them whether you've already applied sharpening or you want them to do it. Too much sharpening can be just as bad as no sharpening.
- Use USM on individual channels. This is especially useful when one channel is noisy or when you're sharpening CMYK files.
- Try converting files to Lab Color and sharpening only the L channel.
- To apply a different blend mode or change the opacity of the USM filter after running it, select Edit > Fade Unsharp Mask and change the settings.

Smart Sharpening

Smart sharpening is a term that Photoshop insiders use for a process that allows you to sharpen image edges without sharpening noise, film grain, pores, or out-of-focus areas. This method may seem like too much trouble, but keep it in mind for those noisy and grainy images and files that are suffering from JPEG artifacts. (Although this technique requires ten steps, it can be scripted to run as an Action, which I have included in Chapter 8 of the book's supplemental Web site.)

⊕▷⤙ **smart_sharpen.atn**

1. Duplicate the Background layer.

2. Duplicate the channel with the highest image contrast. I duplicated the Blue channel, as shown in **figure 8.74**.

figure 8.74

Duplicate the channel with the highest image contrast.

3. Select Filter > Stylize > Find Edges.

4. Invert the channel (Cmd + I)[Ctrl + I].

5. Select Filter > Noise > Median and use a value of 2 to accentuate the edge lines (see **figure 8.75**).

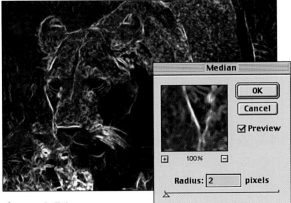

figure 8.75

Use the Median filter to thicken the lines.

6. Select Filter > Other > Maximum and use a value of 4 to spread the edge lines even more (see **figure 8.76**).

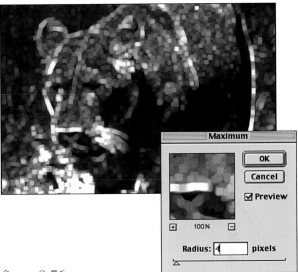

figure 8.76

The Maximum filter spreads the lines further.

7. Select Filter > Blur > Gaussian Blur and apply a value of 4.

8. Return to the composite view (Cmd + ~) [Ctrl + ~] in the Channels palette.

9. Load the channel mask (Cmd + Option + 4) [Ctrl + Alt + 4].

10. Apply the Unsharp Mask filter to sharpen just the edges of the subject while avoiding sharpening noise and grain, as shown in **figure 8.77**.

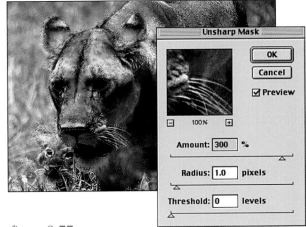

figure 8.77

Use the Unsharp Mask filter as the final step.

Sharpening with Finesse

Not all images will look their best if you sharpen the entire image or use the same sharpening on the image highlights and the shadow areas. For example, you may want to sharpen the main subject of a photograph without sharpening the sky, which would accentuate bothersome film grain. Use the following techniques to control where the sharpening takes place.

Method 1: To sharpen highlights and shadows separately, duplicate the Background layer twice. Use one layer to sharpen the highlights and the second to sharpen the shadow areas. Then use the Blend if layer options to blend the two layers, as shown in figure 8.78.

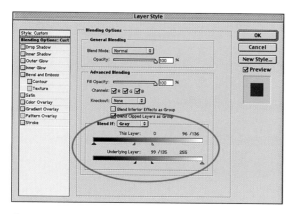

figure 8.78

Use the Advanced Blending feature to blend layers together, one that has been sharpened for the highlights and the other for the shadows.

Method 2: Take a History snapshot before using the Unsharp Mask filter. Run the filter, take a new snapshot, and then use the History brush to paint back and forth between the sharpened and unsharpened snapshots.

Method 3: Duplicate the layer to be sharpened. Run the Unsharp mask filter, add a layer mask to the sharpened layer, and then use a large, soft, black airbrush on the sharpened layer mask to hide the sharpening in areas you don't want to sharpen (such as the sky, large flat surfaces, and people's skin). The beauty of this method is that you can always modify the mask to hide or reveal the sharpening, as long as the layer and layer mask are in place.

High Pass Sharpening

When no matter how careful I am with the Unsharp Mask filter I'm still not happy with the results, I turn to the High Pass filter to enhance image edges. That filter turns all non-edge areas to neutral gray but leaves image edges intact. This, combined with Soft Light or Overlay Blending Modes, yields a sharpening effect that avoids ugly artifacts created when the standard sharpening filters are over-used.

Figure 8.79 shows a before image of a simple garlic and onion still-life taken with the Nikon CoolPIX 990. Figure 8.80 shows the sharpened file created with the High Pass Filter.

figure 8.79

figure 8.80

⊕▷≼ ch8_garlic.jpg

1. Duplicate the Background Layer

2. Select Filter > Other > High Pass and use the Radius slider to bring out the image edges. A very high Radius setting is less effective than a lower setting. Start with a setting between 2–5 and experiment with the Radius slider to increase or decrease the edge enhancement effect, as shown in **figure 8.81**.

3. Change the filtered layer's Blending Mode to Overlay or Soft Light to make the neutral gray disappear while maintaining the edge accentuation, as shown in **figure 8.82**. Using the Overlay Blending Mode adds a bit more contrast to the image than using Soft Light will.

4. If the image is too sharp, decrease the filtered layer's Opacity to achieve just the right amount of sharpening.

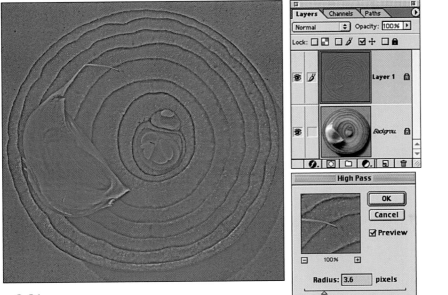

figure 8.81

Use the radius slider to bring out edge differences.

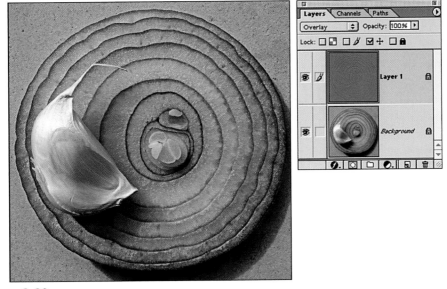

figure 8.82

Changing the Blending Mode and opacity offers tremendous control of the strength of the sharpening effect.

Emboss Sharpening

I learned this method from Greg Vander Houwen, a very talented digital artist and illustrator in Seattle. Greg has devised a method to bring soft-focus images like **figure 8.83** into focus; it creates faux edges that fool the eye into seeing a sharper image, as seen in **figure 8.84**. This technique works best for images that were shot with a soft-focus filter or are slightly out of focus.

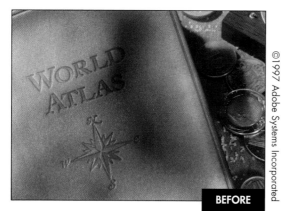

figure 8.83

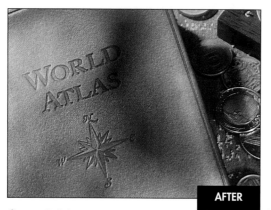

figure 8.84

1. Duplicate the Background layer.
2. Select Filter > Stylize > Emboss. Set the Angle to mimic the direction of light in the image, keep the Height between 2-4, and keep the Amount near 100% (see **figure 8.85**). Click OK.

figure 8.85

Use the Emboss filter on a duplicate layer.

3. Change the embossed layer's Blending Mode to Overlay. The edges are accentuated, as shown in **figure 8.86**. It's a Photoshop miracle!

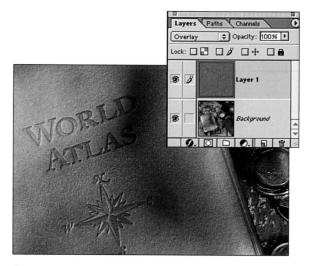

figure 8.86

Change the embossed layer's Blending Mode to Overlay.

Custom Sharpening

The Custom filter features a 5×5 matrix of edit boxes, into which you type numbers ranging from +999 to -999. It's hardly obvious what numbers you should type to achieve a desired result, or what will result from a given matrix of numbers. Chris Tarantino, who specializes in high-end catalog color correction and retouching, has spent many hours investigating the Custom filter to develop brightening, softening, and sharpening filters for high-end prepress file preparation. As Chris explains, "The advantage of the Custom filter is that I can sharpen without adding artifacts or halos, and if need be, I can brighten and sharpen in one fell swoop."

The Custom filter calculates pixels against one another in response to the typed-in values. In the following figures, I've shown you some of Chris's most useful Custom filter settings. Use these values as a starting point for your investigation of the Custom filter. **Figure 8.87** is the original scan that Chris started with. After masking out the individual image areas (sweater, scarf, purse, and background), Chris used his own Custom settings to bring out each image area, as shown in **figure 8.88**. **Figure 8.89** shows a Custom setting for strong brightening and sharpening. **Figure 8.90** shows a Custom setting for subtle sharpening.

🌐▷← **ChrisCustomKernels**

figure 8.87

figure 8.88

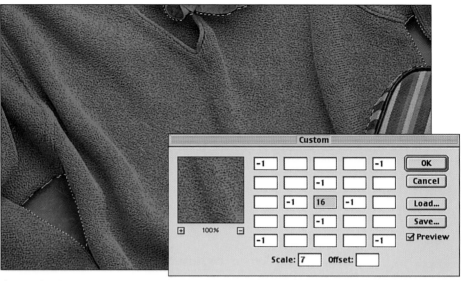

figure 8.89

A Custom filter setting that increases both brightness and sharpness.

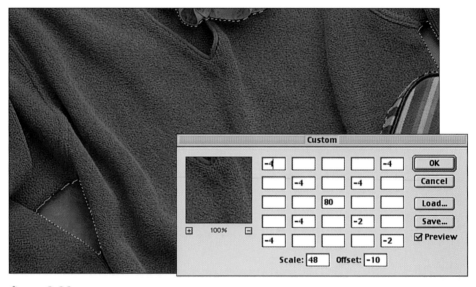

figure 8.90

A Custom filter setting for sharpening without brightening.

Once you've experimented with Chris's Kernels and found settings that work for your purposes, remember to click the Save button and save your settings into Photoshop's Filter folder. This way you can save, load, and share Custom filter settings. To make your Custom settings compatible across platforms, save them in the 8dot format—an eight-letter filename with the file extension .acf, such as bright.acf.

CLOSING THOUGHTS

All in all, digital tools and techniques give you tremendous control and creative possibilities. The most important thing to do is to duplicate your Background layer, and then go to town with these techniques to interpret your images to your creative heart's content.

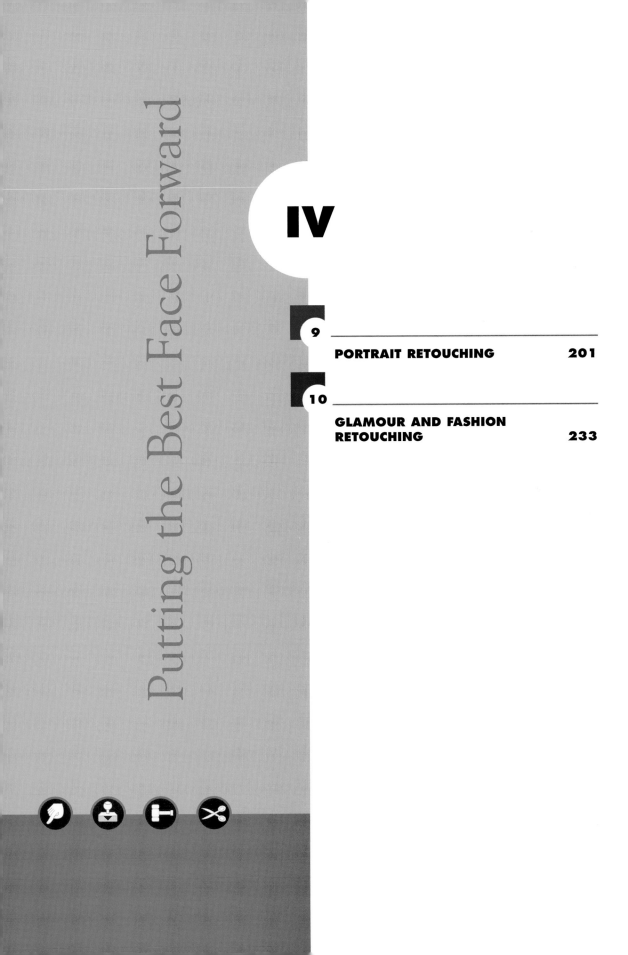

IV

Putting the Best Face Forward

9

PORTRAIT RETOUCHING

The first step of successful portrait retouching is to identify the character of the person and which facial features you can accentuate or minimize to help that person shine through the picture. Imagine you had to retouch three portraits: a fashionable teenager, a professional athlete, and a successful senior executive. Each of these people has different characteristics to recognize and enhance. The teenager's skin might need to be cleaned up, whereas the professional athlete's sweat and muscle tone could be accentuated for greater effect. In the senior executive's portrait you wouldn't want to take out every wrinkle or gray hair because lines in the face and gray hair are signs of wisdom and experience. Before you pick up the mouse, take a moment to look at the portrait and recognize what type of person you're working with.

As a retoucher, it's your job to bring out the best in each person. In this chapter we'll learn to work with contrast, color, and detail to make each person look their best. The areas we'll concentrate on in this chapter are

- Improving skin texture
- Accentuating the eyes
- Polishing a portrait with light

As a portrait retoucher your role is to accentuate the person's natural features while minimizing the blemishes that can detract from a pleasing portrait. Most importantly you want to maintain the individuality of the person. Not every person will have the Hollywood ingenue's flawless skin or a lion's head of hair. So study the character of the person in the picture and decide which attributes to accentuate and which to minimize before you begin to click your mouse.

N o t e

If by chance you jumped to this chapter first, please understand that the very first step to working with any digital image is to apply global exposure and color correction, as explained in earlier chapters. When those problems are solved, you can move on to correcting and enhancing selective areas as described in this chapter.

LEVELS OF RETOUCHING

Retouching a person's face can be a very sensitive undertaking. You don't want to take away important characteristics or accentuate less-than-flattering features. Additionally, you don't want to put time and effort into a portrait retouch that the client isn't willing to pay for. Before you begin any retouching it is imperative that you discuss with the client exactly what they want done to the portraits.

Clients may have a hard time envisioning the possibilities of retouching. To avoid any confusion or miscommunication, create a sample portfolio of your retouching services. As clients page through the portfolio, explain that you can remove blemishes and wrinkles for X number of dollars; if they would like additional retouching as seen in your more advanced examples, it will cost them X dollars. Not all clients will want the full treatment, and knowing this before you begin will save you time, effort, and money.

Rick Billings (www.photowave.com) has developed a three-level approach to retouching, shown in **figure 9.1** through **figure 9.4**:

- Level 1: Removes obvious blemishes, wrinkles and distractions with a process similar to applying a little make-up.
- Level 2: Continues where Level 1 stops and uses lights and darks to create volume and shape; this draws the viewer's eye into the subject's face.
- Level 3: Finely sculpts the face with contrast, color, and detail to accentuate the eyes, lips, and facial contours just as a classic painter would use light and shadow to define important details.

A three-level approach enables you to develop a plan as to the amount of retouching you will do, which in the end determines how much you will charge the client. A straightforward blemish removal or subtle wrinkle reduction can be accomplished in ten to fifteen minutes, whereas applying chiaroscuro lighting requires a master's time and touch—both of which will add much more to the final bill. Communicating with your client and knowing what your final outcome will be before lifting a mouse will help you to work economically and efficiently.

Looking Behind the Curtain Costs Extra

In the movie *The Wizard of Oz*, the great and wondrous wizard insisted that no one look behind the curtain, because that would reveal that he was really just a bunch of hot air and noisy machinery. Digital retouching is not smoke and mirrors, but it is magical, and I highly recommend that you keep the process magical for your clients.

Don't let the client watch while you're retouching. Letting clients see how quickly you can work and the magic you can create with Photoshop is a sure way to deflate your position and have them ask for more and more retouching for possibly less money. I've heard it over and over: "Oh, you make it look so easy! While you're at it, can't you just straighten out my nose or remove the dark circles under my eyes?" Well the answer is of course you can, but doing it quickly while they watch will cheapen your value and skills.

Clients seem to forget that you had to practice long into the night to develop your skills or that you may still be paying for your equipment. In addition, you can work much more efficiently without having a nervous client watching or distracting you. The only clients that I permit to watch me are the art directors hired and paid for by the client or agency to direct a project.

T i p

Retouching is more than a skill; it is an art form. Don't rush through any job, and try to avoid working when you're over-tired. You're working with a person's face and identity—something that requires your full concentration and empathy.

figure 9.1

Original Portrait

figure 9.2

Level 1 retouch with exposure improvement and blemish removal.

figure 9.3

Level 2 retouch with shaping face and smoothing of skin by modeling the lights and darks.

figure 9.4

Level 3 finish using painterly techniques to model the face and draw attention to the eyes.

WORKING WITH CONTRAST, COLOR, AND DETAIL

Our eyes are attracted to contrast, color, and detail. By accentuating these image attributes you can draw a viewer's eye toward the important parts of a portrait. Conversely, by reducing them you are creating areas that are less interesting to look at. What are the most important attributes of a portrait? Usually it's the person's eyes and then the mouth. By increasing the contrast, color, and detail in these areas you can draw the viewer's attention to the portrait's eyes and mouth. On the other hand, most people don't want you to look at or see every single pore, facial blemish, or wrinkle. By reducing the contrast, color, and detail of these less-appealing areas, you give the eye less to notice. While you are

retouching, keep contrast, color, and detail in the back of your mind. Work with them to emphasize the important areas of the portrait or to take away attention from the unimportant areas.

IMPROVING SKIN TEXTURE

Most people are self-conscious about their skin. Perhaps we suffered through the teenage years of acne, we're older and can already see the first crow's feet, or we didn't get enough sleep and look puffy and pale. It's a wonder we even get out of bed at all! Improving the appearance of skin in a portrait can be as simple as covering a few blemishes or as global as softening the entire portrait and then using the History Brush to paint back areas of selective focus.

Skin Blemishes... The Teenage Years

Why is it that blemishes seem to pop up when you're about to have your picture taken, need to go for a job interview, or about to have a first date? Photoshop can't help you with the job interview or the date, but removing blemishes in a photograph is a snap.

Cloning Good Over Bad

This method of removing blemishes such as those in **figure 9.5** is similar to removing dust or mold from an old photograph (and there were plenty of examples of those problems in Chapter 5, "Dust and Mold Removal"). By working on an empty layer you can work without the fear of cloning in problems rather than taking them out, as seen in **figure 9.6**.

BEFORE

figure 9.5

AFTER

figure 9.6

© Rick Billings, PhotoWave.com

⊕⊳≿ **ch09_blemish1.jpg**

1. Add an empty layer and name it Blemish Removal.

2. Set the Clone Stamp tool to Use All Layers and lower the opacity to 50%–75%, as shown in **figure 9.7**.

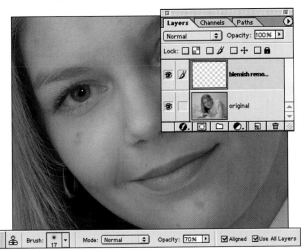

figure 9.7

Working on an empty layer to remove blemishes guarantees you the ability to back off, erase, or throw away the retouch and start over again if necessary.

3. Make the Blemish Removal layer active. Set your clone source by (Option + clicking)[Alt + clicking] near the blemish to sample good skin tones that have similar color, texture, and brightness values to the area you're concealing.

4. After moving the Clone Stamp tool over the blemish, click 2–3 times to build up the retouch, as seen in **figure 9.8**.

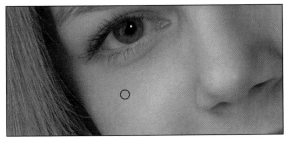

figure 9.8

The blemish removal is completely invisible, effective and yet hardly adds anything to the file size.

5. If you slip or if the blemish removal is too obvious, use the Eraser tool to erase areas and then resample and reclone with the Clone Stamp tool.

🔍 **Tip**

To minimize the ghostly softness that the soft-edged brushes can introduce, change the hardness of the brush to 40–70 (see **figure 9.9**). Higher resolution images can handle higher hardness settings. See "Building Your Own Brushes" later in this chapter for additional information.

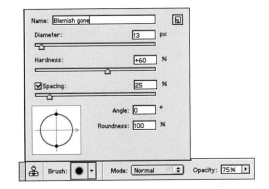

figure 9.9

When using the Clone Stamp tool, increasing the hardness of the brushes reduces the soft edges that can ruin film grain structure or skin texture.

🔍 **Tip**

When cloning over blemishes, do not move the clone source. Instead, sample a good area, move the Clone Stamp to the blemish and click the mouse button or tap the stylus two or three times to cover up the blemish. Clicking instead of brushing avoids disrupting the grain or skin structure.

Dust & Scratches Filter and History Brush Technique

The following method is especially useful in those situations where there are many small blemishes, such as those in **figure 9.10**. As you can see in **figure 9.11**, the blemishes have vanished. With this method, you'll need to run the Dust & Scratches filter twice—once for the large blemishes and once

for the smaller ones. Thanks to Dan Caylor from
www.thinkdan.com for this straightforward
technique.

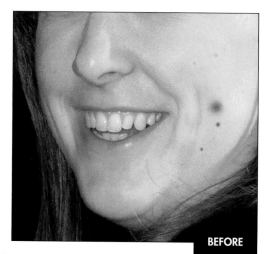

figure 9.10

figure 9.11

 ch09_blemish2.jpg

1. To remove the large blemish, select Filter >
   Noise > Dust & Scratches and use a high
   enough Radius and low enough Threshold to
   obliterate the large blemish (see **figure 9.12**).

2. (Option + click)[Alt + click] the Create New
   Snapshot icon and name the snapshot Big
   Blemish DS.

3. Select Edit > Undo to undo the Dust &
   Scratches filter.

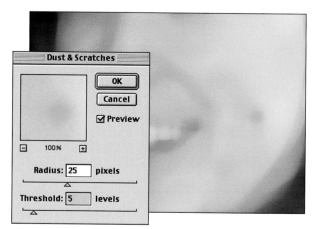

figure 9.12

*Using the Dust & Scratches filter to blur the large blemish
out of the picture.*

4. Repeat the procedure to take care of the
   small blemish. Select Filter > Noise > Dust &
   Scratches and use a lower Radius and
   Threshold to obliterate the smaller blemishes
   as seen in **figure 9.13**.

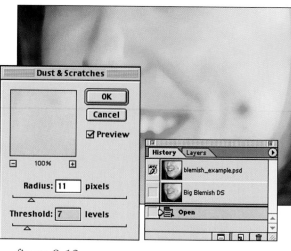

figure 9.13

*After undoing the first blur and taking a History Snapshot,
use the Dust & Scratches filter to blur the small blemish out
of the picture.*

5. (Option + click)[Alt + click] the Create New
   Snapshot icon and name the snapshot Little
   Blemish DS.

6. Select Edit > Undo to undo the Dust &
   Scratches filter.

7. Select the History Brush tool and set the History Source to the Small Blemish DS snapshot. Working with a soft brush, click over the small blemish.

8. Set the History Source to the Big Blemish DS snapshot and tap over the larger blemishes to achieve the results seen in **figure 9.14**.

Tip

Setting the brush to Lighten will replace only the lighter pixels and leave more of the original grain in the image undisturbed.

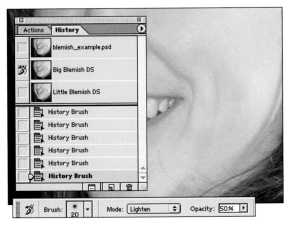

figure 9.14

Set the History source to the appropriate History Snapshot and tap over all blemishes to be removed.

9. In some cases (especially with larger blemishes), you might need to polish up the results with a bit of help from the Clone Stamp tool, but in the long run, this method is every teenager's fantasy.

Building Your Own Brushes

Often, using the soft brushes with the Clone Stamp or History Brush tools seems to add more problems around the edges of the newly cloned areas than are taken away. **Figure 9.15** shows a sample of noise and four strokes made with the Clone Stamp tool. Working from left to right, I made the same stroke but varied the Hardness and Spacing of the brush. The softness on the leftmost stroke causes soft, ghostly edges when using the Clone Stamp tool. On the far right is a brush with

75% Hardness and 10% Spacing—it has a slightly soft edge without any jitter problems. Increasing hardness and decreasing spacing creates a soft-edged brush without creating the dreaded ghostly-edges. Experiment to find a balance between the hardness setting and the spacing. Lower spacing yields a smoother stroke but can also slow down the painting stroke as Photoshop "sprays out" more information.

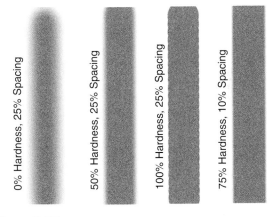

figure 9.15

From left to right: varying hardness and spacing to fine-tune the brush behavior.

Photoshop 6.0 includes the Preset Manager (shown in **figure 9.16**) to manage, rename, and access brushes according to names, thumbnails, or large lists, as seen in **figure 9.17**.

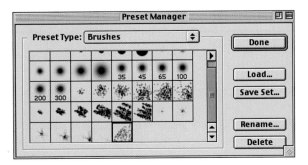

figure 9.16

Find the Preset Manager under the Edit menu. Use it to organize brushes, color swatches, styles, and patterns.

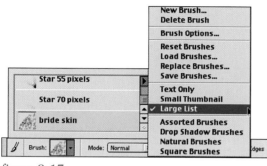

figure 9.17

You can view and access the brushes in lists or as thumbnails.

To create your own brush for retouching, follow these steps:

1. Use the Elliptical Marquee to select an area with image, skin, or film grain texture, as seen in **figure 9.18**.

figure 9.18

Selecting the image texture.

2. Copy and paste the selection into a new document, flatten, and convert to Grayscale mode.

3. Use Levels to crank up the contrast, as seen in **figure 9.19**.

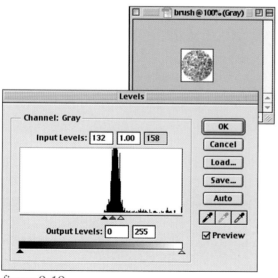

figure 9.19

Increasing contrast to bring out texture.

4. Select all. Choose Edit > Define Brush. The Naming Brush dialog box pops up, in which you can custom name your brushes.

Tip

To modify an existing brush, activate the brush and (Control + click)[right click] to select Edit Brush. You can also click on any brush in the Brush options bar to edit diameter, hardness, spacing, and tilt. A lower spacing applies the paint more steadily but can slow the brush down, whereas higher-spaced brushes have a tendency to add a stutter effect.

Reducing the Marks of Time

As people get older, gravity, sun exposure, and changes in skin structure cause wrinkles. Every wrinkle is not created equal, and rather than removing all of them I suggest you remove only the most distracting ones. Horizontal lines, such as the lines on our foreheads when we raise our eyebrows in surprise, are friendly and require the least amount of work. Vertical lines are caused by age and worry; if they are dark or deep they should be removed. Diagonal lines make a person look tense and anxious, and these are the wrinkles you should reduce the most.

In a photograph, a wrinkle is not a wrinkle; it's actually a dark area against a lighter area. By lightening the wrinkle you are reducing the contrast of that part of the face and are therefore reducing the visual interest that the viewer will have. Their eyes will seek out areas in the portrait that have more contrast, detail, and visual interest.

As people age, their wrinkles become longer and deeper. By shortening the length of the wrinkle you can "take off" a few years without making the person look as if they had plastic surgery. To reduce the length of the wrinkle, start at the youngest and narrowest end, not its origin (see **figure 9.20**), and use the techniques described in the following text to turn back the clock.

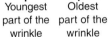

Youngest   Oldest
part of the   part of the
wrinkle   wrinkle

figure 9.20

For effective wrinkle reduction, retouch wrinkles from the youngest part in toward the older part of the wrinkle.

In the portrait of a retiring judge, Joel Becker of Becker-Cline Digital Photography used a Kodak DCS 460c digital camera to take the original picture. **Figure 9.21** shows a cropped view of the original portrait and **figure 9.22** shows the retouched version. Notice that after retouching and reducing the wrinkles the judge still looks experienced and wise, without looking plastic or fake.

I have devised three methods to remove or reduce wrinkles—using a duplicate layer, a neutral overlay layer, or a layer with its Blending Mode set to Lighten—and I usually end up using a combination of these three techniques to melt the years away.

🌐▷✕ **ch09_judge.jpg**

Working on a Duplicate Layer

1. Duplicate the Background layer (or the layer with the person's face).

2. Set the Dodge tool to 5%–15% Exposure and the range to Midtones.

3. Set the brush size to match the width of wrinkle to be removed.

BEFORE

figure 9.21

AFTER

figure 9.22

4. Zoom in on the wrinkle, and, starting at its youngest end, dodge inward toward the origin of the wrinkle. Reduce the newest, narrowest part of the wrinkle first because this is the part that appeared most recently. As you can see in **figure 9.23**, the judge is looking less imposing.

figure 9.23

Using the Dodge tool on the youngest part of the wrinkle makes it appear shallower and softer.

Working on an Overlay Neutral Layer

Working with an Overlay neutral layer has three advantages. If you over-lighten an area, you can paint over problem areas with 50% gray and then rework the area again with the 3%–5% white Brush. Adding a neutral layer does not double the file size as does duplicating the background layer in the first method. Finally, the Overlay neutral layer enables you to lighten up darker areas, such as the shadow areas of the judge's eyelids.

1. (Option + click)[Alt + click] the New Layer icon on the Layers palette.

2. Select Overlay from the Mode menu and click Fill with Overlay-neutral color (50% gray) as seen in **figure 9.24**.

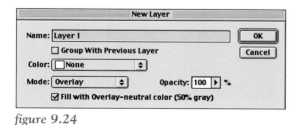

figure 9.24

Setting up the Overlay neutral layer.

3. Set the Foreground color to white, the Paintbrush tool to 3%–5% Opacity, and the brush size to match the width of the wrinkle to be reduced.

4. To lighten the dark areas of the wrinkles, paint with white on the Overlay neutral layer with the Paintbrush tool set to a low opacity (see **Figure 9.25**). Start the wrinkle-removal process at the end of the wrinkle to lessen the youngest part of the wrinkle first. **Figure 9.26** shows only the Overlay neutral layer.

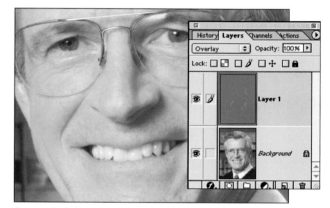

figure 9.25

Use the Paintbrush tool with white paint and a soft brush on the Overlay neutral layer to reduce the darkness and contrast of the wrinkles.

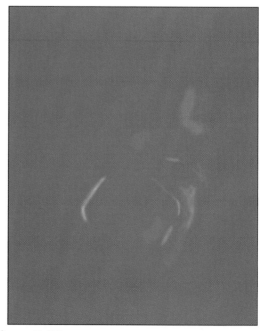

figure 9.26

The white brushstrokes on the Overlay neutral layer.

Working on an Empty Lighten Layer

A third option to remove wrinkles is to work on an empty layer that has been set to Lighten blending mode. I especially like this method because I can control the wrinkle removal by lowering the opacity of the Clone Stamp tool or the layer's opacity.

1. (Option + click)[Alt + click] the New Layer icon on the Layers palette and under mode select Lighten.

2. Set the Clone Stamp tool to Use All Layers and between 15%–35% opacity. Use a lower setting for smaller or younger wrinkles and higher settings for deeper, darker wrinkles.

3. With the Lighten layer active, sample lighter skin areas next to the wrinkle and paint over the wrinkle, as shown in **figure 9.27**. Once again, work from the end of the wrinkle inward.

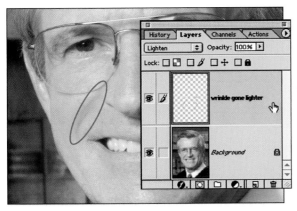

figure 9.27

Using the Clone Stamp tool on the Lighten layer is another effective method of reducing wrinkles.

In extreme instances a wrinkle can be so deep or its lighter edge so apparent that you need to darken the highlight. Use the Lighten method with a Darken layer and continue as before to darken the lighter edges of the wrinkle.

 N o t e

Removing blemishes and wrinkles requires a careful hand, and it is better to apply a little bit of good retouching than to overpower the portrait with a lot of bad retouching.

Improving Overall Texture and Tone

For years portrait photographers have used soft-focus filters to soften a person's skin. In the television and film industry, special cameras are used to make the actors or newscasters look younger by reducing the contrast and thereby reducing their wrinkles. In Photoshop you can add softness to portraits or product shots and, best of all, you can control exactly where the softness takes place with Layers, layer masks, or the History Brush tool.

Working with Gaussian Blur and Layer Masks

The black-and-white portrait in **figure 9.28** was taken very late in the evening, and as you can see the woman is attractive, yet tired and without make-up. Her skin texture needs softening and the areas under her eyes need to be lightened to achieve the fresh look seen in **figure 9.29**. (As a final touch, I'll retouch her eyes in the next section, "Accentuating the Eyes".)

ch09_BWportrait.jpg

1. Duplicate the Background layer.

2. Use the Gaussian Blur with the radius set between 1.5 and 3.0 to soften the duplicated layer as shown in **figure 9.30**.

3. Add a layer mask to the blurred layer and paint with black using the Airbrush tool set to 50% Opacity on the mask in the areas you want to bring back the sharp image areas. To reveal more of the sharpened image underneath, you'll need to paint more than once over an area. Most likely this will include the eyes and mouth, and in this case I also brought back some hair and eyebrows as they are on the same focal plane as the eyes and mouth (see **figure 9.31**).

figure 9.28

BEFORE

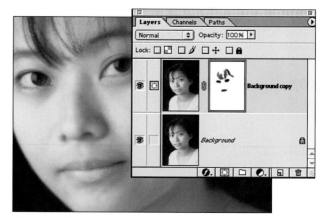

figure 9.30

After duplicating the Background layer, use the Gaussian Blur filter to soften the portrait.

figure 9.29

AFTER

figure 9.31

Add a layer mask and paint on it with a black Airbrush over the eyes, eyebrows, and mouth to hide the blurring on those areas.

4. To lighten the dark areas under her eyes and to fill the shadow next to the nose, first add a new layer and change its Blending Mode to Overlay.

5. To lighten image areas without being obvious, use a very low opacity setting of 1%–4%. In this instance, paint over the darker areas with white using the Paintbrush tool set to 3% pressure as seen in **figure 9.32**. Work smoothly, as if you were brushing make-up concealer onto a real person's face.

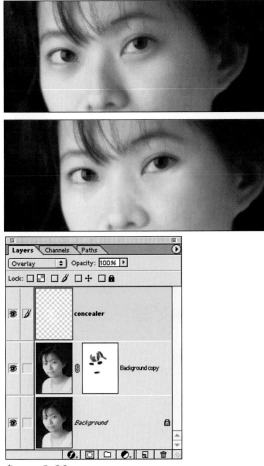

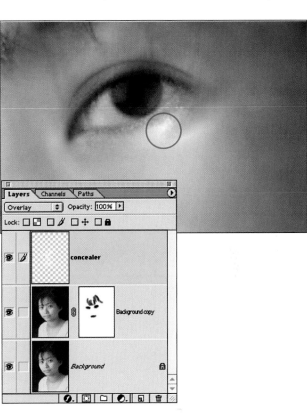

figure 9.33

Use the Eraser tool to erase the overspray in areas that are over-lightened.

figure 9.32

The bottom image shows areas improved by painting with a soft white brush on the Overlay layer to hide the dark circles under her eyes.

6. If parts of the image get too light or are affected by over-spray (see **figure 9.33**), use the Eraser tool to erase away over spray and reapply the concealer with the Airbrush.

Caution

When using this Overlay layer method on a color portrait, do NOT use white to lighten dark areas. It's very important to sample the person's skin and paint with that color on the Overlay layer.

Tip

If you don't use make-up or are unsure how to apply digital concealer as explained in this example, go to a department store make-up counter with a friend, girlfriend, or wife and watch how a professional applies make-up. Notice which facial areas are lightened or darkened, how colors are used, and which brushes the make-up artist uses. Then take your newly made-up model out for a nice dinner to say thank you.

Using the History Brush and Blending Modes

I learned this method from Eddie Tapp (www.eddietapp.com). It combines the Gaussian Blur filter, History Brush tool, and Blending Modes to enhance a portrait. His technique will take you from the original shown in **figure 9.34** to the enhanced version in **figure 9.35**. This method requires that you do the first three steps in the exact order described in the following text.

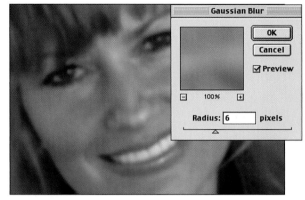

figure 9.36

Use the Gaussian Blur filter to soften the entire portrait.

2. Take a History Snapshot by clicking the Create New Snapshot icon. Naming the History Snapshots is very helpful when using the History Snapshots later in the process.

3. Undo the Gaussian Blur by selecting Edit > Undo Gaussian Blur.

4. Select the History Brush tool and set the Blending Mode to Darken at a very low opacity, usually 10%–15%. Set the History Source to the Gaussian Blur Snapshot.

5. Use the History Brush tool to apply a foundation only to the face and neck areas. Make sure to avoid areas such as the hair, lips, teeth, and eyes because you'll want to retouch them separately. Multiple brush strokes will allow you to build up this foundation, but don't expect to see too much change yet, as seen in **figure 9.37**.

BEFORE

figure 9.34

©Eddie Tapp, Model: Lisa Jane Murphey

AFTER

figure 9.35

🌐 📂 **09_colorportrait.jpg**

1. Run the Gaussian Blur filter over the entire portrait with a high enough setting to smooth the skin and tones, as seen in **figure 9.36**.

figure 9.37

Use the History Brush set to Darken at 15% Opacity as a soft foundation for the portrait.

6. When you've completed the foundation, change the History Brush's Blending Mode to Lighten and a very low Opacity. As in Step 5, apply a foundation only to the face and neck areas. Now you'll start to see some remarkable changes building up, as seen in **figure 9.38**. Eddie warns, "Avoid the temptation to use higher opacity brushes to speed up the effect. I recommend repeating this entire process several times to build up the make-up effect."

figure **9.38**

Use the History Brush set to Lighten Blending Mode at 15% Opacity to further refine the skin.

7. After the skin tone is enhanced, Eddie uses the Clone Stamp tool with the Lighten Blending Mode at 10%–15% to reduce deeper wrinkles or blemishes.

8. You might want to soften the entire portrait slightly to match the hair and clothing with the retouched skin. Select the subject's eyes and mouth with a feathered lasso, as seen in figure 9.39.

9. Inverse the selection, to select everything except the eyes and mouth.

10. Make sure that the Gaussian Blur snapshot is still selected in the History palette.

11. Choose Edit > Fill and select History in the Contents menu. Change the Blending Mode to Lighten and start with 55%–65% opacity as shown in **figure 9.40**.

figure **9.39**

Selecting the model's eyes and mouth.

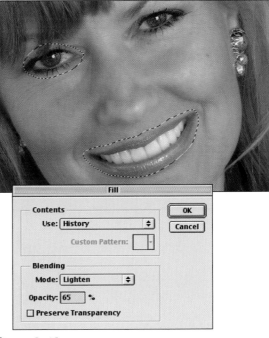

figure **9.40**

After inversing the selection, use a History Fill with Lighten to quickly add a hint of softness to the rest of the portrait.

12. Repeat the History Fill, but this time change the Blending Mode to Darken and start with half the opacity as used for the Lighten step

13. Adding a touch of overall softness to the portrait balances out the face with the image background.

The best part about using the History Brush and History fill method is that you can selectively paint back sharp or soft information as needed. Set the History source to the original for sharp or to the blurred snapshot to access the softer version. Use a 35% History Brush set to Soft Light to bring back some sharpness if needed.

Caution

When working with the History palette, you must finish the retouch process before closing the file. The History States and Snapshots are forever purged if you close the file or quit Photoshop or if the computer crashes. You can salvage some of this work by saving your file with a new name at various stages of the retouching process.

ACCENTUATING THE EYES

We look into a person's eyes to see their soul, to see if they are speaking the truth, and to make one-on-one contact. The eyes are the most important aspect of most portraits and require special care. Accentuating a person's eyes can make the portrait more intriguing, and by increasing contrast, color, and detail in a person's eyes you also draw the viewer's eye away from less interesting aspects of the portrait. I use a variety of methods to retouch a person's eyes. In the following examples, we'll work with layers and the Dodge and Burn and painting tools to bring out the very best in a person's eyes.

Eyeball Fundamentals

Our eyes are spheres and you should avoid overworking them with over-zealous cloning or lightening of the whites or darkening of the iris. Being heavy-handed in the eyes will flatten them out and make them appear lifeless. Before you retouch a person's eyes, take a moment to study the light origin so that you can work with the light and not against it. **Figure 9.41** shows that the lightest part of the eye whites are in the lower half of the eyeball and that the lightest part of the iris is always opposite the primary light source. To keep the eyes lively and interesting, it is essential to maintain moisture and highlights and to keep the red tones in the corners by the tear ducts.

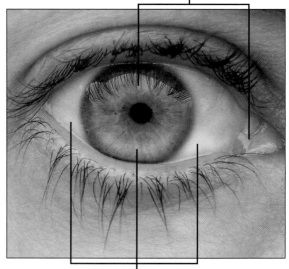

Make sure to keep moisture and highlights in the eye.

The lightest areas of eye whites and iris are opposite the main light.

figure 9.41

Our eyes are round and translucent and light plays off and through them.

Accentuating Contrast with the Dodge and Burn Tools

The skin tone of the black and white portrait we worked with earlier has been improved significantly (see **figure 9.42**). The next step is to accentuate this subject's beautiful eyes by lightening the eye whites and carefully darkening the eyelids—just as if we were applying eyeliner or mascara to her eyes (see **figure 9.43**).

Whenever you lighten or darken an aspect of a person's features, you can strengthen the effect by using the opposite tone in the adjacent area. For example, if you lighten the eye whites, you should also darken the iris (as described in the example after this one) or accentuate the eyelashes with a bit of digital mascara to contrast the lighter eye areas.

 ch09_BWeyes.jpg

1. Activate the layer that has eye information for you to accentuate. In this example, I had to select the original Background layer. Generously select the eyes with the Marquee tool as seen in **figure 9.44**.

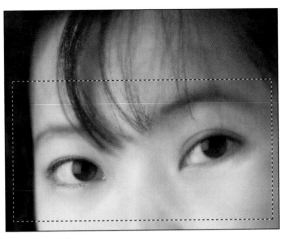

figure 9.44

Select the eyes with the Marquee tool.

2. Select Layer > New > Layer via Copy to place the eyes onto their own layer.

3. Select the Dodge tool and set the exposure to 5% and Range to Highlights.

4. Zoom in on the eyes and carefully lighten the eye whites. As you can see in **figure 9.45**, the left eye is already brighter and more interesting to look at than the right eye that hasn't been retouched yet. Don't over lighten or take out every bit of tonality to avoid the frozen in the headlights look, as seen in **figure 9.46**.

figure 9.42

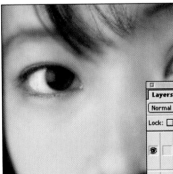

figure 9.45

Working on the eye layer, use the Dodge tool to carefully lighten the eye whites. In this example the eye on the left has been enhanced and the eye on the right is still in its original state.

figure 9.43

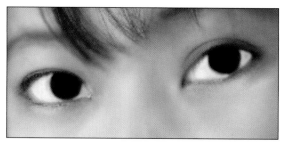

figure 9.46

Being heavy-handed with either lightening or darkening will make the eyes look lifeless and dull.

5. Use the Dodge tool on the other eye to balance out the eye whitening effect.

![hand icon] C a u t i o n

When using the Dodge and Burn tools, use a very low exposure (5%–10%) and build up the effect slowly. The default setting of 50% is like trying to retouch with a sledgehammer.

6. Working on the same eye layer, select the Burn tool and set it to Shadows and 10%.

7. Use a brush that is the same size as the edge of the eyes you are going to apply eyeliner to and carefully trace the edges of the eye, as seen on the left eye in **figure 9.47**.

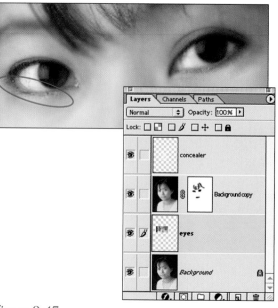

figure 9.47

Use the Burn tool to gently outline the eyes.

8. Carefully apply similar darkening to the other eye.

9. If the retouch is too strong, you can erase overdone areas and reapply the digital eye-whitening or eyeliner, or better yet, reduce the opacity of the eye layer to create the desired effect.

Careful clean-up

The Dodge and Burn tools as previously described can also be used on color portraits. If the eyes need more aggressive clean up, use a combination of the painting and Clone Stamp tools as described here. In the color portrait by Eddie Tapp, the woman's eyes are blood-shot and her contacts are too apparent, as seen in **figure 9.48**. With careful cloning and a bit of painting you can clean up a person's eye whites and enrich the natural color without making the eyes look artificial, as seen in **figure 9.49**.

figure 9.48

figure 9.49

1. Select the eyes with the Marquee tool and select Layer > New > Layer via Copy to place the eyes on their own layer.

2. Zoom in on the eye so that you can see every detail. I usually work at 200%–400% view when retouching eyes.

3. Retouching a person's eyes impacts the entire portrait. To see the progress and impact of the eye retouch on the entire face, use a second view as seen in **figure 9.50** to monitor your progress. Select View > New View to create another view of the same file that you can watch as you retouch.

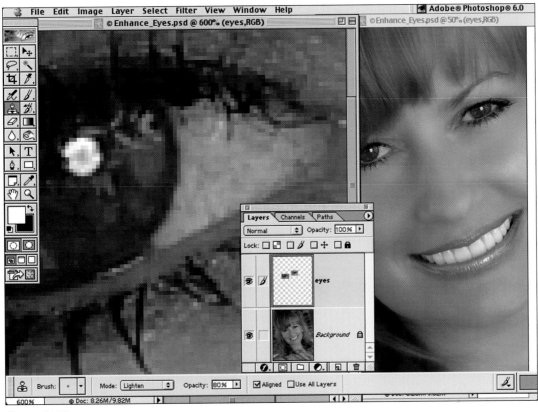

figure 9.50

Use a second view to see how working on the eyes is impacting the portrait.

4. Set the Clone Stamp tool to Lighten and 80% Opacity and carefully clone over the blood lines in the eye. Don't try to make the eye whites perfect—eyes have shape, contour, and some texture. Making eye whites too perfect will make the person look like a B-movie alien.

5. To accentuate the color of the iris, use the Sponge tool set to Saturate with a 10% Pressure and carefully brush over the iris. This will intensify the color, as seen in **figure 9.51**.

Tip

Keep highlights and single catchlights in the eyes—they make the person look lively and upbeat. Eyes without the highlights caused by natural moisture and reflections are flat and unappealing.

figure 9.51

Saturating the iris with the Sponge tool adds a hint of depth and interest to the eye.

Painterly Accentuation

The final method I use to accentuate eyes takes a painterly approach that emphasizes the play of lights, shadows, and colors. The best aspect of this technique is that all of the enhancements are built up on separate layers, giving you tremendous control over the intensity of the retouch. As you can see in **figure 9.52**, the original eyes are attractive, while the enhanced ones in **figure 9.53** have a romantic painterly quality to them. With the following technique you will lighten the eye whites and rim and enhance the iris, fine-tune the catchlights, darken the eyelashes, and warm the eyes to draw the viewer's eye in.

figure 9.52   *figure 9.53*

 ch09_coloreyes.jpg

1. Zoom in to 200% on the eye to be retouched, create and position a new view, and make sure the Layers palette is visible, as shown in figure 9.54.

2. Add a new layer.

3. Set the Airbrush tool to work at 10% Pressure and make sure that the foreground color is set to white. The brush should be almost as large as the individual eye whites.

4. Puff in a hint of white on to the eye whites to the left and right of the iris (see **figure 9.55**). Don't worry about staying "inside the lines" because you can use the Eraser tool to clean up any overspray.

figure 9.54

Take a moment to set up the new view and arrange your working area.

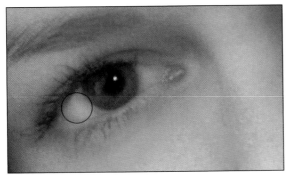

figure 9.55

By adding a hint of white to either side of the iris, her eyes become lighter and clearer.

5. Add another new layer and use the Airbrush tool with black paint and a small brush to carefully trace the rim of the iris, as seen in **figure 9.56**.

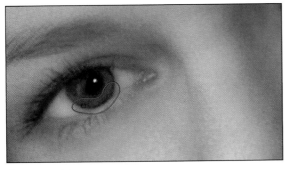

figure 9.56

On a designated layer, trace the rim of the iris with the Airbrush tool set to 10% Pressure.

Tip

Naming the layers will help you to identify a layer that might need further refinement. It only takes a split second to name the layer but it saves you minutes of frustration as you hide and reveal layers to track down the layer with the problems.

6. Add a new layer. Use the Clone Stamp tool set to Use All Layers to remove any bother-some catchlights. In this example, the small catchlight in the woman's pupil is distracting.

7. On the same layer, paint in a soft light that mimics the larger catchlight in the upper-left side of the iris (**figure 9.57**)

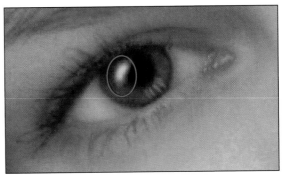

figure 9.57

Simplify the eyes by removing any harsh and distracting catchlights.

Note

Eyes are translucent spheres and light travels through them. Adding a touch of white on the opposite side of the primary light source accentuates the roundness and liveliness of the eye.

8. As shown in **figure 9.58**, use a very small white Brush set to 20% Opacity to add a hint of the highlight on the iris opposite the catchlight. I often soften these lines with a touch of the Smudge or Blur tools.

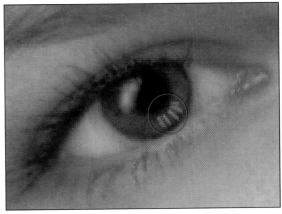

figure 9.58

Opposite the main catchlight, draw in hints of light and use the Blur or Smudge tools to soften them.

9. To accentuate the natural color of the eyes, sample the color of the iris, open the Color palette and switch the palette to HSB mode. Boost the Saturation by 30%–50% and the Brightness by 15%–25%. HSB is a very useful color mode to work in to strengthen colors without shifting them.

10. Add a new layer and paint over the iris with the Airbrush tool set to 10% Pressure with a large soft brush. Change the Blending Mode of the iris color layer to Color to make the color translucent and natural (see **figure 9.59**). Use the Eraser tool to clean up any color spill.

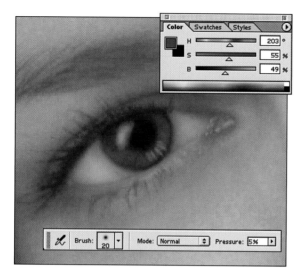

figure 9.59

Brighten the eyes by painting with a more saturated and brighter version of the original color.

11. Not all portraits will need to have the eyelashes accentuated, but in many cases framing the eye with darker eyelashes adds a heightened contrast in relationship to the eye whites.

12. Add a new layer and name it eyelashes. Use a 10% opacity, soft, black Airbrush to swoop around the entire eye.

13. Use a smaller Eraser to erase any spill in the eyes and to separate the lashes. Lower the opacity of the eyelash layer to your liking for results like those shown in **figure 9.60**.

Note

For more realistic eyes, warm the tear ducts with a touch of red. As Jane Connor-ziser, a classically trained painter and retoucher who has been working digitally for over a decade, explains, "In some cases, retouching the eye can make the image too cool and unfriendly. You can offset this by dabbing just a touch of red into the tear duct area."

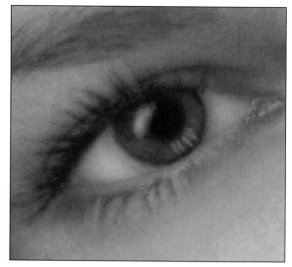

figure 9.60

Use the Airbrush and Eraser tools on new layer to make the eyelashes darker and thicker.

14. Add a new layer and name it tear ducts.

15. Choose a bright red from the swatch window. Jane likes the default warm red in the upper-left corner of the Swatches palette, as shown in **figure 9.62**.

16. Use the Brush tool to daub a hint of the red over the tear ducts and in the outside corners of the eyes. Clean up any overspill with the Eraser tool and reduce the opacity of the layer if need be, as shown in **figure 9.61**.

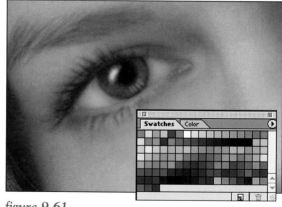

figure 9.61

Adding a touch of red to the small corners of the eye adds warmth to the eye and the portrait.

17. Finally, look away from the portrait for a few moments to clear up your visual memory and to refresh your eyes. Look at the portrait again and check your work with contrast, color, and detail in mind.

Tip

Get a second opinion. After working on a portrait, you become very familiar with it and might not even notice problems or areas that are overworked or don't look right. Ask someone to take a look at the portrait and tell you what he or she notices or thinks about the image.

Removing Reflections in Glasses

Removing reflections in glasses can be as straightforward as simply reducing them with a bit of burning and cloning as Joel Becker did in the portrait of the judge (see **figure 9.22**). Or it can be as intensive as using good information from one part of the face to hide the reflections. In the example in **figure 9.62**, the photographer's softbox is much too apparent in the man's eyeglasses. In **figure 9.63**, I covered the reflections by duplicating and cloning good forehead information over the bothersome reflections.

1. Start by studying the image—notice where the light is coming from and where there is information you can take advantage of to hide the reflections.

Tip

Portrait photographers take more than one exposure. Ask your client for these additional exposures—they might contain information you can use to rebuild the image.

2. To keep the cloning, pasting, and painting inside of the glasses, I made a selection for the inside of each lens. Because eyeglasses are so smooth, I prefer to use the Pen tool to outline the inside of each lens (see **figure 9.64**).

BEFORE

figure 9.62

AFTER

figure 9.63

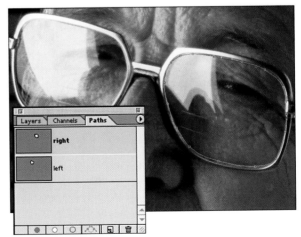

figure 9.64

Use the Pen tool to outline the individual lens.

3. I turned the path into a selection and used the Marquee tool to move the active selection to select good information, as shown in **figure 9.65**.

figure 9.65

Turn the path into a selection and use it to select good image information.

4. After copying this information, I activated the original lens selection by making the path into a selection, and selected Edit > Paste Into to paste the borrowed information into the lens. The overlapping information can look rather bizarre (see **Figure 9.66**).

figure 9.66

The Paste Into command keeps your copied information within the selected lens, but covers up the original image entirely.

5. Photoshop automatically creates a layer mask based on the active selection. Painting with black on the mask hides the extra eyebrow and the skin that is covering the man's eye, as shown in **figure 9.67**.

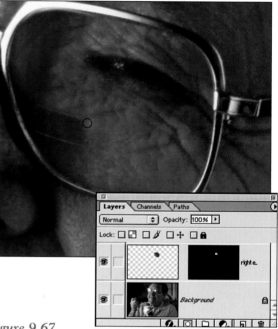

figure 9.67

Paint on the layer mask to hide and reveal the replacement information.

Tip

Lowering the just-pasted layer's Opacity to 50% is a great aid when painting on the mask to see where to hide or reveal image information because you can see through it to know where to paint. When you're done modifying the mask, pull the layer's Opacity back up to 100%.

6. I added a new layer and used the Clone Stamp tool set to Use All Layers to clone over any stray reflections.

7. I zoomed out and inspected the work in progress to double-check the contrast, color, and detail.

8. I added a hint of white to the eyes to make them more lively and interesting. I added a new layer and used the Airbrush tool set to 20% Pressure to dab a few highlights into the eye whites (see **figure 9.68**).

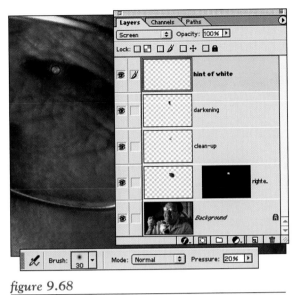

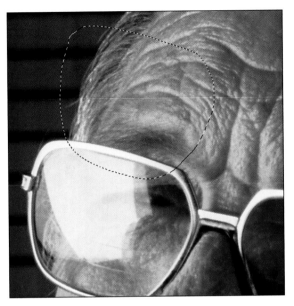

figure 9.68

Add a bit of white to lighten up the eyes.

9. In Photoshop 6, layer sets allow you to man-age your layers. To create a layer set, link all layers you would like in a set and then select New Set from Linked from the Layers palette menu, as shown in **figure 9.69**.

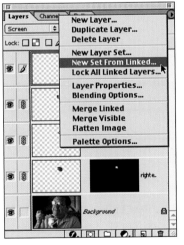

figure 9.69

Group layers that are used for a particular retouching task into one layer set to manage the layers palette.

10. Working on the man's left eye is similar to the process used for the right one. I borrowed good information from just above his eye and made sure to include some hair and background, as seen in **figure 9.70**, because those areas will be visible through the lens.

figure 9.70

Using good information for the left eye includes taking some hair and background.

11. As the Layers palette in **figure 9.71** shows, I masked, cloned, and used shading as previ-ously described to build up a believable eye.

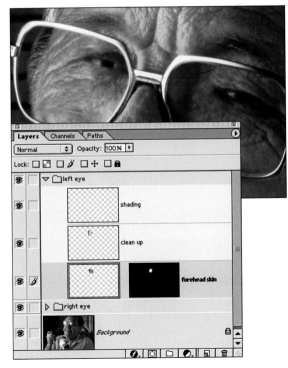

figure 9.71

The layer set for the left eye reflection reduction.

Note

Taking out reflections is similar to repairing damaged photographs as described in Chapter 6, "Damage Control and Repair." It involves begging, borrowing, and stealing information from other parts of the person's face, the image background, and in some cases, other images.

Removing Redeye... or Becoming a Digital Exorcist

Redeye occurs when the flash bounces off the back of the eyeball. Redeye makes people and pets look as if they are possessed by Linda Blair demons. Redeye has a higher chance of occurring if the flash is on the camera or very close to the lens. This is the case for most consumer point-and-shoot or low-end digital cameras. It is also more likely to be a problem if the subject is in a dark room and the pupils are wide open. Taking it out is one of the most common retouching jobs.

Avoiding Redeye

To prevent redeye, use any or all of following photographic techniques:

- Move the flash off the camera or use a secondary flash with a sync cable.
- Move the subject into a better-lit position—that way you might not need the flash at all, and the pupils will shrink, reducing the possibility of redeye.
- If your camera offers a redeye reduction mode, use it to have the flash prefire, which closes the pupils and then fires another flash to take the picture. Personally I'm not a huge fan of this preflash because, when used, people think that you've just taken the picture and have a tendency to look away.

As every Photoshop user knows, a number of different ways are often available to accomplish the same thing. The following text outlines three different techniques to remove redeye. Though the results are similar, I offer all three techniques so you can pick the one that works the best for you. Experiment with combining these techniques to save the world from red-eyed aliens.

Figure 9.72 shows Maija, daughter of Myke and Vivienne Ninness, looking like a true dragon child; a little Photoshopping, and the demonic redeye is removed in **figure 9.73**.

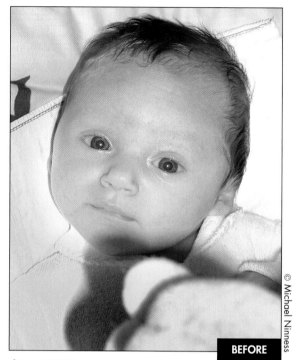

figure 9.72

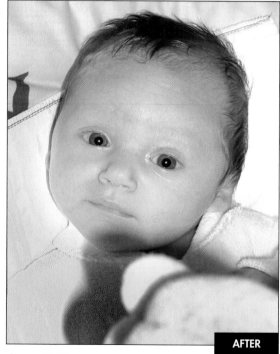

figure 9.73

Select and Desaturate

This method quickly removes the offending redeye. I'm often asked when to use each method and as you can imagine there are no hard and fast rules. Experiment with each one and I'm sure you'll develop techniques of your own that work well for each image scenario.

ch09_redeye.jpg

1. Zoom in on the eyes and press Q to enter Quick Mask mode.

2. Use the Airbrush tool with black paint and a brush that is a bit smaller than the pupil. Hold the Airbrush over the pupil. Because the Airbrush keeps pumping out paint you'll see that the black circle enlarges toward the edges of the pupil. Repeat on second pupil (see **figure 9.74**).

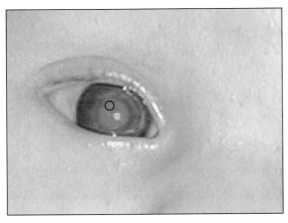

figure 9.74

Working in Quick Mask mode, use a black Airbrush to paint over the redeye.

3. Press Q to activate the selection and inverse (Select > Inverse) the selection.

4. Add a Hue/Saturation Adjustment Layer.

5. Move the Saturation slider all the way to the left, to draw out all of the color (see **Figure 9.75**). In many cases this will at least look better, but the pupils may now look washed out. By changing the Blending Mode of the Adjustment Layer to Multiply, Photoshop will darken the desaturated layer to a rich, dark tone.

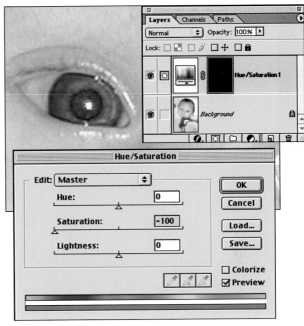

figure 9.75

Desaturate the redeye with a Hue/Saturation layer set to -100 saturation.

6. Adjust the opacity to taste, to the point that the pupils are enhanced without looking unnatural.

Painting on Individual Channels

Photoshop builds RGB color images by combining three black-and-white channels. Wherever a channel is light, more color shines through. In the case of redeye, the Red channel will be very light (in the pupils), which lets the red shine through. By painting with black directly on the Red channel in the pupil area, you can offset the lightness in the channel and block out the red.

1. Zoom in on the eyes. Open the Channels palette and make the Red channel active. Press ~ so you are working on the Red channel but viewing the composite.

2. Use the Brush tool with black paint set to 100% Opacity to paint directly over the pupil in the Red channel, as shown in **figure 7.76**.

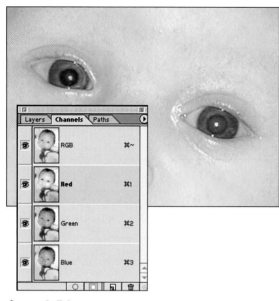

figure 9.76

With the Red channel active, turn on the view column to see the effect on the composite image.

3. If the pupil is discolored or looks greenish or bluish, make the Green channel active and paint the same pupil area. Repeat the painting on the Blue channel, as seen in **figure 9.77**.

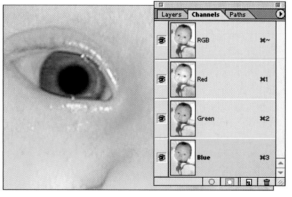

figure 9.77

Paint out the redeye on the Green and Blue channels.

4. One problem with this technique is that it also paints out the catchlight that makes the eyes lively. To offset this, add a new layer, and use a small white brush to dab in the catchlight (see **figure 9.78**).

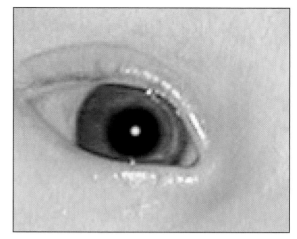

figure 9.78

Add in a new catchlight to maintain liveliness in the eye.

Select and Substitute

The following method takes a bit more work but I think it is the best because it maintains both pupil texture and catchlights.

1. Open the Channels palette and go to the channel with the best (the darkest) pupil. It will most likely be the Green channel—it will definitely not be the Red channel.

2. Use the Elliptical Marquee tool to select one of the pupils. Hold down the Shift key to select the second pupil, as seen in **figure 9.79**.

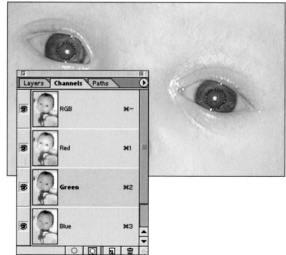

figure 9.79

Find the channel with the best information and select both pupils.

3. Choose Select > Feather and use a setting of 1 to slightly soften the edge of the selection.

🔍 T i p

Saving the selection (by clicking the Save Selection icon on the Channels palette) will save the selection to an alpha channel. You can then activate the selection at any time.

4. Copy the selected pupils. With the selection active, click the Red channel and choose Edit > Paste Into. This will paste the good green pupil into the bad red pupil.

5. Make the Blue channel active and repeat the Paste Into command as seen in **figure 9.80**.

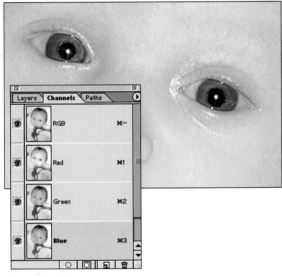

figure 9.80

Repeat the Paste Into the Blue channel.

POLISHING A PORTRAIT WITH LIGHT

Faces are defined by the contours of light and shadow. Retouchers can model a person's face with subtle placement of light to add sparkle and liveliness to a portrait. Jane Conner-ziser says, "By contouring the edges of the lighting, the skin is smoothed and polished. If an area looks flat, by identifying what light is missing or causing the problem you've identified what light needs to be refined."

As Jane explains, "The *Five Lights of Nature* are always in relationship to one another":

- Specular Highlights: Brightest points of light, found in the catchlights in the eyes, the forehead, cheekbones, nose, and chin. The sharpness of the edges of this light indicates how shiny the surface is.

- Diffuse Highlight: Mid-tone area of the face. This base tone area tells you the correct color and texture of the object. If you match it in the highlights and shaded sides, you will leave the subjects with their characteristic pore structure.

- Shaded side: Appears opposite of the specular highlights. They need to be handled gently so the person's face doesn't look dirty or muddy. Painting with the brush set to Color with a very transparent red will warm the complexion and make the subject appear healthy.

- Refracted Light: Kicked-in fill light used to open up shadows or reduce contrast. Rims the edges of the shades side and adds dimension.

- Shadows: Cast by objects and provides information as to where the objects are in relation to the surrounding areas. For instance, the nose casts a shadow on the face. The shape of the shadow follows the contour of the upper-lip area if that's how the lighting is set up. Photographers frequently use nose shadows to identify the type of lighting they are using, such as butterfly, short lighting, or loop lighting.

When I studied photography and studio lighting, I learned that light-skinned faces are defined by shadows and dark-skinned faces are defined by highlights. Either way, faces without highlights or shadows are flat and uninteresting. In **figure 9.81**, you see the original portrait of a young man, and **figure 9.82** shows the final retouched version in which the subtle addition of highlights invites your eye to look at his face.

figure 9.81

1. To add a hint of light to a portrait, start by adding an Overlay neutral layer. (Option + click)[Alt + click] the New Layer icon on the Layers palette. Set the Mode to Overlay and click Fill with Overlay-neutral color (50% gray).

2. Set the foreground color to white and use the Airbrush tool with a large soft brush set to 2% Pressure on this neutral layer to add highlights to the subject's face, as seen in **figure 9.83**.

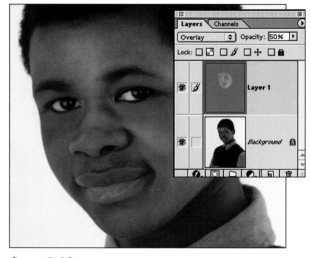

figure 9.83

Working with a very subtle white brush to lighten up the highlights of the face.

3. Adjust the Opacity of the Overlay layer to refine the effect.

The additional retouching on this portrait was achieved by using the Clone Stamp tool on empty layers and retouching the eyes with the Dodge and Burn tools as described earlier.

Painterly Light

Noses, cheekbones, chins, and foreheads are our prominent features, and they catch more light. Accentuating these protruding areas with light adds a painterly quality to a portrait. In **figure 9.84**, you see a portrait by Rick Billings that has been retouched to take out a few minor blemishes. **Figure 9.85** shows how Rick used painterly techniques as described previously to accentuate the contrast, color, and detail of the eyes and lips. Painting with white on the prominent spots on the woman's face on a new layer creates area of light that enhances the portrait.

figure 9.82

© Sally Buck

Lighting with an Overlay Neutral Layer

Sculpting a portrait with light and shadow can give depth and drama to a flat image. By working on Overlay neutral layer you can experiment freely, and if you overdo any lighting additions it's easy just to throw away the offending Overlay neutral layer and start over.

🌐🗶 **ch09_shaping.jpg**

ch09_lightpainting.jpg

figure 9.84

figure 9.85

© Rick Bilings, PhotoWave.com

Shaping the Hair with Light

After retouching a subject's face, take a few minutes to shape the hair by adding highlights and shadow to the natural form of the hair. **Figure 9.86** is yours truly at the end of a long conference day, and **figure 9.87** shows me with improved skin, eyes, and hair with sparkle and life to it.

Enhancing highlights and shadows adds dimension and liveliness to hair. This technique is called *wedging*, and you can use it to add tonal depth to hair or a person's clothing. It only takes a few seconds, but makes the final portrait look richer.

figure 9.86

figure 9.87

© Jim Schmelzer

⊕▷⟨ **ch09_hairshaping.jpg**

1. To accentuate highlights, add a Color Dodge neutral layer by (Option + clicking)[Alt + clicking] the New Layer icon on the Layers palette. Select the Color Dodge Mode and check Fill with Color-Dodge-neutral color (black).

2. Because you want to work very subtly and build up the contouring, use the Airbrush tool with a large soft brush with white paint set to 2%–5% Pressure to trace the contours of the natural hair highlights, as seen in **figure 9.88**.

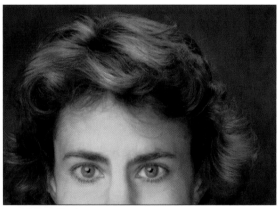

figure **9.88**

Working on a neutral Color Dodge layer painting with the Airbrush tool with a large soft brush emphasizes the highlights.

3. To accentuate shadows, add a Color Burn neutral layer by (Option + clicking)[Alt + clicking] the New Layer icon on the Layers palette. Select the Color Burn Mode and check Fill with Color-Burn-neutral color (white).

4. Use the Airbrush tool with a large soft brush with black paint set to 2%–5% Pressure to accentuate the contours of the shadows, as shown in **figure 9.89**.

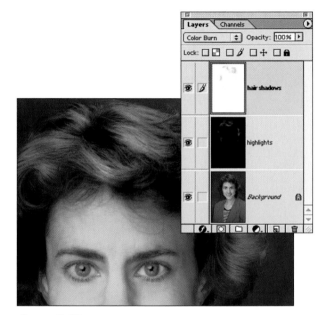

figure **9.89**

Working on a Color Burn neutral layer painting with the Airbrush tool with a large soft brush emphasizes the shadows.

CLOSING THOUGHTS

Retouching a portrait is the most challenging type of retouching you can do. Remember to work with the contrast, color, and detail of the image. Before we move onto the "Glamour and Fashion Retouching" in Chapter 10, I'd like to give you one last hint. When you are retouching a person's face, keep their mother in mind. Try to see the retouching as she would. If it were too obvious, she would notice it and, most likely, not like it. If Mom can see the retouching, then she can't see her child and if her child isn't in the picture, then you've overworked the portrait.

10

GLAMOUR AND FASHION RETOUCHING

We've all seen pictures of super models, actors, and the so-called beautiful people and have been astounded by their blemish-free skin, sparkling eyes, perfectly balanced faces, and cellulite-free thighs. I've always wondered whether those people eat anything, have a bad hair day, or ever get a pimple?

The glamour and fashion business creates an illusion of perfection. It is an ideal that is unachievable without genetic good fortune, a bevy of make-up artists, professional photographers, and highly skilled digital retouchers. The glamour and fashion industry relies on Photoshop to remove the slightest imperfections in make-up, to straighten professionally coifed hair, and to make an already beautiful face perfectly symmetrical.

This chapter shows the techniques used to make the beautiful perfect, and the less than perfect beautiful. It is important to me to show you that without extensive help the ideal is unattainable and shouldn't be chased after by anyone—especially teenage girls and boys. Am I against digital retouching? Of course not, but we do need to learn to recognize, cherish, and appreciate the natural beauty of each individual.

In this chapter you'll learn how to

- Fix make-up and hair
- Open and balance eyes
- Straighten noses and enhance lips
- Go on the digital diet

I am indebted to the talented Helene DeLillo (www.dancingicon.com) and photographer Lee Varis (www.varis.com) who have allowed me to watch, learn, and share their techniques with you.

DEVISE A WORKING STRATEGY

Before you pick up the mouse to retouch a glamour or fashion photograph, devising a retouching plan with the client will save you hours of unnecessary work, haggling, and redos. To be able to talk knowledgeably with the client, research the person or product in the picture before your first meeting. For example, a portrait of a gritty blues musician requires a completely different approach than a picture of the latest teenage pop singer. By knowing about the person or product in the picture, you can emphasize the important, positive aspects while minimizing the less-important or less-flattering aspects. Research helps you communicate with the client and, in the end, deliver the best results.

The Big Picture

The first time you look at a picture, sweep around the image with your eyes. Don't focus on the details, but rather follow the line of the image and notice any distractions. As Helene DeLillo, a photographer, retoucher, and principal of Dancing Icon in New York City, explains, "Listen to your initial feelings and reactions when looking at the image for the first time. What stands out, in both a positive and negative manner?" Some of the issues that Helene keeps in mind when evaluating an image for the first time include

- Is the image color balanced?
- Is the lighting working?
- Are the contours of the image smooth?
- Is the environment helping or distracting?
- Is everything correctly in or out of focus?

The closer the retoucher works with the photographer, the more these big-picture issues can be addressed during the initial photo shoot. However, as you can imagine, during a location fashion shoot, some details may slip by the wayside as the photographer rushes to capture the evening light as the sun sinks beneath the horizon.

The Details

Next look at the details—zoom in to 100% or 200% view and note all the details that require your attention.

- Does the image need dust removal?
- Is the make-up applied evenly?
- Is the skin texture appealing?
- Do the eyes need cleaning up?

- What blemishes, wrinkles, or shadows need to be removed?
- Are the lips full, round, and attractive?

The longer you retouch and the more images you look at, the faster this process becomes. The goal is for the viewer to be able to get the image's message as quickly as possible. After you remove the distractions, the viewers will see the message as quickly as they can turn the pages of the latest fashion magazines.

Get It in Writing

After researching and evaluating an image, make sure that you establish what needs to be accomplished and, more importantly, that the client agrees with the retouching to be done. Use a combination of Photoshop layers and a work-order form to note what needs to be done. **Figure 10.1** shows a file that Helene is about to retouch. The red marks are scribbled onto an empty layer, and Helene refers to them to make sure that she is on track with the client's wishes. Additionally, she'll use a text layer to make notes on what needs to be done.

In Photoshop 6 you can also add written or voice annotations to a file. This is incredibly useful when emailing files back and forth—rather than trying to describe something in writing, a client can just add an annotation right on the file that needs the work.

figure 10.1

Make notes and annotations directly on the file to record what needs to be improved or changed.

With each file, you should include a work order or job ticket. This form should list what needs to be done and include the client's initialed approval when the job is complete. As you can see in **figure 10.2**, the form starts with the usual job tracking information and then addresses the retouching requirements—from global to specific, from color and contrast to blemishes and wrinkles. I've posted a generic order form (orderform.pdf) on the www.digitalretouch. org Web site. Use it as a reference when developing your own work-order forms.

DIGITAL RESTORATION AND RETOUCH REQUEST

WORK ORDER #: _____

COPYRIGHT INFORMATION

CLIENT INFORMATION

All that appears on the enclosed medium (including, but not limited to, floppy disk, modem transmission, removable media) is unencumbered by copyrights. We, the customer, have full rights to reproduce and retouch the supplied content.

Contact Person: _____
Company: _____
Address: _____
City, ST, Zip: _____
Office Phone: _____
Home Phone: _____
E-mail: _____

Signature: _____
Date: _____

ORIGINALS:	TYPE	NUMBER	SIZE

DELIVERY INFORMATION

Chrome:

Deliver ____   Hold For Pickup ____   Call When Complete ____

Negative:

Delivery Address: _____

Print:

City, ST, Zip: _____

Removeable Media:

TURNAROUND INFORMATION

Normal ____   Rush ____   Emergency ____
Date/Time In: _____ Date/Time Out: _____

Image number:

Image Description:

CLIENT INITIALS	OVERALL RETOUCHING INSTRUCTIONS	CLIENT APPROVAL
_____	Exposure Correction _____	_____
_____	Contrast Correction _____	_____
_____	Color Correction _____	_____
_____	Cleanup _____	

RETOUCHING INSTRUCTIONS: FACE AREA

_____	Skin/Blemishes _____	_____
_____	Forehead _____	_____
_____	Eyes _____	_____
_____	Nose _____	_____

figure 10.2

Use a job ticket or order form to ensure that you and the client are in agreement with the work to be done.

THE SUBTLE DIGITAL BEAUTICIAN

The techniques discussed in Chapter 9, "Portrait Retouching," form the foundation for many of the following fashion and glamour retouching techniques. Key techniques for retouching include working on empty layers, using neutral layers to lighten or darken areas, and (of course) never changing the Background layer because it is as valuable as your original file. Helene also recommends making a backup copy of the original scan and storing it in a safe place. For additional information on workflow and file organization please see Chapter 1, "The Tools and Essential Navigation."

In this section, we'll follow Helene as she cleans up a professional portrait by retouching the hair, removing skin blemishes, refining the eyes, enriching the lips, and applying selective contrast to insinuate a beautiful hint of sharpness. **Figure 10.3** shows the original photograph and **figure 10.4** is the retouched portrait.

BEFORE

AFTER

© Helene Delillo, Dancing Icon

figure 10.3

figure 10.4

FINE-TUNING THE HAIR

To smooth away the stray hairs on the left side of the portrait, Helene painted over them with the background color that she had sampled with the Eyedropper tool. Because the background was a simple gray and the original image was captured with the high-resolution Phase One LightPhase digital camera back mounted on a Hasselblad 555 ELD, Helene was able to simply paint over the flyaway hair (compare **figure 10.5** to **figure 10.3**). If the background had been patterned or the film grain very apparent, you would have to use the Clone Stamp tool to cover the stray hairs to smoothly shape the person's head.

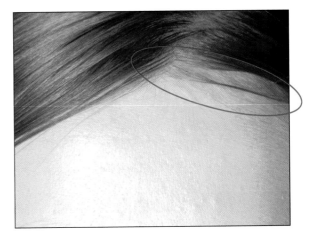

figure 10.6

Study the person's hair and look for gaps or distracting hairs that need to be concealed or removed.

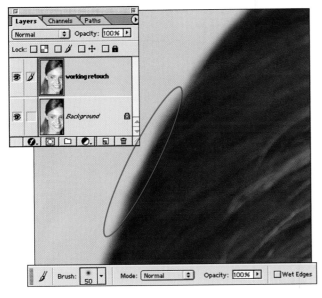

figure 10.5

Painting or cloning over flyaway hair smoothes the contours of a portrait.

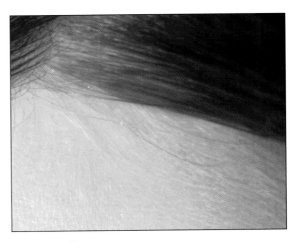

figure 10.7

Use 75%–80% opacity Clone Stamp tool to reform the hairline and let some of the skin tone shimmer through.

As you can see in **figure 10.6,** there are a few gaps in the model's hairdo near her forehead that need to be restyled with a bit more hair. Skin tone often shows though very short hair or hair near the part or the forehead. To clean up the slight gap in the hairline on the right side of the model's face, Helene used a 75% opacity Clone Stamp tool. The slightly lower opacity makes the original skin tone perceptible, adding realism to the added strands of hair, as shown in **figure 10.7.**

The stray hairs on the model's forehead and ear (see **figure 10.8**) need to be removed because they are dark on light and our eyes are drawn to the distracting contrast. By increasing the hardness of the brush (see **figure 10.9**), you can avoid the ghostly edges that can ruin film or skin texture when using the Clone Stamp tool. (See "Building Your Own Brushes," in Chapter 9, "Portrait Retouching," for additional information.) In **figure 10.10** you see the attention to detail that glamour retouching requires as every hair is brought into place.

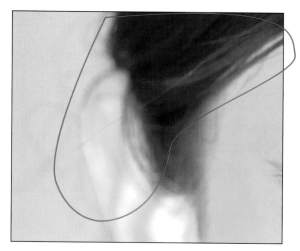

figure 10.8

The exacting nature of glamour retouching means that the tiniest hair out of place must be cleaned up.

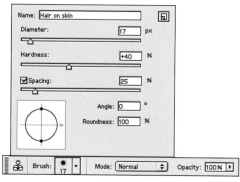

figure 10.9

Increase the hardness of the Clone Stamp brushes to decrease the soft ghostly edges that can ruin film grain and skin texture.

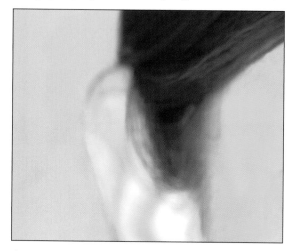

figure 10.10

The improved file has fewer distractions to the viewer's eye.

Removing Skin Blemishes and Hot Spots

Even this attractive young model has a few skin blemishes (see **figure 10.11**). Helene uses the Clone Stamp tool set to Lighten at 100% Opacity with a brush that is a bit larger than the blemish. Being careful to sample good skin that has the same lighting and texture as the blemish to be removed, Helene clicks over the blemishes. Please note—she clicks, not drags, over the blemish. Doing this helps keep the skin texture and film grain intact. Clicking instead of dragging also helps avoid creating repetitive patterns in the cloned area that could be noticeable. (For more information on removing blemishes, see "Improving Skin Texture," in Chapter 9, "Portrait Retouching.")

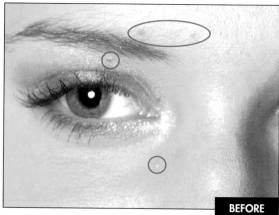

figure 10.11

figure 10.12

Of course, not all blemishes need to be lightened. For lighter blemishes, set the Clone Stamp tool to Darken (see **figure 10.13**), as is the case with three tiny blemishes on the model's nose and chin.

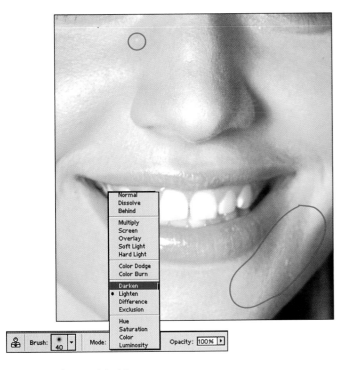

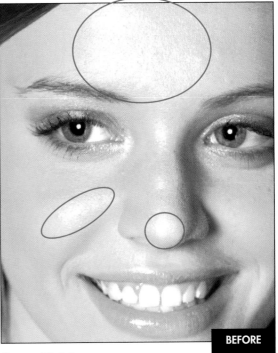

figure 10.14

figure 10.13

Depending on the lightness or darkness of the blemish, change the Blending Mode of the Clone Stamp tool to the opposite to conceal the blemish.

Depending on the lighting, exposure, make-up, and the tendency of a person's natural skin to be oily, there may be some hot spots that need to be toned down, such as those in **figure 10.14**. Helene used a large, soft Clone Stamp tool set to Darken at 20%–50% opacity to tone down these areas, as seen in **figure 10.15**. Most hotspots occur on the forehead, cheeks, chin, and nose—all areas that are more prominent, which causes them to catch more light. Be careful not to be overzealous, because toning down all the hot spots will make the portrait look flat.

figure 10.15

Step-by-Step Eye Retouching

Helene breaks the eye into five areas—eye whites, iris, lashes, brows, and make-up. Lightening the eye whites and darkening the iris draws the viewer to the model's eyes. (For additional eye retouching techniques please see Chapter 9, "Portrait Retouching.")

1. Using the Clone Stamp tool set to 25% Opacity and Lighten Mode, Helene carefully removes any bloodshot veins.

2. She carefully rims the edge of the iris with a 10%–15% Exposure Burn tool and adds a bit of striation to the iris.

3. Then Helene cleans the darker area under the model's eyes with the Clone Stamp tool set to 25%–50% Opacity and Lighten Blending Mode (see **figure 10.16** and **figure 10.17**).

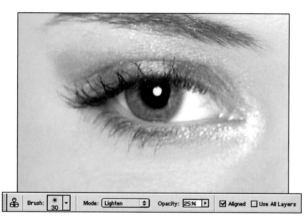

figure 10.16

figure 10.17

4. To lengthen and darken the eyelashes, use the Burn tool at 10%–15% Exposure and follow the natural curve of the lashes, as seen in figure 10.18.

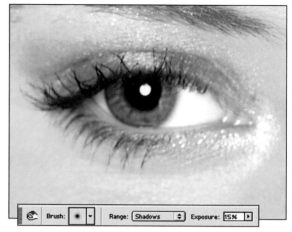

figure 10.18

Use the Burn tool to enhance the eyelashes.

5. If the subject's eyelashes aren't very thick, you can thicken them by selecting the Airbrush tool, clicking the Brush Dynamics Icon at the far right of the Options bar, selecting Fade from the Pressure menu, and entering a number of steps (see **figure 10.19**). Then, you can brush in extra lashes.

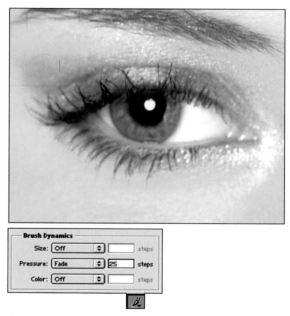

figure 10.19

Set the Airbrush's pressure to fade over a number of steps to paint in more thickness.

When working with a pressure sensitive tablet, you can automatically alter the pressure just by increasing or decreasing the pressure with the stylus.

5. To form the eyebrows, Helene uses a Clone Stamp tool set to Lighten at 75%–100% opacity and carefully forms the eyebrows by cloning skin over the stray brows.

The Lips

After filling in some of the hotspots on the model's lips with the Clone Stamp tool, Helene needed to saturate the lip color for more impact.

1. Using a Color Balance Adjustment Layer, she added a touch of magenta, as seen in **figure 10.20**, which gave the entire image a magenta tone.

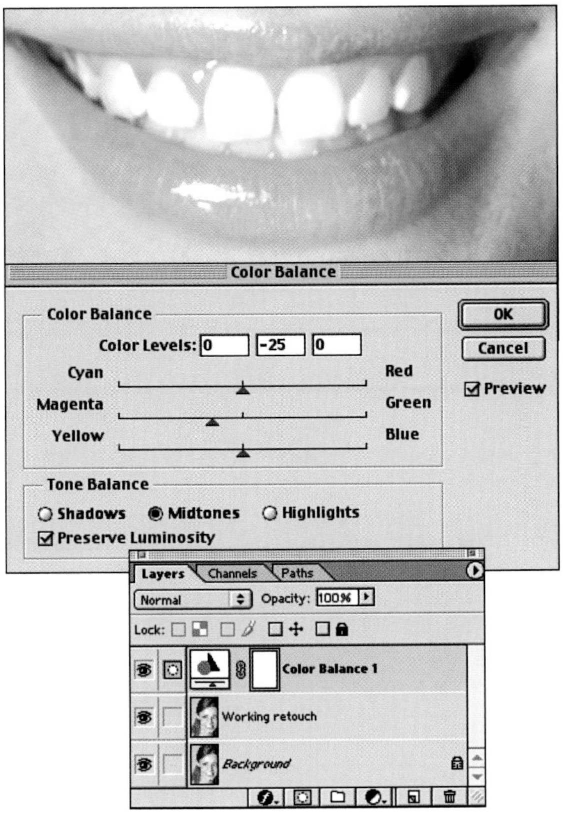

figure 10.20

Toning the entire image with magenta.

2. Helene then filled the Adjustment Layer layer mask with black and used a soft 50% white Brush to paint on the lip area (see **figure 10.21**). This limited the application of the magenta to the lip area.

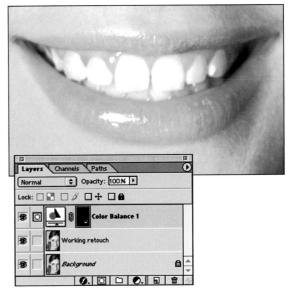

figure 10.21

Hiding the color change with a mask and then painting over the lips brings the color back exactly where you want it.

When enhancing lip color as described here, you can also begin with a selection of the lips. When you add the adjustment layer, it will change only the lip area, not the entire image. Without the selection, it may be difficult to see the change to the lips in relationship to the entire image. After making the adjustment, return to the layer mask to finesse the contours and edges of the color.

Selective Contrast Enhancement

To add more emphasis to a person's eyes, lips, and contours, Helene showed me a technique that I'd never seen before. She drastically boosts the contrast of the entire image with a Levels Adjustment Layer, which she then blocks out by filling the layer mask with black. Then she paints back the enhanced contrast to guide the viewer's eye to the eyes, lips, and some hair detail. This is a wonderful and innovative use of working with adjustment layers and an example of artful painting.

1. Add a Levels Adjustment layer and boost the contrast by bringing in the shadows and highlights, as seen in **figure 10.22**.

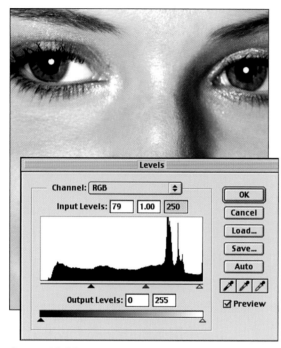

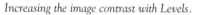

figure 10.22

Increasing the image contrast with Levels.

2. The image will look contrasty and dark, almost ruined. Fill the Adjustment Layer layer mask with black and use a small, white, hard-edged brush to paint over the model's eyelashes and iris. This will add a touch of darkness and increase the tonal differences.

3. With a larger softer white brush at 35% opacity follow the contours of the subject's eyebrows, lips, and a few strands of hair to frame the face.

4. **Figure 10.23** shows the strokes that Helene used on the mask to add a touch of contrast to the eyes, lips, and hair.

Tip

You can view a Layer Mask by (Option + clicking)[Alt + clicking] the layer mask's icon in the Layers palette. To return to full-color view of the image, click the thumbnail of the layer or the eyeball next to a layer in the layer's palette.

figure 10.23

The mask Helene used to selectively paint in the Levels contrast.

Client Approval

When the retouch is done, it's time to show the client the fruits of your labor. Helene shows the client the final retouched version and asks whether any additional work is required.

Tip

Make a print of the retouched file before showing the client. I often catch details that need touching up on the print that I didn't notice on the monitor.

1. With the final retouched version visible, Helene hides all the Photoshop interface by using the Tab key. She switches to Full Screen Mode (shown in **figure 10.24**) by pressing F twice.

2. She has the client examine the file and asks whether anything needs to be changed. If the client isn't happy or asks for additional work, Helene tactfully refers to the original notes and work order to see whether the newly requested change was on the original work order. If the additional requests were not on the original work order, she does the additional work for an additional fee. For example, when the client is looking at the retouch and says, "Oh you forgot to change her eyes from blue to green," referencing the work order enables Helene to double-check to see whether she forgot to do something or if the client is adding extra work to the image.

figure 10.24

Hiding the Photoshop interface while showing the finished work to the client cuts down on any distractions or visual clutter.

3. Finally, Helene flattens the file and gives the client the original film or scan, the retouched version, and a proof print. She does not give the client the layered file. This reduces the possibility of someone else changing the file and ruining her work.

 T i p

Study the latest fashion and glamour magazines to learn the latest make-up and fashion trends. Issues to look for are color and amount of make-up used for eyes and lips, shape of eyebrows, and hairstyles.

DIGITAL MAKE-UP

Even with the skills of a professional make-up artist, make-up has a tendency to fall off, become smudged, or wear off during a photo shoot. As you can see in **figure 10.25**, the make-up artist applied ornate make-up to transform the model into a mysterious character. While taking the photograph, Helene noticed that bits of the glitter were already falling off. Rather than stopping the photo shoot, she continued photographing and then took the file into Photoshop to clean up the make-up to create the final portrait as seen in **figure 10.26**.

BEFORE

figure 10.25

AFTER

figure 10.26

Figure 10.27 shows the original portrait, and figure 10.28 shows the transformations that are possible with the application of digital make-up and hair styling. After studying and planning the portrait, I decided on the strategy scribbled onto an empty layer, as shown in figure 10.29. The five areas of concentration are enrich and smooth the complexion, clear eyes and raise eyebrows, clean hairline, add missing crystals, remove dress straps, and smooth neck and shoulder contours.

figure 10.27

figure 10.28

figure 10.29

Production notes used to plan the retouch give you a guide to follow as you work.

Improving the Complexion

The goal is to smooth her skin and remove any wrinkles and blemishes. For more information on these techniques, please refer to Chapters 8 "Refining and Polishing the Image," and 9, "Portrait Retouching."

1. I set up my workspace with a new view and use the second view as a reference to monitor how the retouching process is affecting the overall image.

2. I duplicated the Background layer and immediately changed its Blending Mode to Overlay. I applied the Gaussian Blur filter. As you can see in **figure 10.30**, the Overlay Blending Mode enables me to use a fairly high Radius setting of 12.5 pixels to soften and enrich skin tones.

3. In some instances, using the Overlay Blending Mode on skin adds red tones. I used a Hue/Saturation Adjustment Layer to selectively edit the reds (see **figure 10.31**). If needed, I can also adjust the range of colors affected by dragging the sliders under the color bar.

figure 10.30

Blurring the duplicate layer softens the skin.

figure 10.32

The Lighten layer covers up the darker blemishes and the Darken layer conceals the lighter blemishes.

figure 10.31

Subtracting the red saturation from the softened layer.

4. Here is a technique that uses a two-layer approach to conceal tiny blemishes and wrinkles. I started by adding an empty layer and immediately changed its Blending Mode to Lighten. Working with a small Clone Stamp tool set to 75%–100% Opacity and Normal Mode, I carefully cloned over all the blemishes or wrinkles that are dark. The layer's Lighten Blending Mode will restrict the Clone Stamp tool to the darker wrinkles and scars. This is similar to changing the Clone Stamp tool's Blending mode and painting. You can use whichever technique you're comfortable with.

   Conversely, to conceal the few blemishes that are lighter, add a new layer and change its Blending Mode to Darken and clone over them, as shown in **figure 10.32**.

5. To help organize the project and layers, I linked the three skin layers (foundation, blemishes lighten, and blemishes darken) and chose New Set from Linked from the Layers palette menu.

Eyes and Eyebrows

The model's eyes are beautiful, but the area under her eyes needs to be lightened, her eye whites need to be cleaned up, the catchlights removed, and her eyebrows need to be raised and shaped. The eyebrows frame the entire face. By lifting and shaping them, you make a person look attentive and often younger.

1. I added a new layer and changed its Blending Mode to Lighten, then used the Clone Stamp tool (as described previously in "Improving the Complexion") to apply under-eye concealer to hide the darkness and wrinkles under her eyes.

2. I made a generous selection with the Marquee tool, as seen in **figure 10.33**, and selected Edit > Copy Merged, which copies all the visible layers, and then selected Edit > Paste. Photoshop will insert the copied eye information into the exact same position. This gives me a separate layer to work on.

3. I used the techniques described in the previous section or in Chapter 9, "Portrait Retouching," to clean up her eye whites, accentuate the iris, accentuate her lashes, and remove the confusing catchlights in her pupils, as shown in **figure 10.35**.

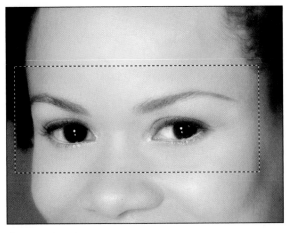

figure 10.33

Select the eye area that you want to copy and paste onto its own layer.

BEFORE

figure 10.34

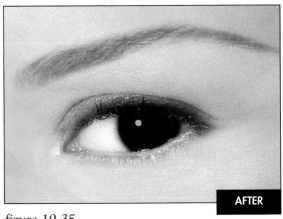

AFTER

figure 10.35

4. Working on the separate eye layer, I selected the eyebrows with a two-pixel feathered Lasso, as seen in **figure 10.36**. Don't try to make an exact selection of the eyebrow—grab some skin around it too.

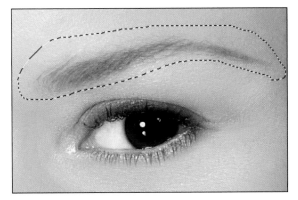

figure 10.36

Selecting the eyebrow.

5. I selected Layer > New > Layer via Copy (Cmd + J)[Ctrl + J] to place the selected eyebrow on its own layer.

6. I selected the Move tool and used the up arrow to nudge the eyebrow up. In this instance I moved the right eyebrow up by ten pixels.

7. I returned to the eye layer and repeated Steps 4–6 on the other eye.

8. Often, just moving the eyebrow up slightly is enough to make the person look more alert. In this instance, I also decided to stylize her eyebrow by shaping it with the Liquify feature.

9. With the right eyebrow layer active, I selected Image > Liquify. I used a small, low-pressure brush to nudge the center portion of the eyebrow up (see **figure 10.37**) and repeated the Liquify command on the left eyebrow.

Tip

When using Liquify to push or distort a small image area such as the eyebrow, make a selection before selecting Image > Liquify. This will make the Liquify interface show just the selected area and speed up the distortions.

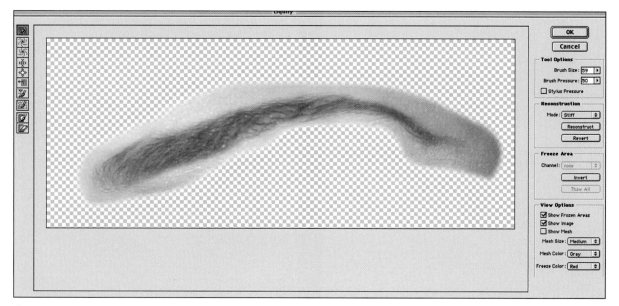

figure 10.37

Use the Liquify command to shape the eyebrow.

10. As **figure 10.38** shows, pushing the eyebrow up may leave a telltale remnant of the original eyebrow. I used the Clone Stamp tool to clean it up.

11. A great trick that I learned from Helene will help you remove any unnecessary skin in the copied layer. As shown in **figure 10.39**, I changed the eyebrow layer's Blending Mode to Difference to reveal all the pixels that are different between the eyebrow layer and the eye layer beneath it. I used the Eraser tool to erase unnecessary skin from the separate reshaped eyebrow layer. Removing unnecessary skin information from added layers is useful to maintain the original texture.

12. Finally, I linked all the eye layers and made a Layer Set from Linked before moving on to the hair section.

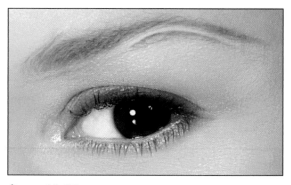

figure 10.38

After pushing the eyebrow up, you'll need to remove traces of the old eyebrow.

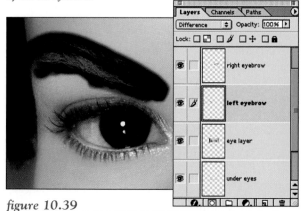

figure 10.39

By changing the eyebrows layer's Blending Mode to Difference, you can see where to erase excess information.

The Hair Stylist

This model has great hair that makes her look very hip and lively. It doesn't need a lot of work except that the Overlay Gaussian Blur layer darkened her hair too much (see **figure 10.40**), her hairline needs a bit of contouring, and oddly enough, the stylist didn't have enough crystals.

Rather than making a complex hair mask to solve the problem of the too-dark hair, I opted to use Photoshop's Advanced Blending options to lighten it.

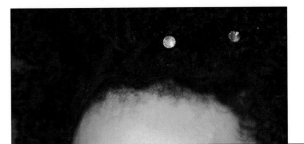

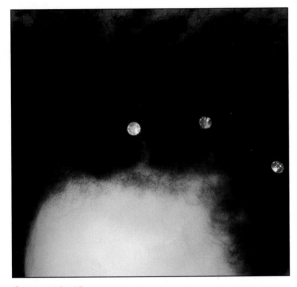

figure 10.40

The softened Overlay layer darkened the hair too much.

1. To access the Advanced Blending options, double-click the layer you want to modify. In this case, I opened the skin layer set and double-clicked on the Overlay Foundation layer. In the Blend If area, I moved the black This Layer slider to the right to tell Photoshop to drop out the darkest tones on that layer. As you can see, this affects the entire layer and yields a very harsh cutout look, as shown in **figure 10.41**.

2. To soften the blend's transitional area, I held down (Option)[Alt] and separate the black triangles, as seen in **figure 10.42**. The distance you move the two sliders apart depends on your image.

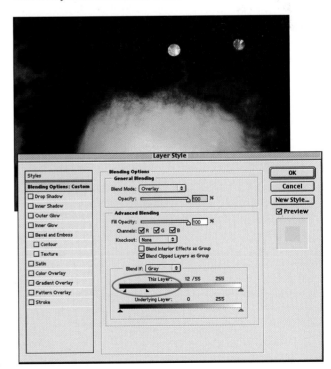

figure 10.41

Using the Advanced Blending feature without a transition adds a very harsh cut between tonal areas.

figure 10.42

Adding a transition smoothes the tonal areas to blend with one another.

3. To protect the work I've done so far, I added a new layer on top of all the working layers and Layer Sets. Holding down (Option)[Alt], I selected Merge Visible from the Layers palette menu and then renamed the layer WIP (for Work In Progress). (Holding down the modifier key keeps your layers separate and just duplicates the information in the new layer.)

4. To form the new hairline, I used the Pen tool to draw in an arch, as seen in **figure 10.43**. If you're uncomfortable with the Pen tool you can also use the Lasso tool to draw in the hairline.

figure 10.43

Using the Pen tool to plan the contour of the hairline.

5. On the Paths palette, I renamed the path and saved it. I chose Make Selection from the Path palette menu and, in the Make Selection dialog box, added a Feather Radius of 5 pixels.

6. Working on a new layer, I used the Clone Stamp tool to add hair to create a new hairline contour.

7. I adjusted the opacity of the cloned hairline to let some of the skin show through, as seen in **figure 10.44**.

8. I selected an existing crystal and copied and pasted it onto its own layer.

9. I rotated and sized each new crystal slightly to give each one a unique quality. I kept each crystal in its own layer, as shown in **figure 10.45**.

figure 10.44

After cloning in the new hairline, dropping back the opacity allows some of the natural skin tones to show through.

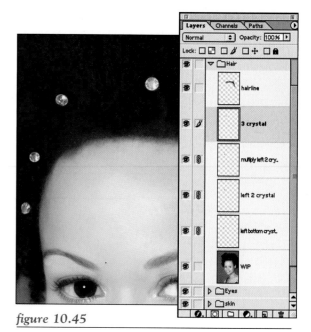

figure 10.45

Placing each crystal on its own layer enables you to position them individually.

Removing Shoulder Straps

Removing or modifying dress or bathing suit straps is a common retouching request and easily done, because they are usually thin and surrounded by plenty of similar skin to copy over them.

1. I started by generously selecting the dress strap as seen in **figure 10.46**, with a two-pixel feathered Lasso tool.

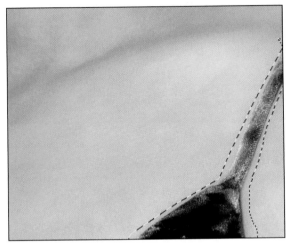

figure 10.46

Selecting the to-be-removed strap.

2. I used the Lasso tool to move the selection over skin, as shown in **figure 10.47**.

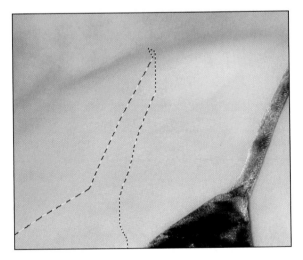

figure 10.47

Moving the selection over to good skin information.

3. I selected Edit > Copy Merged and then Edit > Paste, which drops a piece of skin in the shape of the originally selected strap onto the image.

4. I used the Move tool to position the new skin, and cleaned up the transition between the new skin and the original shoulders with the Clone Stamp tool (see **figure 10.48**).

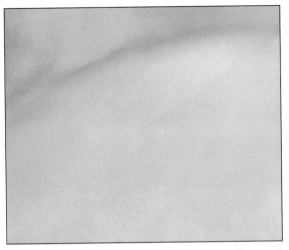

figure 10.48

After cloning, the strap is gone and the skin is smooth.

5. I repeated this process to hide the left strap.

6. Take a moment to study the contours of her neckline, shoulders, and nape. I used the Clone Stamp tool to refine the contours.

7. To tidy up the Layers palette, I linked all shoulder layers and chose New Set from Linked from the Layers palette menu to make a Layer Set.

DIGITAL PLASTIC SURGERY

Photoshop can work wonders to transform a photograph into a beautiful portrait. In this section we'll concentrate on the details of perfecting eyes, noses, and lips.

Tip

Opening eyes, sizing noses, and enhancing lips must be done with a delicate touch and a careful eye. Be sure to work on duplicate layers and save your work in stages so that you can move back and forth between retouch layers until you have created the perfect image.

Opening and Balancing Eyes

Most people's eyes are not the same size—something you usually don't notice until you take a photograph. You can balance eye size with a variety of techniques that range from extending the eye with a duplicate layer to pushing the eye open with the Liquify feature.

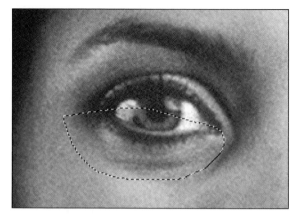
figure 10.51
Select the area of the eye to be moved.

Tip

If one of your eyes is smaller than the other, make sure that the smaller eye is closer to the camera lens when you're being photographed. Having the larger eye farther away from the camera will make it appear smaller and balance your face.

Stretching the Smaller Eye

In **figure 10.49**, you see the original eyes and can see that the eye on the left is smaller than the right. I've opened the left eye just a bit to balance the two eyes (see **figure 10.50**).

BEFORE
figure 10.49

AFTER
figure 10.50

  ch10_eye1.jpg

1. Select the bottom half of the smaller eye with the Lasso tool with a one-pixel feather, as seen in **figure 10.51**.

2. Select Layer > New > Layer via Copy (Cmd + J)[Ctrl + J] to place the selected piece of the eye onto its own layer.

3. Select the Move tool and use the down arrow to nudge the eye layer down two to three pixels. The results of this move are shown in **figure 10.52**.

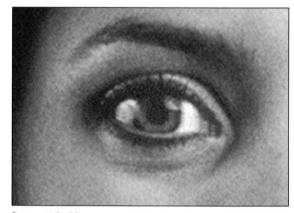
figure 10.52
Nudge the new eye layer down two to three pixels to open the eye.

4. Add a new layer and use the Clone Stamp tool to fix any telltale artifacts that the stretch may have added into her iris and eye whites, as seen in **figure 10.53**.

5. Activate the Background layer, select the right eye, and press (Cmd + J)[Ctrl + J] to copy it onto its own layer. Balance the brightness of the left and right eyes, to one another, as seen in **figure 10.54**.

6. Add a new layer and use the Clone Stamp tool set to Lighten at 50% Opacity and Use All Layers to conceal the darkness under her eyes, as seen in **figure 10.55**.

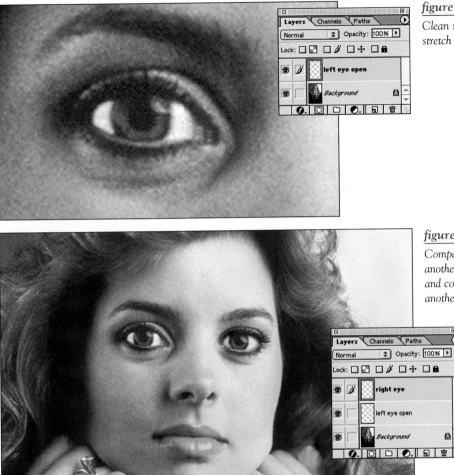

figure 10.53

Clean up any artifacts that the stretch may have added.

figure 10.54

Compare the two eyes with one another and match the brightness and contrast of the eyes with one another.

figure 10.55

Add noise to the layer used to lighten the dark areas under the eyes to maintain textural integrity of the image.

Enlarging an Eye with the Liquify Command

Opening a person's eyes very slightly using Photoshop is the same as having them open them a bit more during the photo shoot. In **figure 10.56** you see the original eyes, and **figure 10.57** shows the same eyes that have been nudged open with the Liquify command.

ch10_eye2.jpg

1. Generously select the eyes with the Marquee tool.

2. Select Layer > New > Layer via Copy (Cmd + J)[Alt + J] to place the selected eyes onto their own layer. Then (Command) [Control] on the new eye layer to load the layer transparency. When you then select Liquify, Photoshop will fill the interface with the selection—making it easier to see what you are doing.

3. Select Image > Liquify and use the Freeze tool to paint over areas that you want to protect from distortion, as shown in **figure 10.58**. The Freeze tool is similar to Quick Mask—wherever there is red the image will be protected from any changes.

4. Select the Warp tool and reduce the Brush Size and Brush Pressure and carefully push the eyes open (see **figure 10.59**). In case you overdo it or don't like the effect, you can either click Reconstruct to revert to the undistorted image (but leave the frozen area) or use the Reconstruct tool to selectively "un-paint" the distorted image.

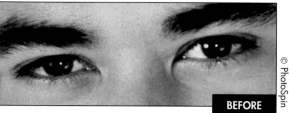

figure 10.56   **BEFORE**

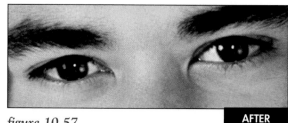

figure 10.57   **AFTER**

© PhotoSpin

Freeze tool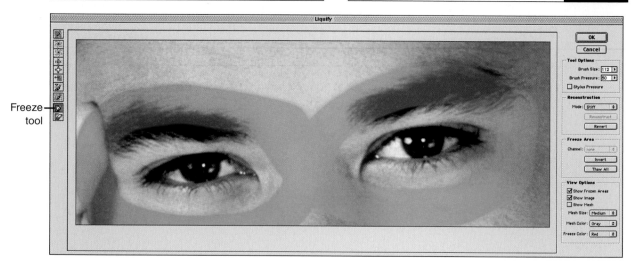

figure 10.58

Use the Freeze tool to lock areas that you do not want to distort.

Warp tool

Reconstruct tool

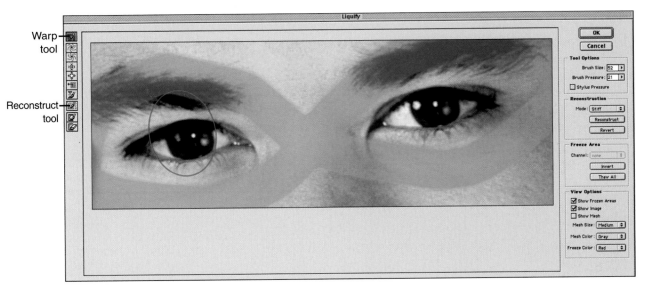

figure 10.59

Carefully open the eye…you won't need much.

Forming Noses and Contouring Lips

Some people's noses are large, some are crooked, and some are just right. When working with noses you want to take the person's real nose and transform it into the desired size and position. In **figure 10.60**, you can see that the Eismann family is not nose shy, but **figure 10.61** proves that I too, can have the perfect nose and fuller lips.

BEFORE

figure 10.60

AFTER

figure 10.61

© Jim Schmelzer

⊕⇗ **ch10_nose.jpg**

1. Generously select the nose with the Lasso tool with a one-pixel feather. Press (Cmd + J)[Ctrl + J] to copy the selected information onto its own layer.

2. Use the Free Transform tool to reduce the width of the nose. In this instance I also narrowed my schnoz with the Perspective command, as seen in **figure 10.62**.

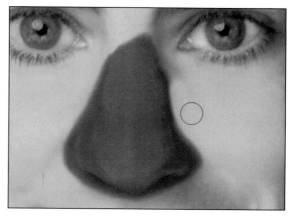

figure 10.63

Changing the layer Blend Mode to Difference enables you to see extraneous information.

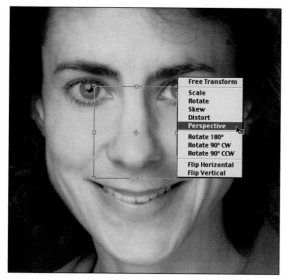

figure 10.62

After placing the nose information on its own layer, use the Transform command to shape, rotate, or straighten the nose.

3. Use Helene DeLillo's technique of changing the new layer's Blending Mode to Difference (covered earlier in this chapter in "Eyes and Eyebrows"), reduce the opacity to 50%, and erase any unneeded skin, as shown in **figure 10.63**. You want to be careful not to get too close to the nostrils or bridge of the nose, as these areas have been replaced and need to be covered up with the new nose.

4. Refine the transitional areas with the Clone Stamp tool and be happy that you just saved me thousands of dollars on plastic surgery.

5. Enhancing lips follows the same technique: select the lips, press (Cmd + J)[Ctrl + J] to copy them to a new layer, and then use Transform to carefully enlarge them, as seen in **figure 10.64**.

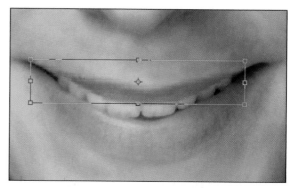

figure 10.64

Transforming the lips to make them fuller.

✒ **N o t e**

The more space the person's face takes up in the photograph, the more information you have to work with and the more time you should spend with the retouch.

THE DIGITAL DIET

In the commercial world of cosmetic, swimwear, and beauty advertising, many models need a nip or a tuck here or there to insinuate that the product shown will make the buyer just as perfect as the imaged model. Thighs, bellies, folds of fat under bra straps, and breasts are reshaped to perfection on the computer on a daily basis. For example, every bathing suit or lingerie model needs to be a C cup—something that not all of them are. Photoshop is used to add additional fullness with cloning and shadow play to create the fullness that isn't there naturally.

Photographic Slimming Techniques

When you're taking the picture, use the following photographic techniques to flatter people and make them look slimmer:

- Use a moderate telephoto lens (85–105mm on a 35mm camera) to flatten features and avoid the unflattering distortion that a wide-angle or normal lens can create.

- Position the camera lens at the level of the model's chest or waist. Shooting up elongates and flatters the body.

- Position the person in a three-quarter view to minimize their width.

- Pay attention to the lighting—use narrow lighting to slim down a heftier person with light and shadow.

Digital Tummy Tuck

There are a myriad of Photoshop techniques to slim a person—from cloning, to stretching, to distorting, to painting with light to accentuate the positive and minimize the less attractive lumps and bumps.

Lee Varis, a digital photographer and illustrator based in Los Angeles, photographed all the component images (see **figure 10.65**) for a Neutrogena ad (see **figure 10.66**) with a Megavision S3 digital camera. Because the woman was lying down during the photo shoot, she looks a bit heavy, as seen in **figure 10.65**. Lee created this image before Photoshop 6.0 was released and he used KPT 6.0 Photo Goo to shape her waistline You can achieve the same effect by using the Liquify command, which was first introduced with Photoshop 6.0.

© Lee Varis, Varis PhotoMedia

© Lee Varis, Varis PhotoMedia

© Lee Varis, Varis PhotoMedia

BEFORE

figure 10.65

AFTER

figure 10.66

🌐▷← **ch10_splashmodel.jpg**

1. To zoom in to the area that needs manipulating and to speed up the application of the Liquify distortions, use the Marquee tool to roughly select the area to be worked on and then select Image > Liquify.

2. Use the warp tool to gently push her waistline in from both sides (see **figure 10.67**). A little bit of Liquify shaves pounds off of her, sculpting her waistline beautifully, as shown in **figure 10.68**.

figure 10.67

After bringing the selected image area into Liquify.

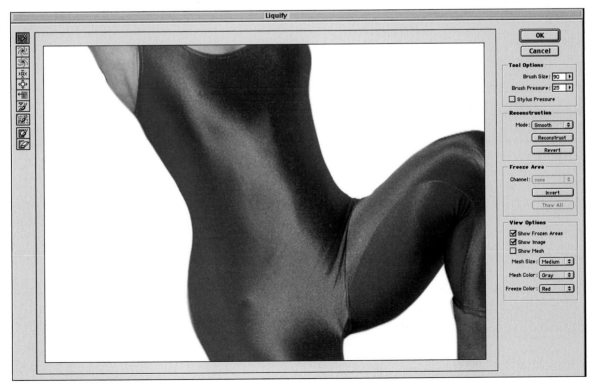

figure 10.68

After using the warp tool to carefully push in her waistline.

Digital Liposuction

In the following example, the very attractive model was caught in an unflattering pose. Her thighs are too prominent—accentuated by the last moment of sunlight illuminating her lower body while her upper body and attractive face are left in the shadow (see figure 10.69). In figure 10.70, the lighting is evened out, her body lengthened, her thighs slimmed, and the washed out sky replaced. In the following section, we'll follow the primary steps used to balance the exposure, lengthen the body, slim the thighs, and darken the background.

BEFORE

figure 10.69

AFTER

figure 10.70

Balancing the Exposure

When balancing exposures, start by adding a Color Sampler to the areas that need to be matched. In this example, I added a point to the thigh (the target exposure) and a point to her shoulder (area to be lightened). As you can see on the top of **figure 10.71**, I changed the Info palette readout to measure in K (grayscale)— this helps when monitoring the exposures.

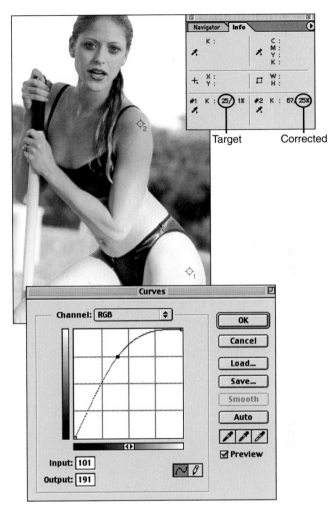

Target   Corrected

figure 10.72

Using Curves to match the tonal values.

figure 10.71

Adding reference Color Samplers.

1. I added a Curves Adjustment Layer.

2. I (Cmd + clicked)[Ctrl + clicked] the area that needed to be changed (in this case, her shoulder) to add a working handle to the curve.

3. I pulled this handle up—and didn't worry that the lower (good) information was changing. Keeping an eye on the Info palette, I used the curve to force the darker exposure to match the lighter target. **Figure 10.72** shows that the target 25% K has been reached on the right side of the Info palette readout for sample point #2 (the shoulder).

4. The exposure is now correct in the shoulder area, but now the lower half of the image is completely blown out (**figure 10.73**).

5. I used the Gradient tool set to black and white on the Curves Adjustment Layer layer mask to balance the exposure. I pulled the blend from the thigh area to her shoulder area to even out the exposure.

6. After changing the Info palette readout to RGB, I color corrected the shoulder area by adjusting the individual channel curves while monitoring the RGB readout, as seen in **figure 10.74**. This process is discussed in more detail in Chapter 4, "Working with Color."

figure 10.73

The exposure Curve corrected the top part of the image but ruined the bottom part.

figure 10.74

Changing the exposure may bring out hidden color casts that need to be removed.

Tip

When using the Gradient tool (in Normal Blending Mode) on a layer mask or an Adjustment Layer layer mask, you can draw the blend over and over without having to undo your last step. When masking an exposure, keep in mind that the black areas are not affected by the Adjustment Layer, and the white areas enable the change to show through.

Lengthening the Body

Stretching a portrait or full body image is an old trick to make a person look taller and slimmer. It offsets the 5–10 pounds that camera distortion can add. There are three methods you can use to stretch a person: transform the entire image, select the entire person and transform her, or select a portion of the person and transform that. I chose to transform the entire photograph, as this would lessen the amount of retouching required to repair the background and edges of the body.

1. I merged the working layers onto an empty layer by creating a new layer and holding (Option)[Alt] key while selecting Merge Layers from the Layers palette menu.

2. I selected Edit > Free Transform and pulled the lower transform handle down. As you can see in **figure 10.75**, in the Options bar I shortened the image by 5% and narrowed it by 4%. Overdoing the initial stretch may distort the face or other body parts.

figure 10.75

Stretching the entire image by 5% lengthens and flatters the model.

Slimming the Thighs

Slimming thighs, reducing waistlines, narrowing arms, and removing love handles can be achieved by going to the gym and eating fewer sweets or by using Photoshop to hide the extra pounds. I'm not promoting poor eating habits or avoiding exercise, but sometimes those last pounds just refuse to melt away. In those cases, a bit of Photoshop reshaping can work wonders. This method starts by drawing the line with the Pen tool to create the slimmed thigh, and then using the Clone Stamp tool to paint scene background to create the new contours.

1. I drew the desired contour with the pen tool, as seen in **figure 10.76**.

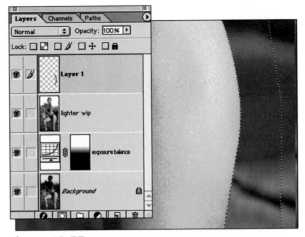

figure 10.77

Cloning background information onto the new layer to cover up the leg.

3. I repeated this procedure for the inner thigh, as seen in **figure 10.78**. Be careful not to overdo the slimming process, and be sure to keep the retouching for each leg on its own layer.

figure 10.76

Use the Pen tool to draw the contours of the slimmer thigh.

2. I added an empty layer, turned the path into a selection with a one-pixel feather, and used the Clone Stamp tool to clone background information over the less flattering body information, as shown in **figure 10.77**.

figure 10.78

Working on the inside of the leg.

Maintaining Edge Detail

When using the Clone tool to contour bodies, you are also covering up the natural texture of the edge, which in most cases includes very fine hair. If the edge texture is essential, for example, when modifying jaw lines or in very high-resolution situations, use the following technique:

1. Use the Pen tool to contour the body, as shown in **figure 10.79**. Turn the path into a selection without a feather.

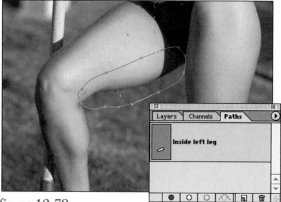

figure 10.79

Make a generous selection of the thigh area with the Pen tool.

2. Select Layer > New > Layer Via Copy (Cmd + J)[Ctrl + J] to place the selected area onto its own layer.

3. Use a combination of the Move tool and Transform to position the thigh area in toward the body, as shown in **figure 10.80**.

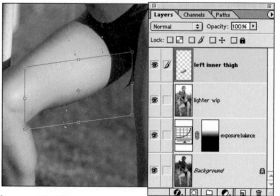

figure 10.80

The Transform command enables you to skew the thigh area to fit.

4. Use a soft-edged eraser and Clone Stamp tool to blend the transitions, as described in the "Forming Noses and Contouring Lips" section and as shown in **figure 10.81**

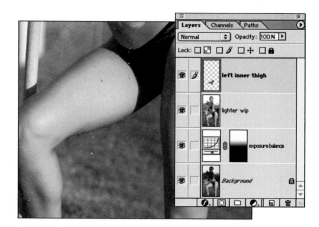

figure 10.81

Erase and clone the transitions to match the original thigh.

Contouring the Body with Light

You can use shading both to draw attention away from the less flattering aspects of a person and to sculpt a person's legs and arms to look more three dimensional. By darkening these contours, you are making them visually less interesting in addition to making her legs look more toned.

1. I made a full body path, as shown in **figure 10.82**.

figure 10.82

The full body path.

2. I added a Curves Adjustment Layer and pulled the curve down to darken the entire image, as seen in **figure 10.83**.

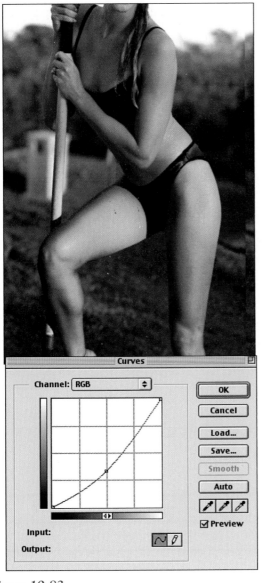

figure 10.83

Darkening the entire image.

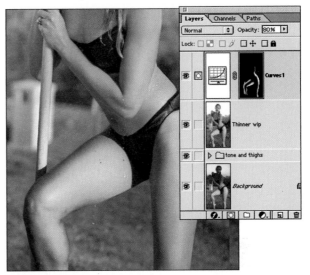

figure 10.84

After filling the Curves Adjustment Layer layer mask with black, painting on it with white enables you to selectively paint the darker tone back onto the image.

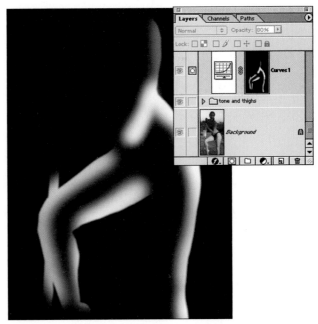

figure 10.85

The lighter areas of the Adjustment Layer layer mask allow the darker Curve values to subtly affect the contours of the model's legs.

3. I clicked the Curves Mask and pressed (Cmd + I)[Ctrl I] to invert the mask. This turns off the entire darkening.

4. I made the path into a selection and used the Airbrush tool at 20% Pressure with white to carefully paint along the edges of her thighs, arms, and waistline, as seen in **figure 10.84**. This contours her body shape with slightly darker tones along the edges. For illustration purposes, **figure 10.85** shows the Curves Adjustment Layer layer mask by itself.

Refining the Details

After cleaning up the background and adding a new sky, I decided to frame the model with darkness to reduce the importance of the background and let the woman stand out more.

1. I merged the working layers up, added a new layer, and turned the full body path into a selection. I then chose Select > Inverse.

2. I set the foreground color to Black and selected the Black to Transparent Gradient Blend, as shown in **figure 10.86**.

figure 10.86

Selecting the Black to Transparent Gradient tool.

3. I drew the blend from the outside of the image in towards the figure, from the top, bottom and each side. The image looks almost ruined (see **figure 10.87**).

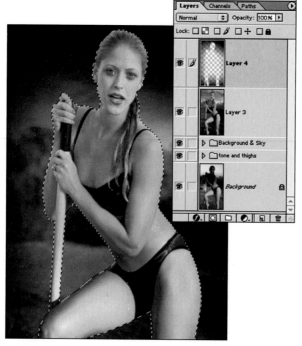

figure 10.87

Applying the blend on the Normal layer makes the image look muddy.

4. I changed the darkening layer's Blending Mode to Soft Light and adjusted the opacity, as shown in **figure 10.88**.

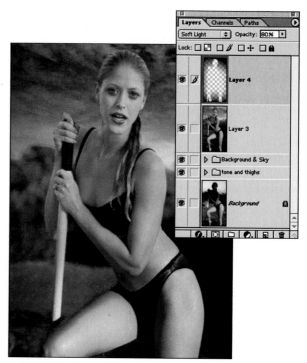

figure 10.88

By changing the Blend Mode to Soft Light you make the darkening effect more effective and subtle.

5. Finally, always inspect the entire image at 100%–200% view. If need be, add a new layer and clone over any remaining dust specks to enhance the final details.

CLOSING THOUGHTS

I hope that the techniques you've seen here help you in a Photoshop sense, but also in a dose of reality sense. To maintain a healthy body and self-image, it is important to separate the reality from the illusion. More often than not, the perfect bodies and faces in the fashion magazines, cosmetic advertising, and swimwear calendars just don't exist—except as a collection of finely tuned pixels on a professional retoucher's hard drive.

APPENDIX A

CONTRIBUTORS

This book would have never come to fruition without the generous sharing of Photoshop knowledge and techniques by these very busy professionals. I thank them all for their time and help.

MARK BECKELMAN

Specialties: Digital Photographic Illustration.
Beckelman Photo Illustration
8 Remer Avenue
Springfield, NJ 07081
973-467-3456
mark@beckelman.com
www.beckelman.com

JOEL F. BECKER

Specialties: Commercial, high-resolution digital capture and imaging.
1332 Meadow Lake Rd.
Virginia Beach, VA 23454-2070
757-481-9940
pix@joelbecker.com
www.joelbecker.com/

RICK BILLINGS

Specialties: Digital Portraiture and Enhancement, Digital Workflow Training and Consulting.
801 Commonwealth Dr.
Warrendale, PA 15086
724-779-7600
rbillings@photowave.com
www.photowave.com

DAN CAYLOR

Specialties: Digital and visual effects.
The New House
48A Queen Street
Coggeshall, Colchester, Essex, England
C06 1UF
dan@thinkdan.com
www.thinkdan.com

JANE CONNER-ZISER

JaneConnerZiser@aol.com

HELENE DELILLO

Specialties: High-end glamour and fashion retouching, digital capture, and workflow-integration consulting.
Dancing Icon Inc.
56 Lispenard Street
New York, NY 10013
212-334-6705
helene@dancingicon.com
www.dancingicon.com

SEAN E. MELNICK

Specialties: Digital imaging, color correction, and restoration for interactive media and print projects.
Rockville Centre, NY 11570
sean@melnick.org

WAYNE R. PALMER

Palmer Multimedia Imaging
Specialties: Photo restoration, film-to-video conversion, photography, and videography.
832 Fifth Avenue
Williamsport, PA 17701-3049
570-321-9660
pmi@palmermultimedia.com
www.palmermultimedia.com

HERB PAYNTER

President
IXSoftware.com, Inc.
770-995-6644
770-995-7497 (fax)
herb@ixsoftware.com

SHANGARA SINGH

Specialties: Graphics, multimedia, Web design.
London, UK
+44 (0)7860 465 857
shangara@oxyopia.co.uk
www.oxyopia.co.uk

EDDIE TAPP

Specialties: Traditional and digital photography.
Digital & Advanced Imaging Committee Chair
PPA
2685 Buena Vista Ave
Doraville, GA 30340
770-925-4482
etapp@aol.com
www.eddietapp.com

CHRISTOPHER TARANTINO

Specialties: High-end catalog color correction and retouching, commercial graphics, graphical interface design, Photoshop consulting on all the above.
70 Murray Lane
Guilford, CT 06437
203-453-5845
Christ3204@aol.com

LAURIE THOMPSON

Specialties: Digital photo restoration, digital art, Photoshop instruction, hand-colored B/W (represented by Swanstock), and infrared photography.
2812 Tanglewood Drive
Sarasota, FL 34239
941-922-9553
941-925-7246 (fax)
istudioart@aol.com or
Laurie@imaginationstudio.com
www.imaginationstudio.com

LEE VARIS

Specialties: Photography and photo-digital illustration.
888-964-0024
varis@varis.com
www.varis.com

DENNIS WALKER

Camera Bits
3705 NW Columbia Ave
Portland, OR 97229
dennis@camerabits.com
www.camerabits.com

JOHN WARNER

Specialties: Studio and location digital photography and QTVR.
Warner Photography, Inc.
60-B Biltmore Avenue
Asheville, NC 28801
828-254-0346
828-254-0390 (fax)
panoman@mindspring.com
www.warnerphotography.com

LLOYD WELLER

Instructor of Photography/Digital Photography and musician
Everett Community College
Department of Photography & Digital Photography
2000 Tower Street
Everett, WA 98201
lweller@evcc.ctc.edu
elleray@mindspring.com